ANNO DRACULA

1895: SEVEN DAYS IN MAYHEM

TITAN COMICS

SENIOR EDITOR
Martin Eden

MANAGING AND LAUNCH EDITOR
Andrew James

COLLECTION DESIGNER
Dan Bura

SENIOR PRODUCTION CONTROLLER
Jackie Flook

PRODUCTION SUPERVISOR
Maria Pearson

PRODUCTION CONTROLLER
Peter James

SENIOR SALES MANAGER
Steve Tothill

PRESS OFFICER
Will O'Mullane

COMICS BRAND MANAGER
Chris Thompson

DIRECT SALES & MARKETING MANAGER
Ricky Claydon

ADVERTISING MANAGER
Michelle Fairlamb

HEAD OF RIGHTS
Jenny Boyce

PUBLISHING MANAGER
Darryl Tothill

PUBLISHING DIRECTOR
Chris Teather

OPERATIONS DIRECTOR
Leigh Baulch

EXECUTIVE DIRECTOR
Vivian Cheung

PUBLISHER
Nick Landau

ISBN: 9781782763000

Published by Titan Comics

A division of Titan Publishing Group Ltd. 144 Southwark St.

London, SE1 0UP

Printed in China.

A CIP catalogue record for this title is available from the British Library.

First edition: November 2017

10 9 8 7 6 5 4 3 2 1

WRITER
Kim Newman

ARTIST
Paul McCaffrey

COLORIST
Kevin Enhart

INKER: (ISSUES #2 - 5)
Bambos Georgiou

LETTERER
Simon Bowland

EDITOR
David Leach

WWW.TITAN-COMICS.COM

Become a fan on Facebook.com/comicstitan

Follow us on Twitter @comicstitan

Email Your Thoughts and Comments to: annodracula@titanemail.com

For rights information, contact: jenny.boyce@titanemail.com

ANNO DRACULA

1895: SEVEN DAYS IN MAYHEM

Titan
COMICS

FOREWORD

First, a couple words about Dracula—DRACULA is the book that changed my life. I read it at an early age and remember thinking "This is it." I'm not sure I knew exactly what "it" was at that time or how far it would take me but I knew it was SOMETHING. Dracula was my introduction to Gothic literature and folklore and it set me on the road to being whatever the hell I am today. And, because my first love was the novel, I'm a bit of a Dracula purist.

So why am I, of all people, writing the foreword to this collection? The short answer is that Kim asked and I was so flattered I had to say yes. But there is also this—

I read the ANNO DRACULA novel shortly after its original publication (sometime in the early 90s) and it immediately became my second favorite Dracula novel. Why? As a Dracula purist shouldn't I hate it? Dracula is hardly in it and when he is… well I think it's safe to say Stoker never imagined anything like that. But it's the world Kim's created, embracing pretty much everything—Historical figures, literary characters, characters from film and television. It's a wild, almost overstuffed thing. It's brilliantly done, smart as hell, but also, most importantly, it's FUN. You don't need to know who all these characters are—I don't (I use Google a lot when reading Kim Newman), but just about everybody seems to be somebody. So, for somebody who loves this kind of stuff (like me) it's almost overwhelming, in the best possible way.

I've read the other novels in the series—THE BLOODY RED BARON (set during Kim's version of World War 1), DRACULA CHA CHA CHA (the 50s), JONNY ALUCARD (the 70s and 80s)—and all are great, but my first love will always be the Victorian Era. So, of course, I've always hoped for a return to that period. So many characters were introduced in ANNO DRACULA and there was just not enough room there to give everybody a chance to shine. And so we come to the comic and my big confession—until being asked to write this foreword I had never actually seen it. Why? I wanted more of this world and here it was, but, the truth is, I wanted another novel. I didn't want to see an artist's version of the world I had imagined. When you really love a book that can be a problem. But Kim was nice enough to ask me to write this and I said yes, so I figured I'd better have a look—and, of course, I'm very glad I did. I know from experience that Kim knows how to write comic (some novelists don't), and here he delivers pretty much everything I could want from a new ANNO DRACULA story. The surprise for me was Paul McCaffrey. I was unfamiliar with his work before seeing it here and now I have I'm a fan. As an artist I feel I should try to say something about why I think Paul's work is so great—I could try, but really all you have to do is turn the page and see for yourself. He's just great. This piece is getting a little long, so let me just say I'm one of those guys who can't read a comic if he doesn't like the art, or thinks the art gets in the way of the story, and yesterday I read the first 4 issues of this series in one sitting and I was left wanting more. So go read it for yourself and enjoy.

And, Kim, thanks for asking me to write this. I hate to think what I would have missed.

MIKE MIGNOLA

Mike Mignola

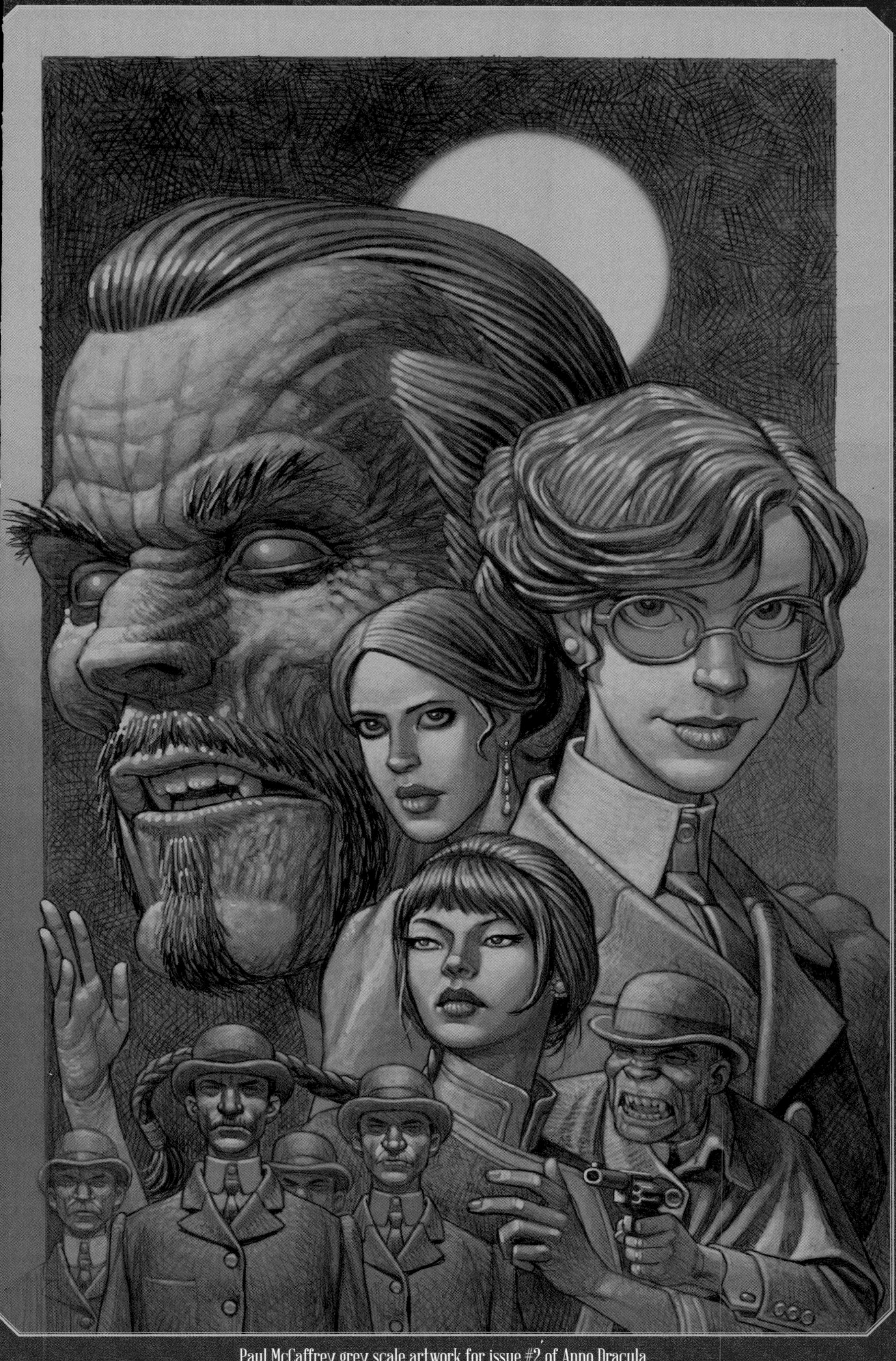

Paul McCaffrey grey scale artwork for issue #2 of Anno Dracula

INTRODUCING SOME OF THE SINISTER

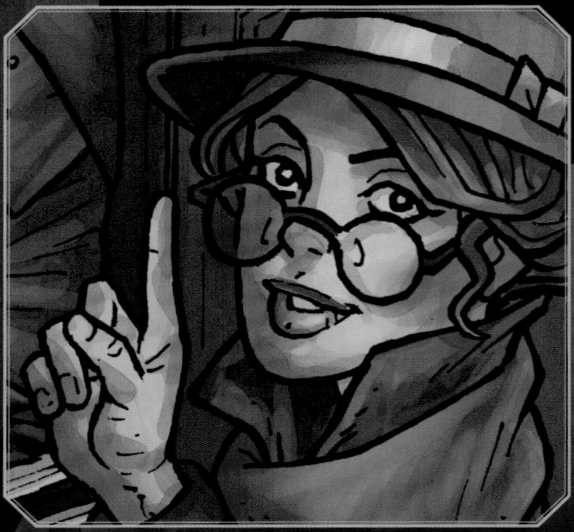

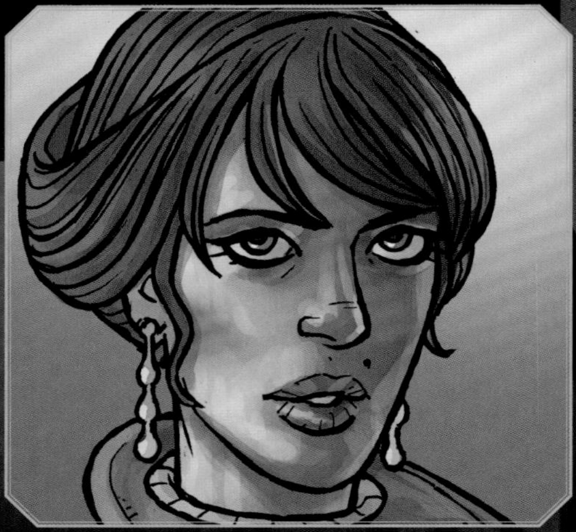

KATHARINE REED. Dublin-born journalist, free-thinker, bicyclist, vampire. Kate is one of the new-born generation of vampires, who turned vampire after Prince Dracula rose to power. A leading member of the insurrectionist underground, writing and campaigning against the rule of Dracula.

PENELOPE CHURCHWARD. Society hostess, gossip, flirt, vampire. Like her childhood friend, Kate, Penny accepted the Dark Kiss early in the reign of Prince Dracula – mostly because she believed vampirism a likely route to social advancement.

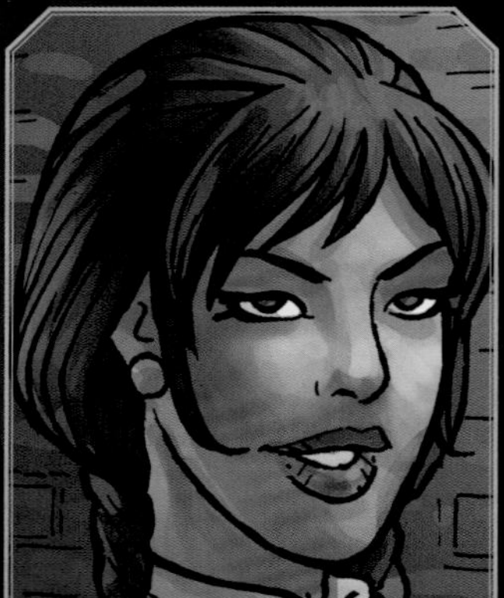

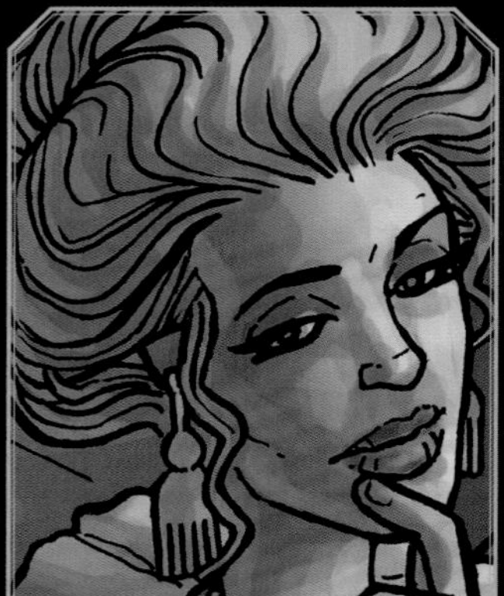

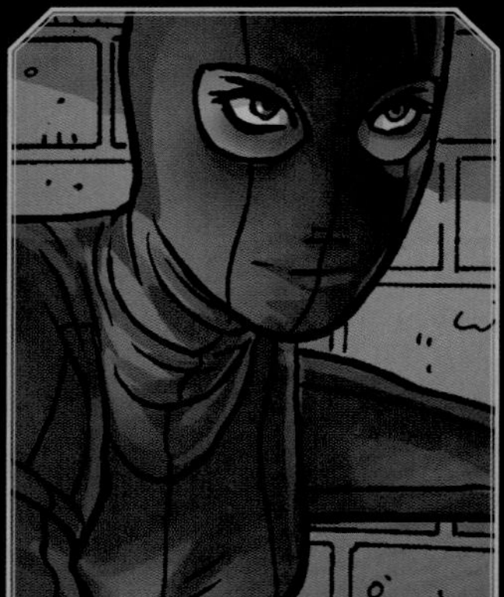

THE DAUGHTER OF THE DRAGON. Also known as Fah Lo Suee. The unworthy child of the criminal mastermind who styles himself 'the Lord of Strange Deaths'. She is a loyal agent for her father's extensive, secret organization – and is also a member of London's leading criminal alliance, the Limehouse Ring.

CHRISTINA LIGHT. A European American schooled by her mother to marry into wealth and a title. She duly married an Italian Prince called Casamassima, who she abandoned to take up with the vampire Count Oblensky who she subsequently left to take up the cause of revolution against Dracula.

IRMA VEP. The anagrammatical adventuress is on loan to the Limehouse Ring from the Parisian criminal Confederation Les Vampires. But does she owe loyalty to anyone but herself? And who is she beneath her mask?

PLAYERS OF OUR TALE.

THE LORD OF STRANGE DEATHS. Father of Fah Lo Suee and head of the Si-Fan tong, a powerful secret society. He commands the loyalty of the lowest criminal scum and some of the most highly-placed persons on three continents. The Si-Fan are linked to cults like the Thugee of India, the Dacoits of Burma and the Freemasons.

THE PRESIDENT (SUNDAY). President of the Council of The Seven Days is a somewhat startling individual – his folder in the Secret Files of the Diogenes Club contains a single sheet of blank paper. What was once written or drawn on it has faded from the memories of those who once knew. He is as mysterious as he is gargantuan.

DRACULA. Also known as Prince Dracula, Count Dracula, Count de Ville, Vlad the Impaler. Undisputed (at present) monarch of the Undead, Crown Prince of Great Britain and Her Empire. Genius strategist and visionary, and the most notable figure of the Age. What was once tentatively known as the Victorian Era must now be viewed as merely the prelude to the Dracula Years.

LORD RUTHVEN. After the Dracula Ascension of 1885, Lord Ruthven took his seat in the House of Lords, before becoming, first, the Leader of the Conservative Party, and later the Prime Minister of Great Britain.

GRAF VON ORLOK. Orlok's official position is Master of the Tower of London – essentially, chief jailer of the kingdom. It is joked (in private) that Orlok was appointed to be the country's supreme bogey man, for those few folk not intimidated by Prince Dracula's terrible visage.

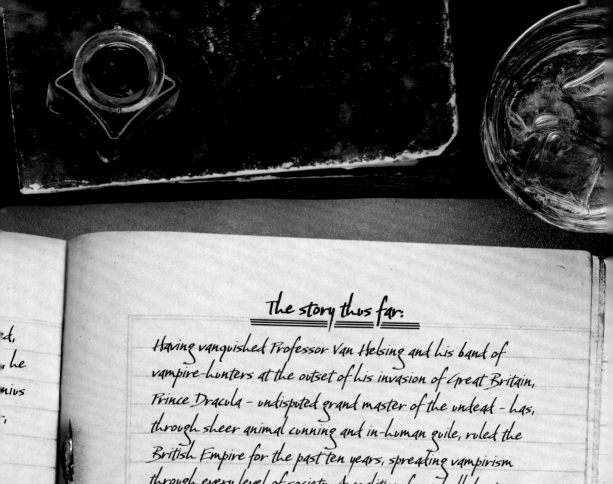

The story thus far:

Having vanquished Professor Van Helsing and his band of vampire-hunters at the outset of his invasion of Great Britain, Prince Dracula – undisputed grand master of the undead – has, through sheer animal cunning and in-human guile, ruled the British Empire for the past ten years, spreading vampirism through every level of society. A coalition force hell-bent on regime change has gathered on the other side of the Channel, amassing the single greatest armada of war ships ever assembled with the express intention of overthrowing Dracula's rule.

Meanwhile, Kate Reed, vampire journalist and free-thinker, has been invited to London to meet the Council of the Seven Days, a radical, anarchist revolutionary group dedicated to the downfall of Dracula through any means necessary. On the streets of London, the Grey Men, Dracula's dreaded secret police force, have recently begun to purge the streets of London of all political undesirables, social malcontents, and those who might wish harm upon the Crown Prince of Darkness.

Now read on.

Your obedient servant, The Editor.

CHAPTER ONE

Illustration by Paul McCaffrey

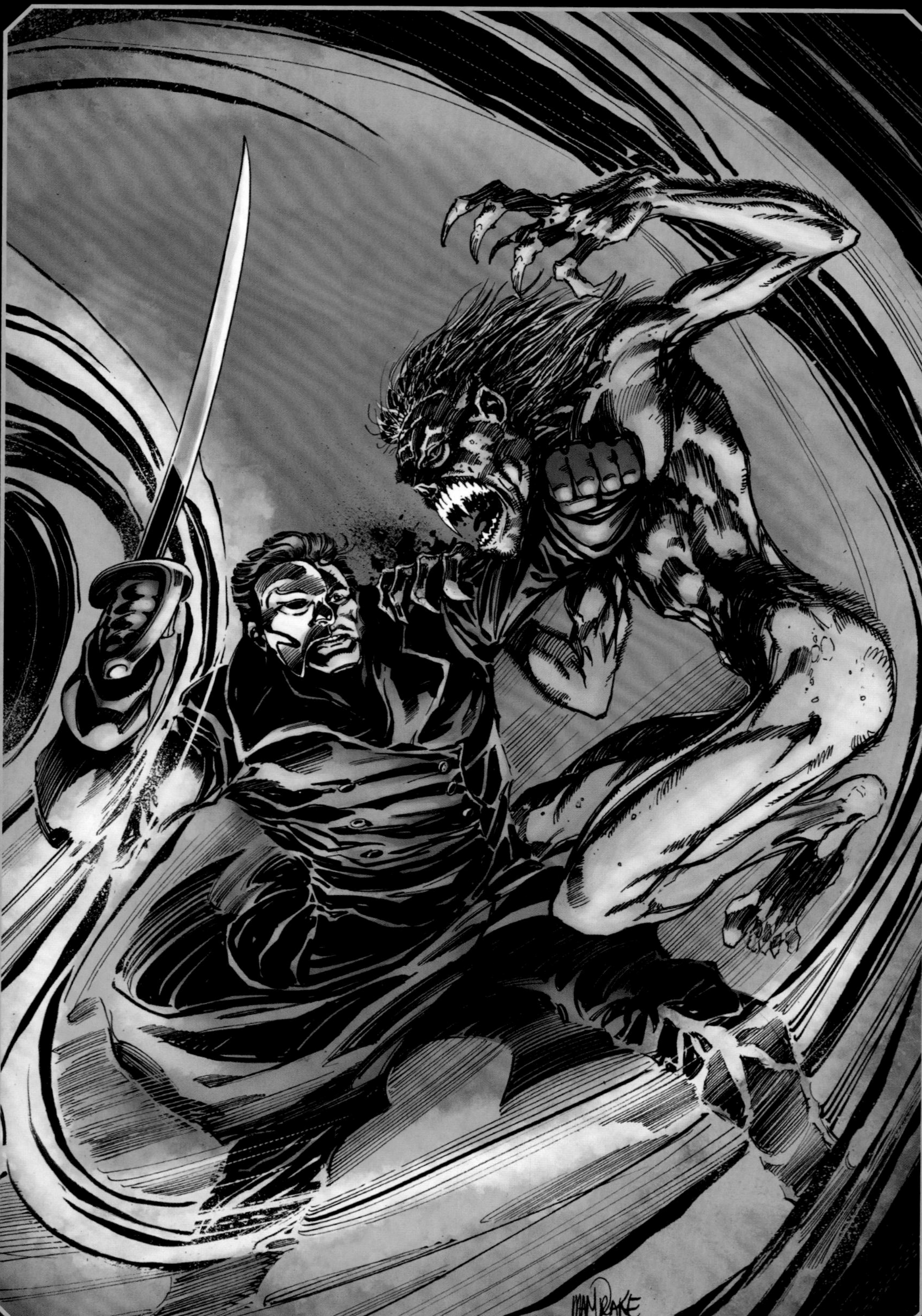
MANDRAKE

Illustration by Tom Mandrake. Colors by Sian Mandrake

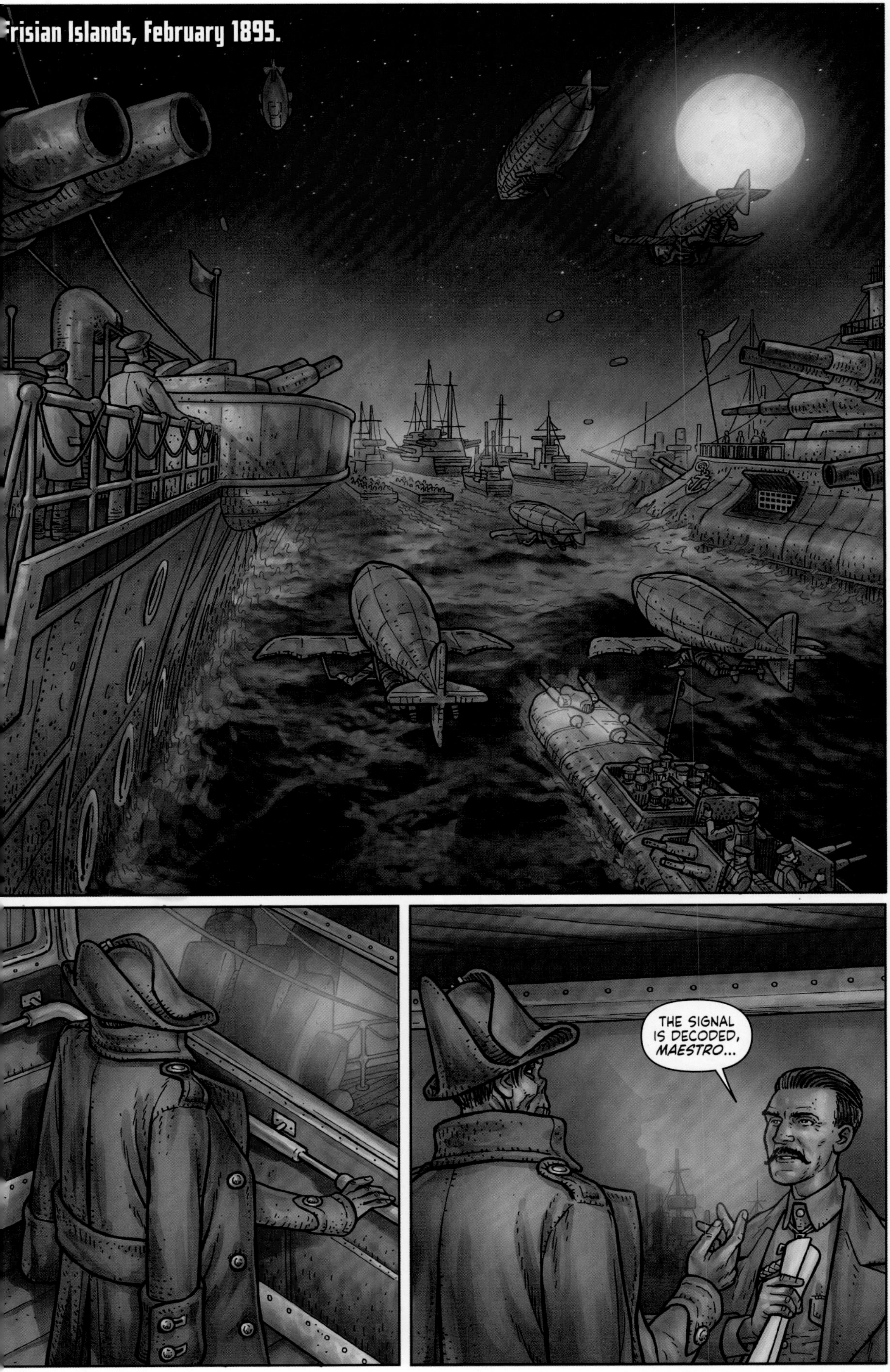
Frisian Islands, February 1895.
THE SIGNAL IS DECODED, MAESTRO...

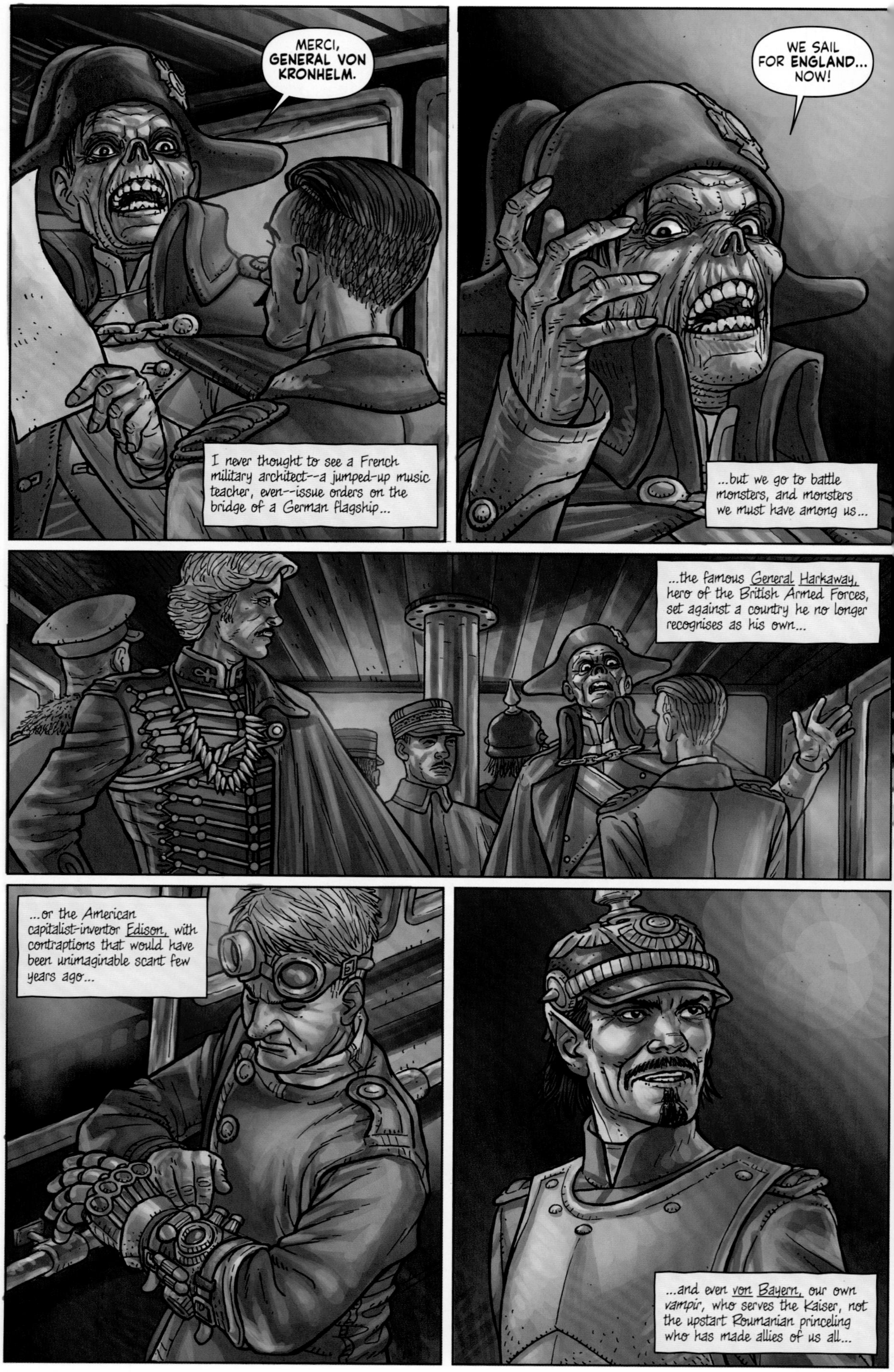
MERCI, GENERAL VON KRONHELM.
I never thought to see a French military architect--a jumped-up music teacher, even--issue orders on the bridge of a German flagship...
WE SAIL FOR ENGLAND... NOW!
...but we go to battle monsters, and monsters we must have among us...
...the famous General Harkaway, hero of the British Armed Forces, set against a country he no longer recognises as his own...
...or the American capitalist-inventor Edison, with contraptions that would have been unimaginable scant few years ago...
...and even von Bayern, our own vampir, who serves the Kaiser, not the upstart Roumanian princeling who has made allies of us all...

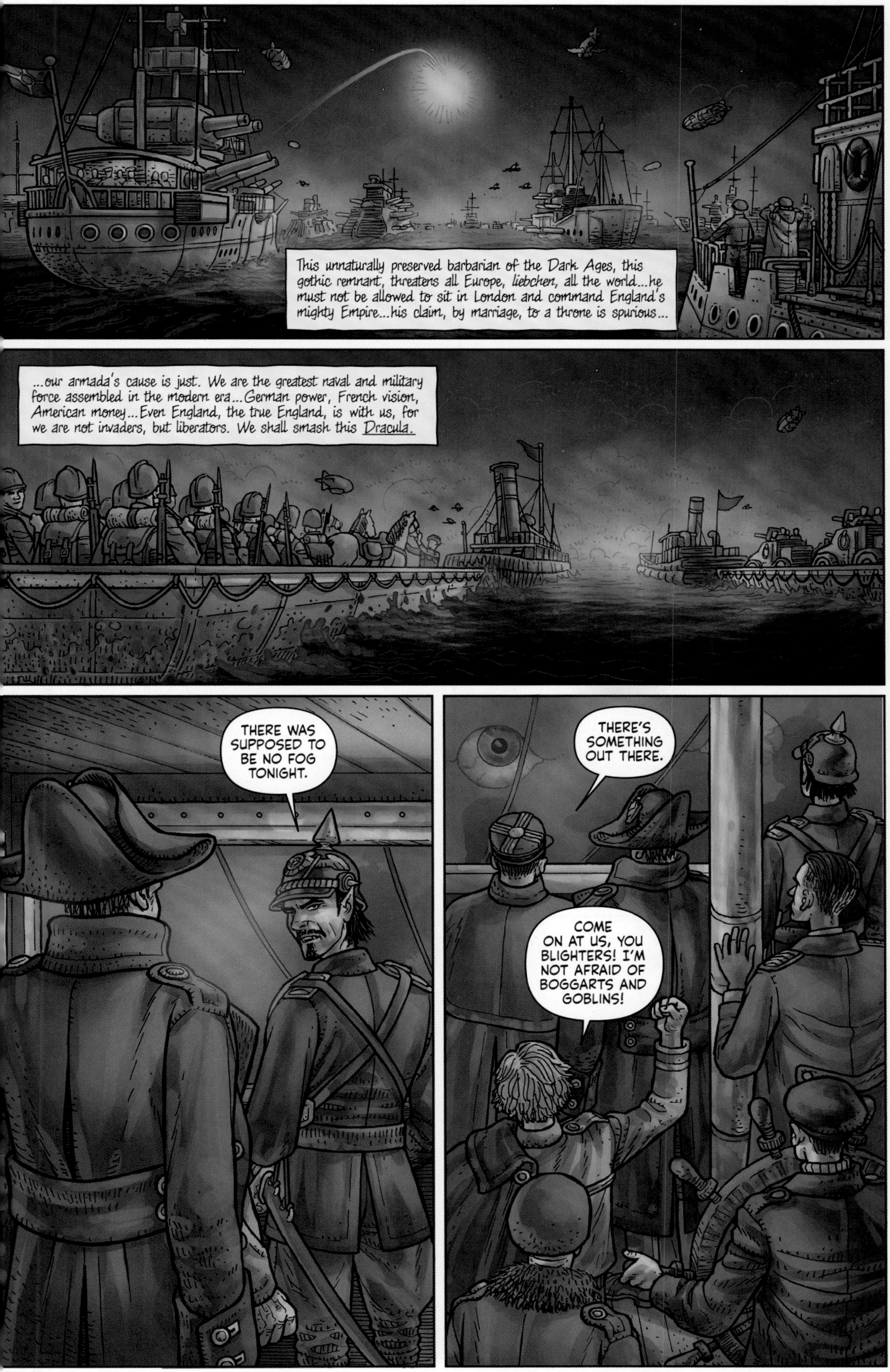
This unnaturally preserved barbarian of the Dark Ages, this gothic remnant, threatens all Europe, *liebchen*, all the world...he must not be allowed to sit in London and command England's mighty Empire...his claim, by marriage, to a throne is spurious...
...our armada's cause is just. We are the greatest naval and military force assembled in the modern era...German power, French vision, American money...Even England, the true England, is with us, for we are not invaders, but liberators. We shall smash this Dracula.
THERE WAS SUPPOSED TO BE NO FOG TONIGHT.
THERE'S SOMETHING OUT THERE.
COME ON AT US, YOU BLIGHTERS! I'M NOT AFRAID OF BOGGARTS AND GOBLINS!

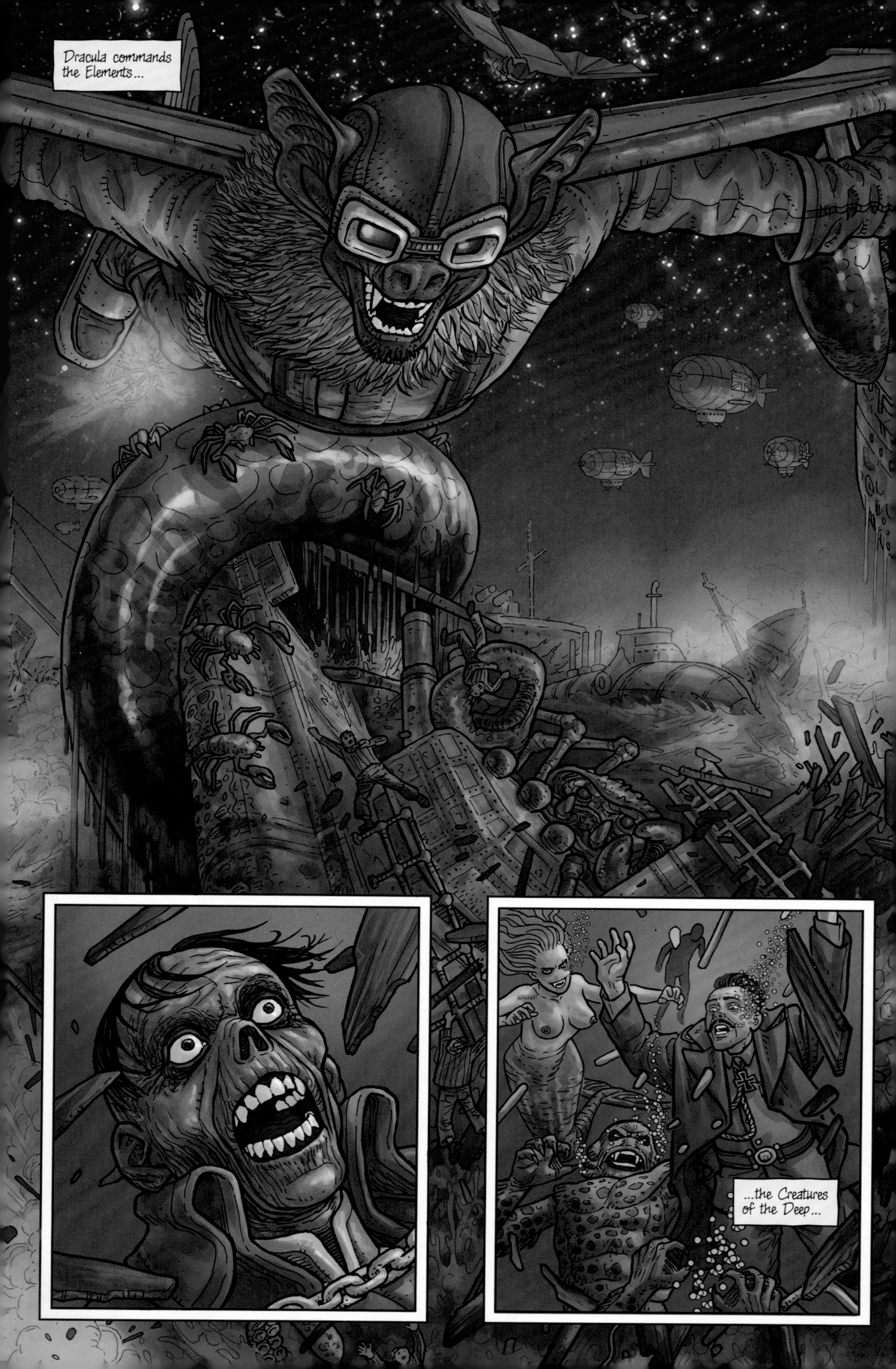
Dracula commands the Elements...
...the Creatures of the Deep...

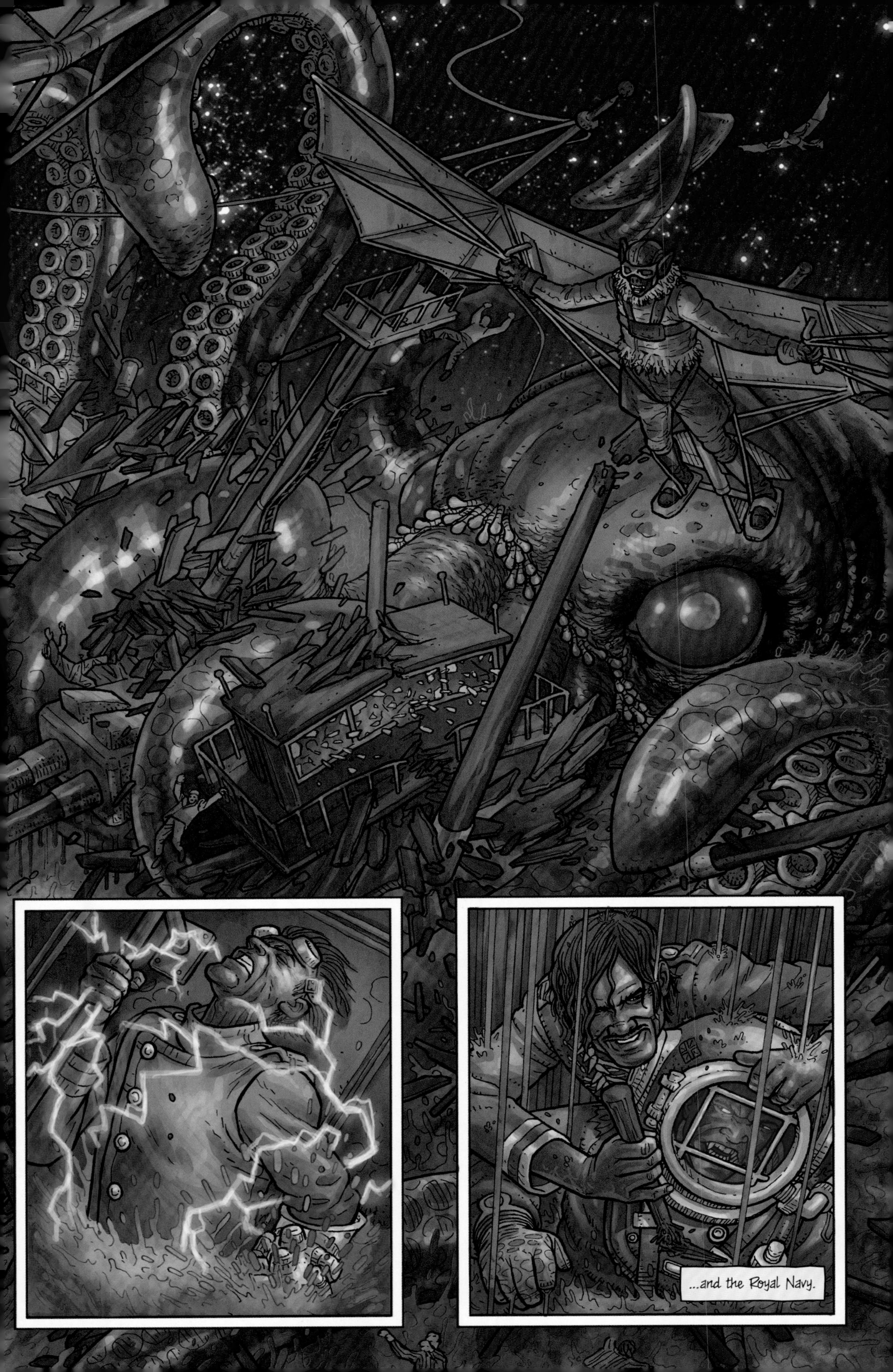
...and the Royal Navy.

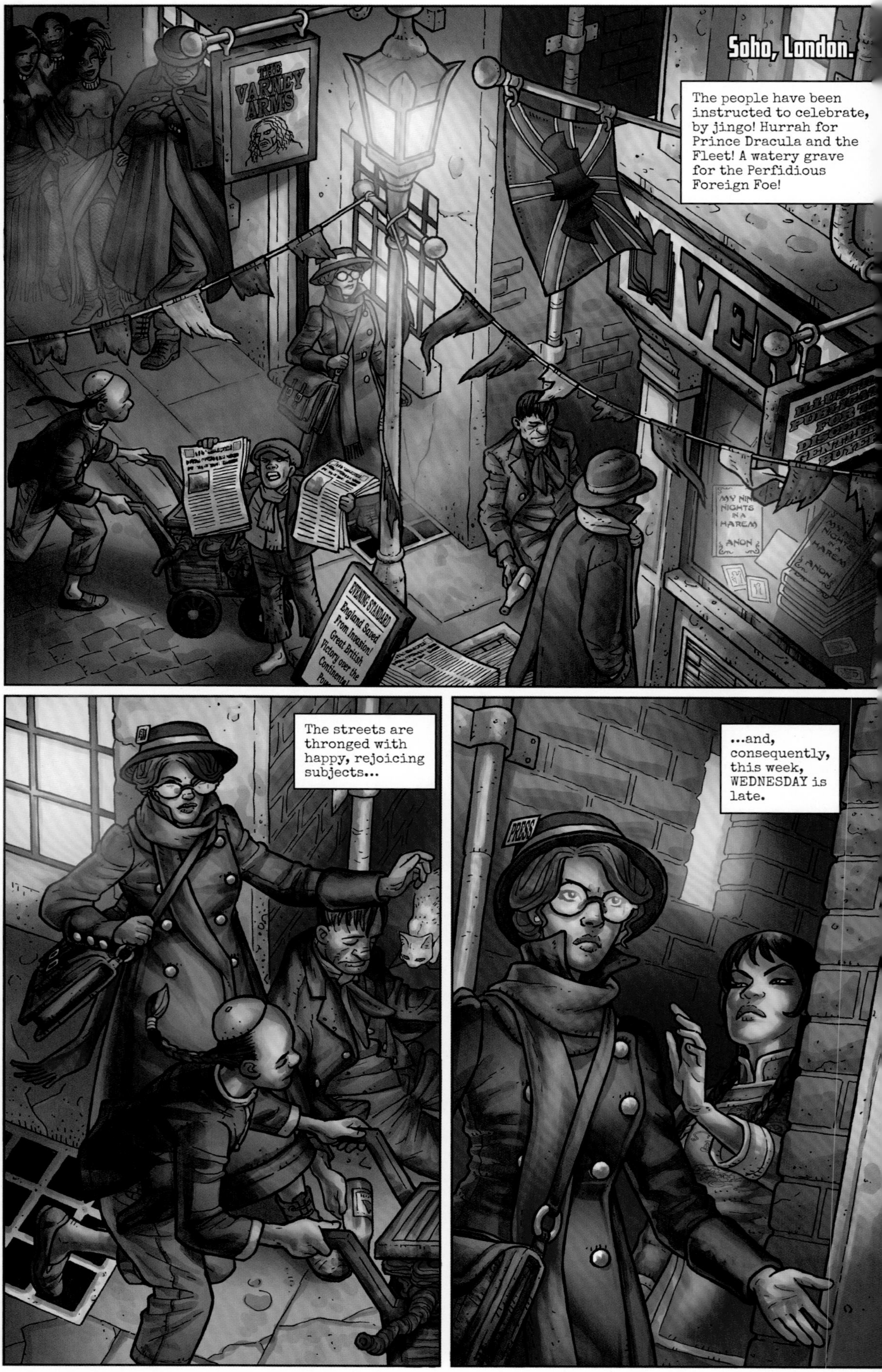
THE VARNEY ARMS
Soho, London.
The people have been instructed to celebrate, by jingo! Hurrah for Prince Dracula and the Fleet! A watery grave for the Perfidious Foreign Foe!
EVENING STANDARD
England Saved From Invasion! Great British Victory over the
HAREM
ANON
The streets are thronged with happy, rejoicing subjects...
PRESS
...and, consequently, this week, WEDNESDAY is late.

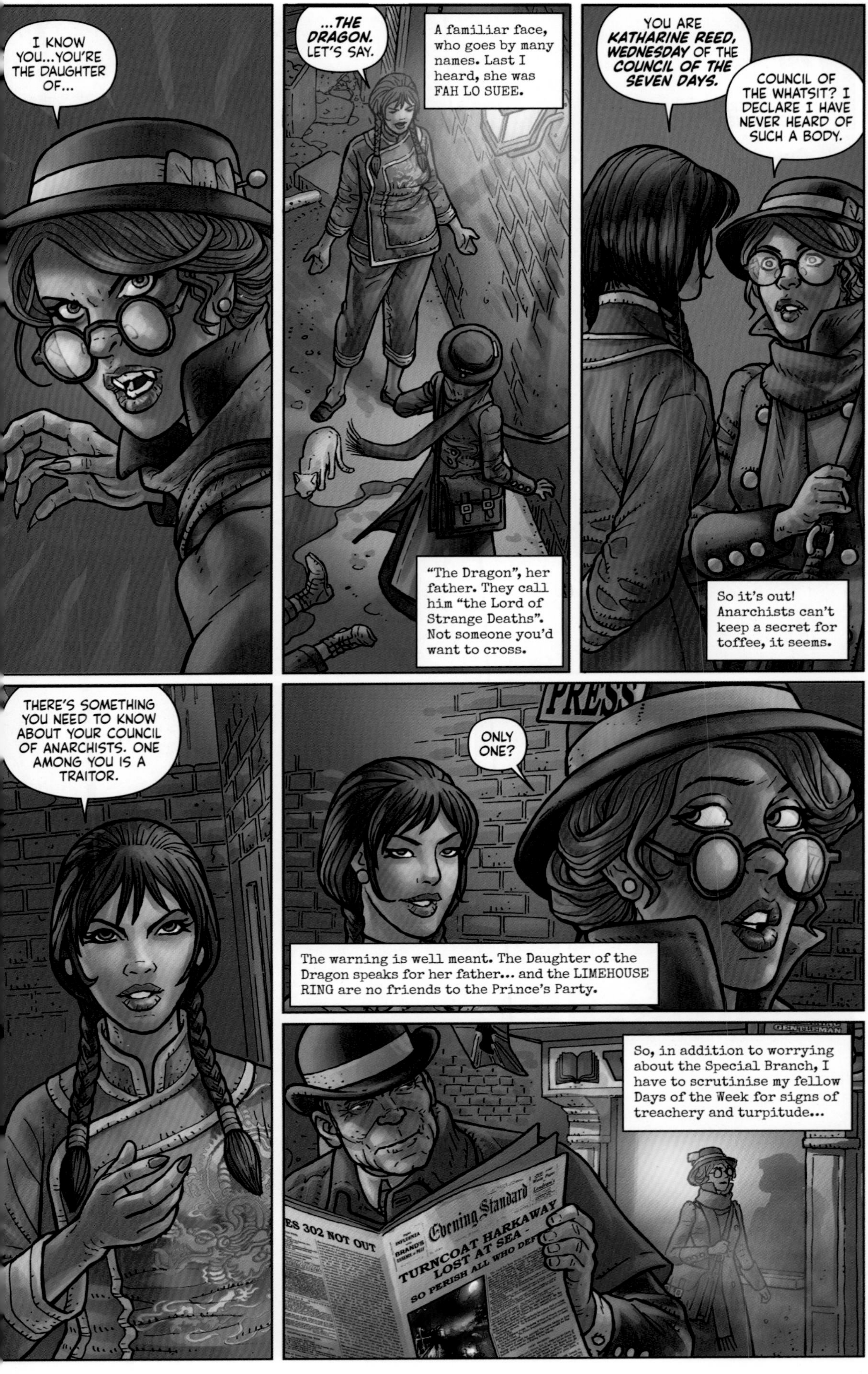
I KNOW YOU...YOU'RE THE DAUGHTER OF...
...THE DRAGON. LET'S SAY.
A familiar face, who goes by many names. Last I heard, she was FAH LO SUEE.
"The Dragon", her father. They call him "the Lord of Strange Deaths". Not someone you'd want to cross.
YOU ARE KATHARINE REED, WEDNESDAY OF THE COUNCIL OF THE SEVEN DAYS.
COUNCIL OF THE WHATSIT? I DECLARE I HAVE NEVER HEARD OF SUCH A BODY.
So it's out! Anarchists can't keep a secret for toffee, it seems.
THERE'S SOMETHING YOU NEED TO KNOW ABOUT YOUR COUNCIL OF ANARCHISTS. ONE AMONG YOU IS A TRAITOR.
ONLY ONE?
The warning is well meant. The Daughter of the Dragon speaks for her father... and the LIMEHOUSE RING are no friends to the Prince's Party.
GENTLEMAN
So, in addition to worrying about the Special Branch, I have to scrutinise my fellow Days of the Week for signs of treachery and turpitude...
Evening Standard
TURNCOAT HARKAWAY LOST AT SEA

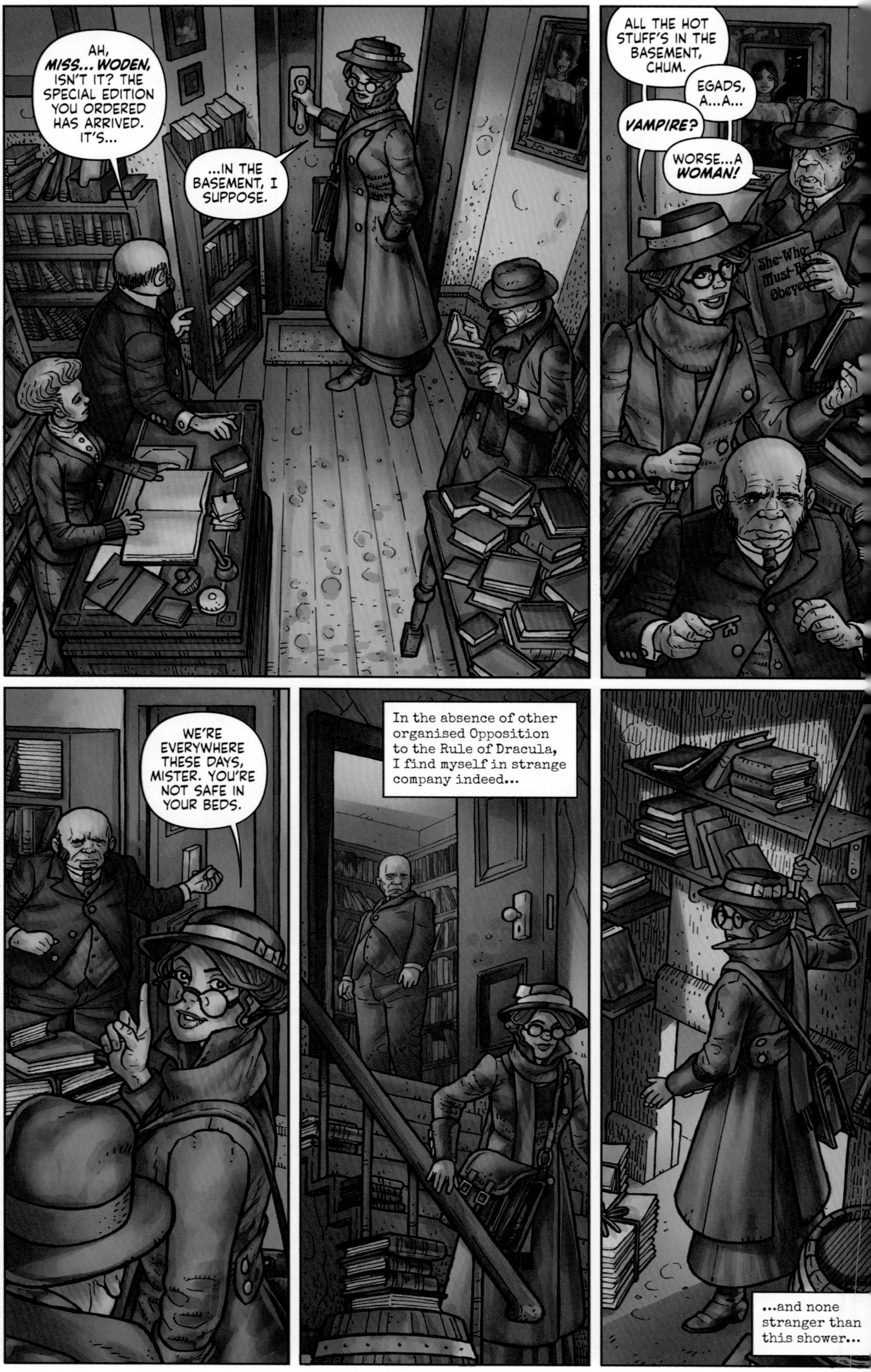
AH, ***MISS... WODEN,*** ISN'T IT? THE SPECIAL EDITION YOU ORDERED HAS ARRIVED. IT'S...
...IN THE BASEMENT, I SUPPOSE.
ALL THE HOT STUFF'S IN THE BASEMENT, CHUM.
EGADS, A...A...
VAMPIRE?
WORSE...A ***WOMAN!***
WE'RE EVERYWHERE THESE DAYS, MISTER. YOU'RE NOT SAFE IN YOUR BEDS.
In the absence of other organised Opposition to the Rule of Dracula, I find myself in strange company indeed...
...and none stranger than this shower...

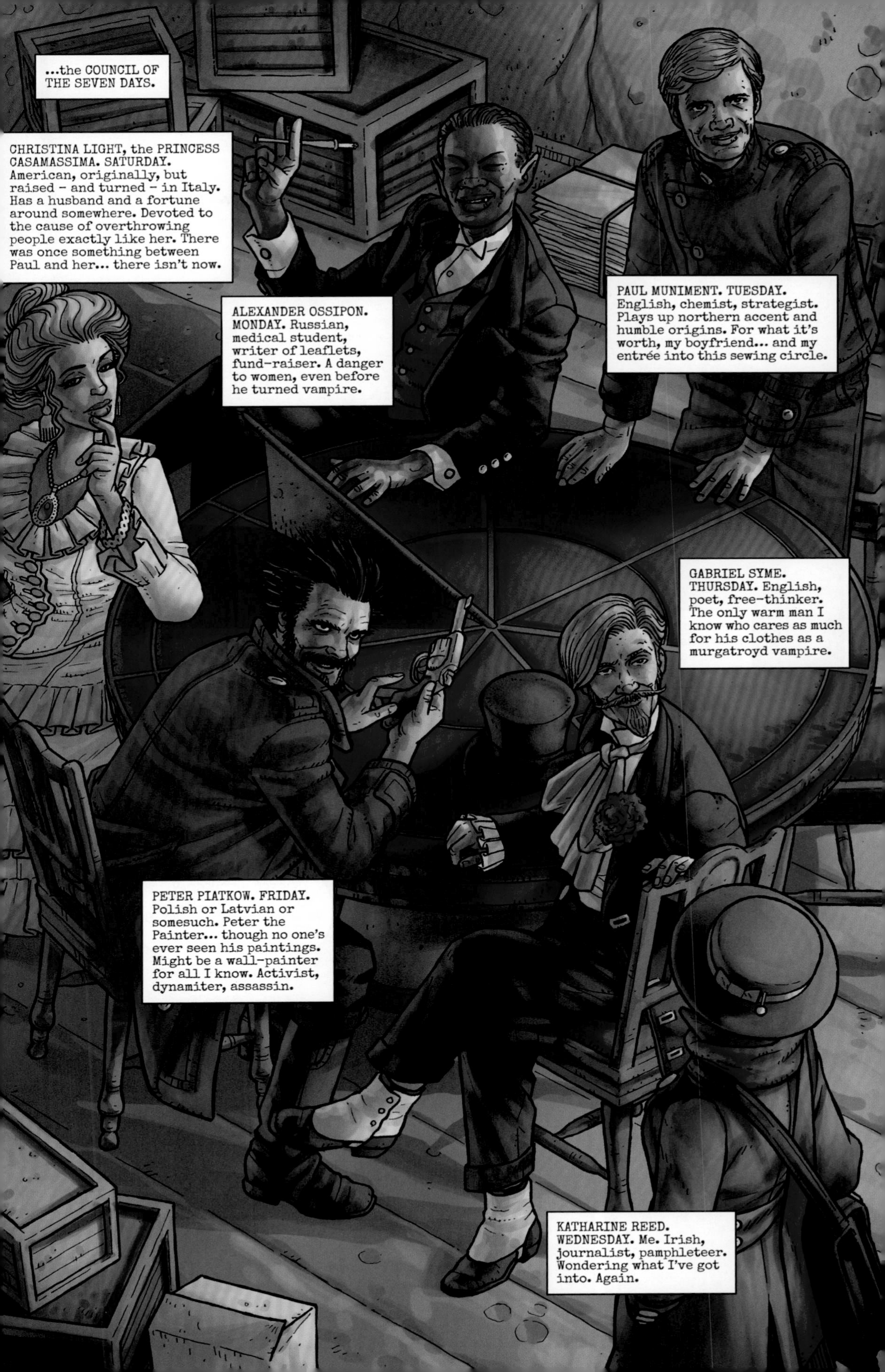
...the COUNCIL OF THE SEVEN DAYS.
CHRISTINA LIGHT, the PRINCESS CASAMASSIMA. SATURDAY. American, originally, but raised – and turned – in Italy. Has a husband and a fortune around somewhere. Devoted to the cause of overthrowing people exactly like her. There was once something between Paul and her... there isn't now.
ALEXANDER OSSIPON. MONDAY. Russian, medical student, writer of leaflets, fund-raiser. A danger to women, even before he turned vampire.
PAUL MUNIMENT. TUESDAY. English, chemist, strategist. Plays up northern accent and humble origins. For what it's worth, my boyfriend... and my entrée into this sewing circle.
GABRIEL SYME. THURSDAY. English, poet, free-thinker. The only warm man I know who cares as much for his clothes as a murgatroyd vampire.
PETER PIATKOW. FRIDAY. Polish or Latvian or somesuch. Peter the Painter... though no one's ever seen his paintings. Might be a wall-painter for all I know. Activist, dynamiter, assassin.
KATHARINE REED. WEDNESDAY. Me. Irish, journalist, pamphleteer. Wondering what I've got into. Again.

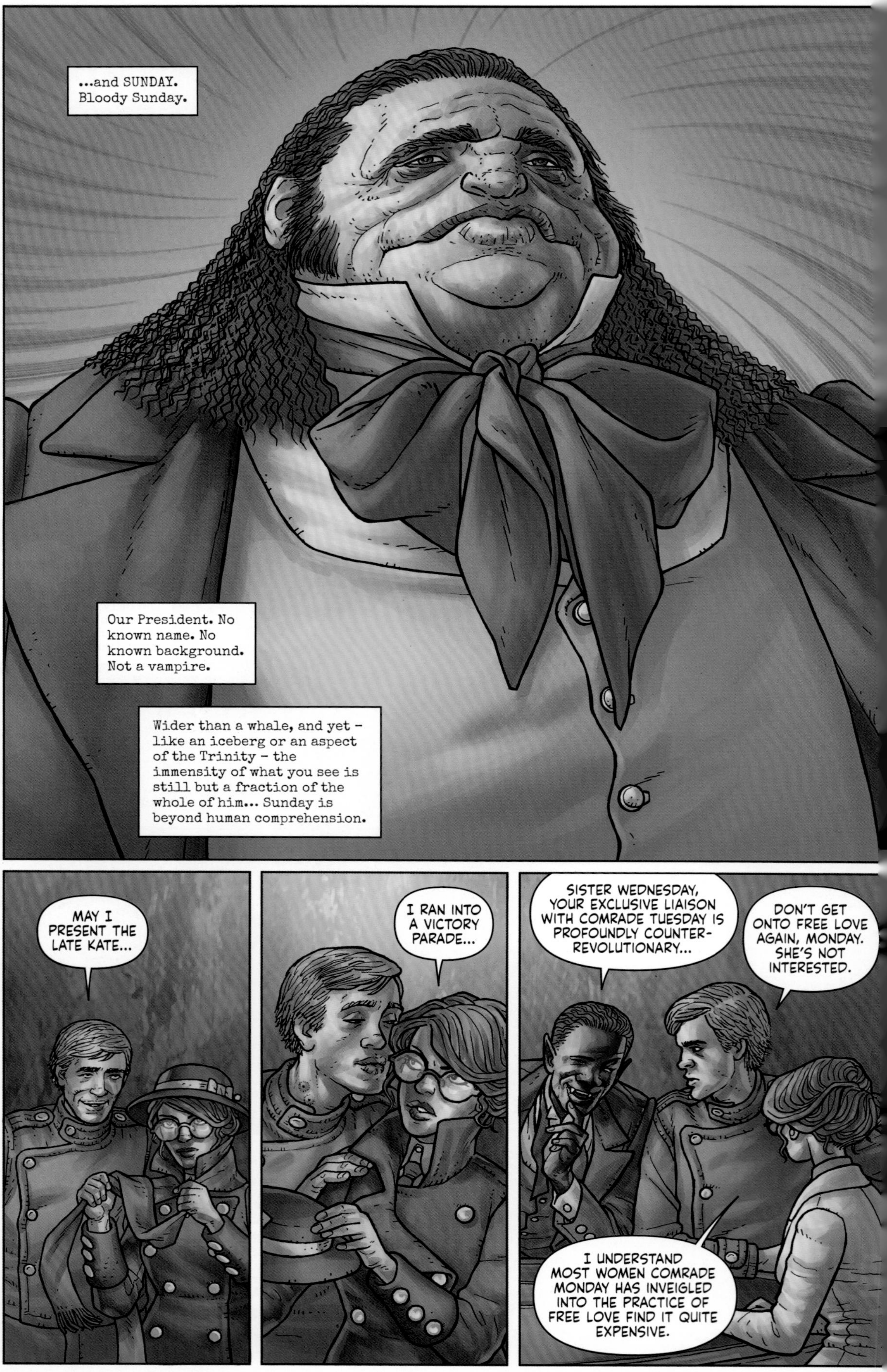
...and SUNDAY. Bloody Sunday.
Our President. No known name. No known background. Not a vampire.
Wider than a whale, and yet - like an iceberg or an aspect of the Trinity - the immensity of what you see is still but a fraction of the whole of him... Sunday is beyond human comprehension.
MAY I PRESENT THE LATE KATE...
I RAN INTO A VICTORY PARADE...
SISTER WEDNESDAY, YOUR EXCLUSIVE LIAISON WITH COMRADE TUESDAY IS PROFOUNDLY COUNTER-REVOLUTIONARY...
DON'T GET ONTO FREE LOVE AGAIN, MONDAY. SHE'S NOT INTERESTED.
I UNDERSTAND MOST WOMEN COMRADE MONDAY HAS INVEIGLED INTO THE PRACTICE OF FREE LOVE FIND IT QUITE EXPENSIVE.

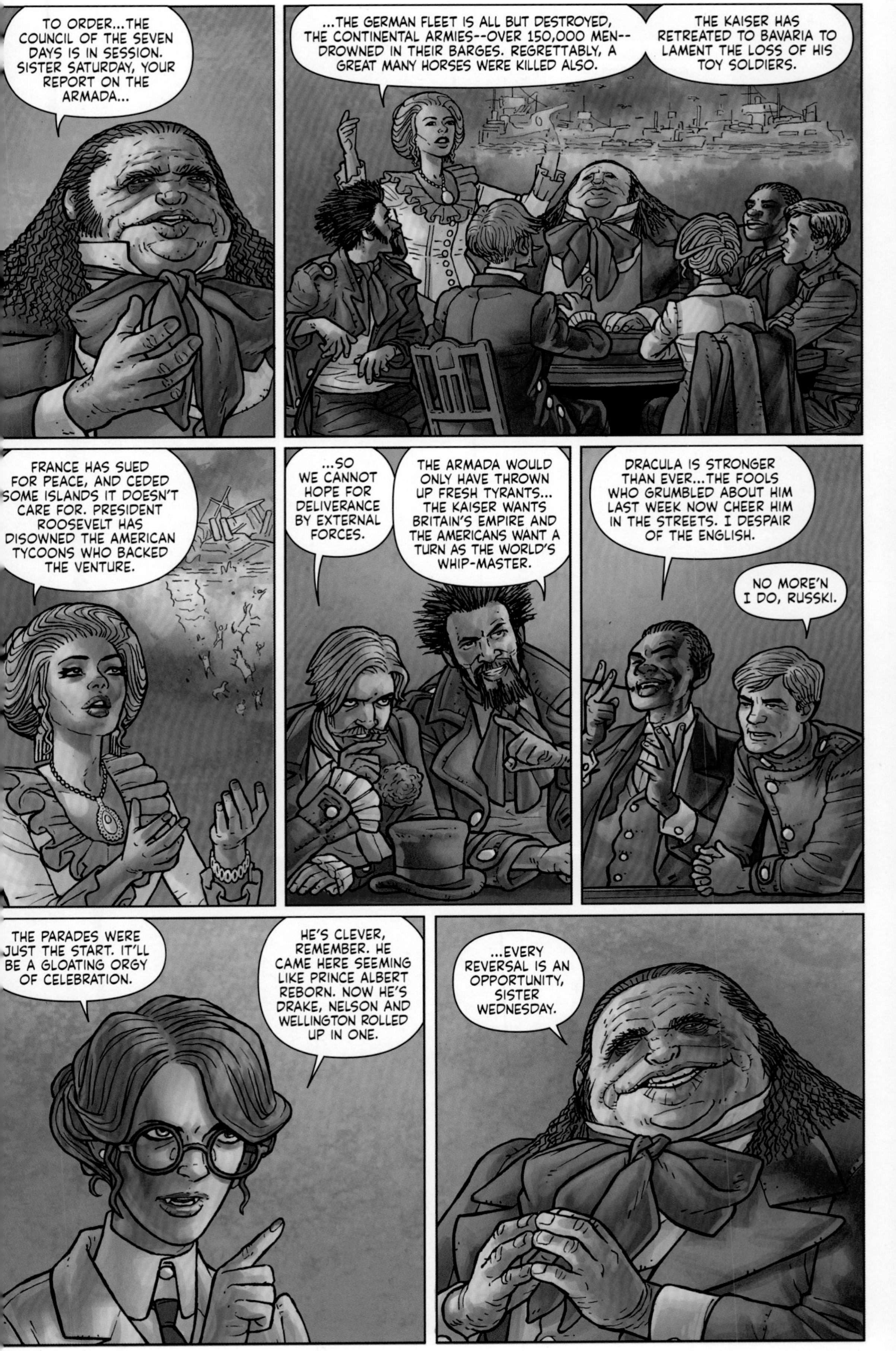
TO ORDER...THE COUNCIL OF THE SEVEN DAYS IS IN SESSION. SISTER SATURDAY, YOUR REPORT ON THE ARMADA...
...THE GERMAN FLEET IS ALL BUT DESTROYED, THE CONTINENTAL ARMIES--OVER 150,000 MEN--DROWNED IN THEIR BARGES. REGRETTABLY, A GREAT MANY HORSES WERE KILLED ALSO.
THE KAISER HAS RETREATED TO BAVARIA TO LAMENT THE LOSS OF HIS TOY SOLDIERS.
FRANCE HAS SUED FOR PEACE, AND CEDED SOME ISLANDS IT DOESN'T CARE FOR. PRESIDENT ROOSEVELT HAS DISOWNED THE AMERICAN TYCOONS WHO BACKED THE VENTURE.
...SO WE CANNOT HOPE FOR DELIVERANCE BY EXTERNAL FORCES.
THE ARMADA WOULD ONLY HAVE THROWN UP FRESH TYRANTS... THE KAISER WANTS BRITAIN'S EMPIRE AND THE AMERICANS WANT A TURN AS THE WORLD'S WHIP-MASTER.
DRACULA IS STRONGER THAN EVER...THE FOOLS WHO GRUMBLED ABOUT HIM LAST WEEK NOW CHEER HIM IN THE STREETS. I DESPAIR OF THE ENGLISH.
NO MORE'N I DO, RUSSKI.
THE PARADES WERE JUST THE START. IT'LL BE A GLOATING ORGY OF CELEBRATION.
HE'S CLEVER, REMEMBER. HE CAME HERE SEEMING LIKE PRINCE ALBERT REBORN. NOW HE'S DRAKE, NELSON AND WELLINGTON ROLLED UP IN ONE.
...EVERY REVERSAL IS AN OPPORTUNITY, SISTER WEDNESDAY.

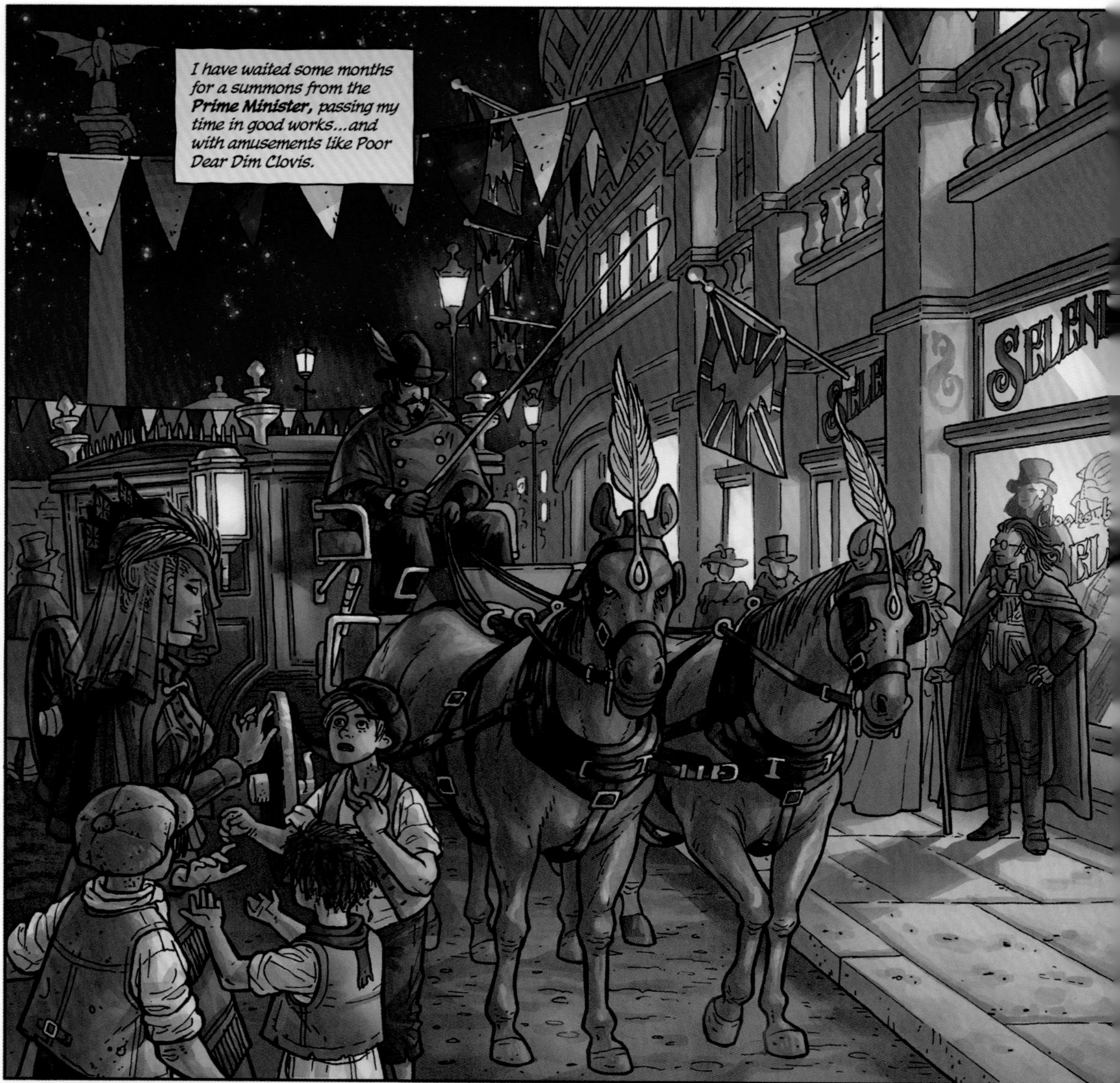
I have waited some months for a summons from the **Prime Minister,** passing my time in good works...and with amusements like Poor Dear Dim Clovis.

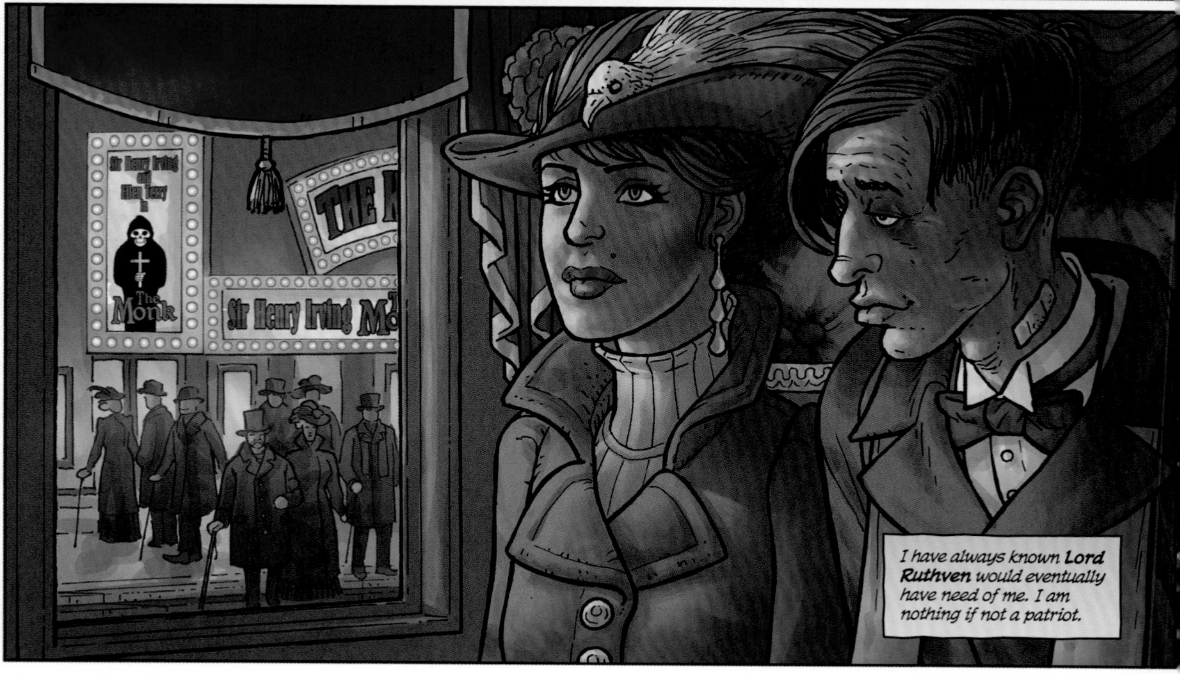
Sir Henry Irving and Ellen Terry in
The Monk
Sir Henry Irving
I have always known **Lord Ruthven** would eventually have need of me. I am nothing if not a patriot.

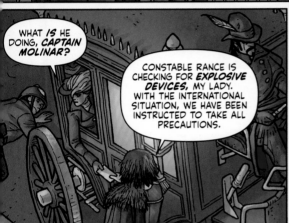

WHAT *IS* HE DOING, *CAPTAIN MOLINAR?*

CONSTABLE RANCE IS CHECKING FOR *EXPLOSIVE DEVICES,* MY LADY. WITH THE INTERNATIONAL SITUATION, WE HAVE BEEN INSTRUCTED TO TAKE ALL PRECAUTIONS.

I DOUBT THE KAISER IS FOOLISH ENOUGH TO TRY TO BLOW UP LORD RUTHVEN.

IT'S NOT KAISER BILL 'E'S WORRIED ABOUT, MISS. IT'S 'IS OWN BACK-BENCHERS.

CLOVIS, STAY...AND TRY NOT TO GET DYNAMITED.

⫽HIC⫽ G'NIGHT, PENNY.

GOOD EVENING, *DIBDIN.*

GOOD EVENING, MA'AM.

GOOD GRIEF--A *SHOT!*

BLAM

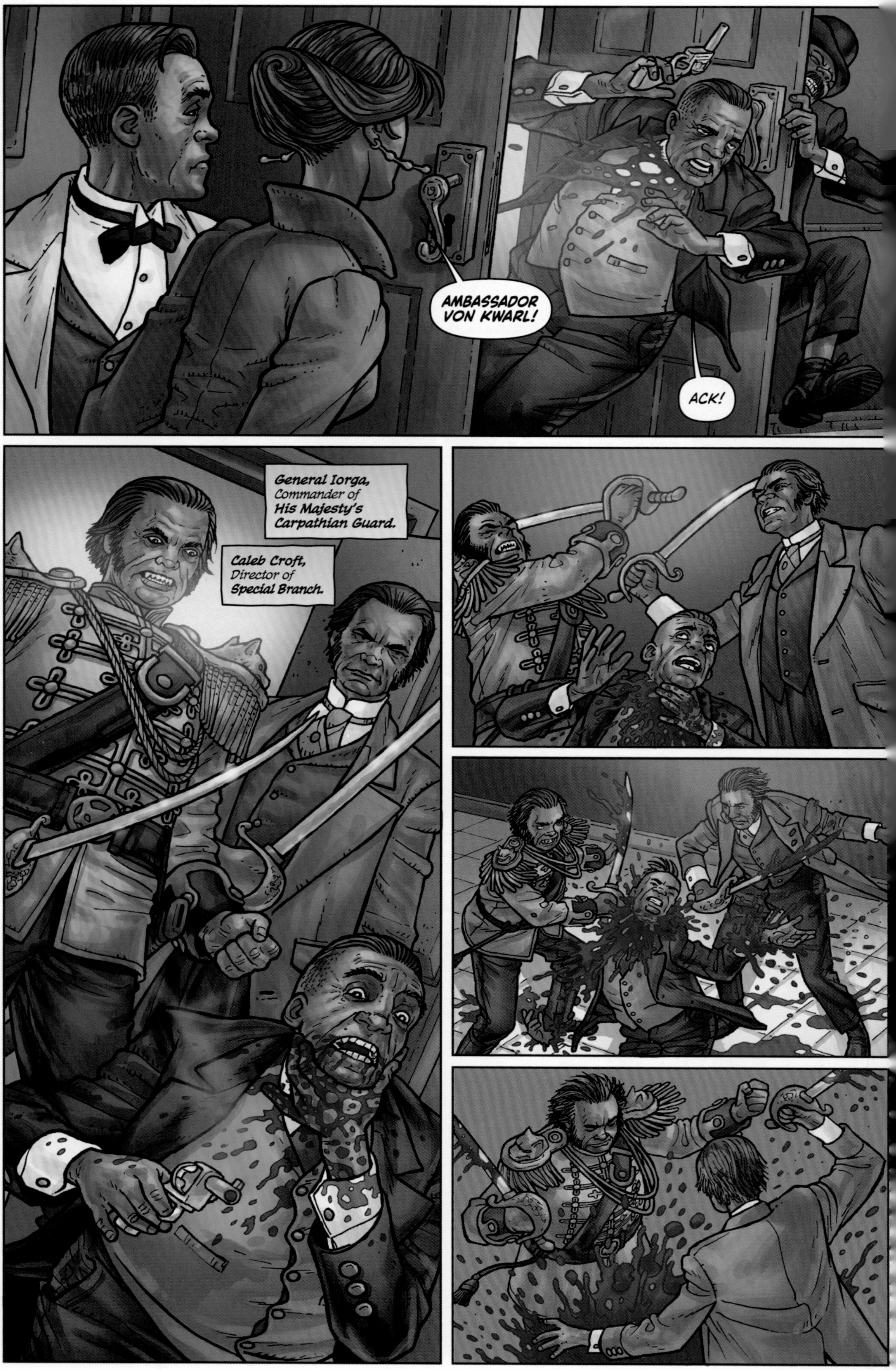
AMBASSADOR VON KWARL!
ACK!
General Iorga, Commander of His Majesty's Carpathian Guard.
Caleb Croft, Director of Special Branch.

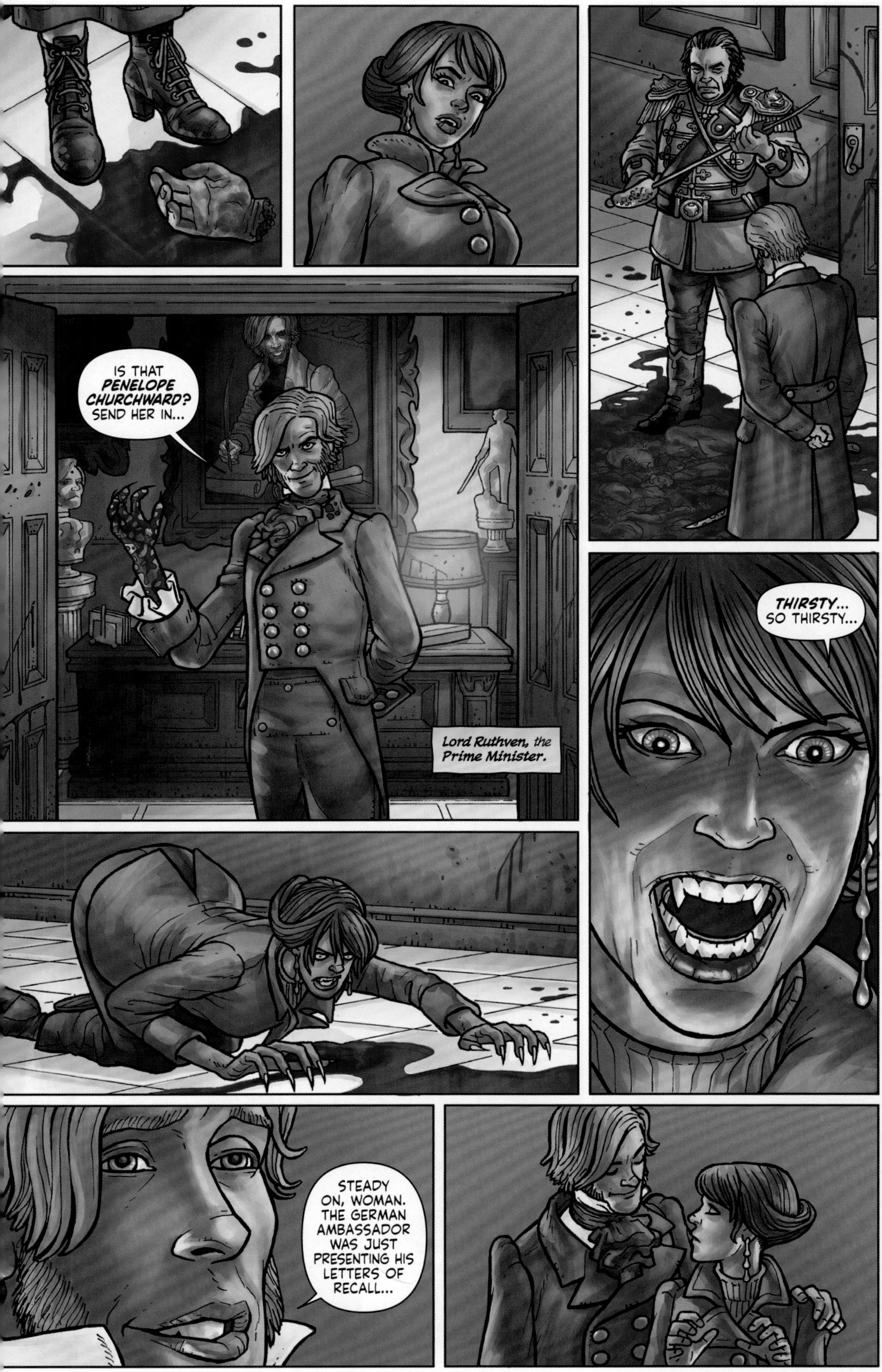
IS THAT *PENELOPE CHURCHWARD?* SEND HER IN...
Lord Ruthven, the Prime Minister.
THIRSTY... SO THIRSTY...
STEADY ON, WOMAN. THE GERMAN AMBASSADOR WAS JUST PRESENTING HIS LETTERS OF RECALL...

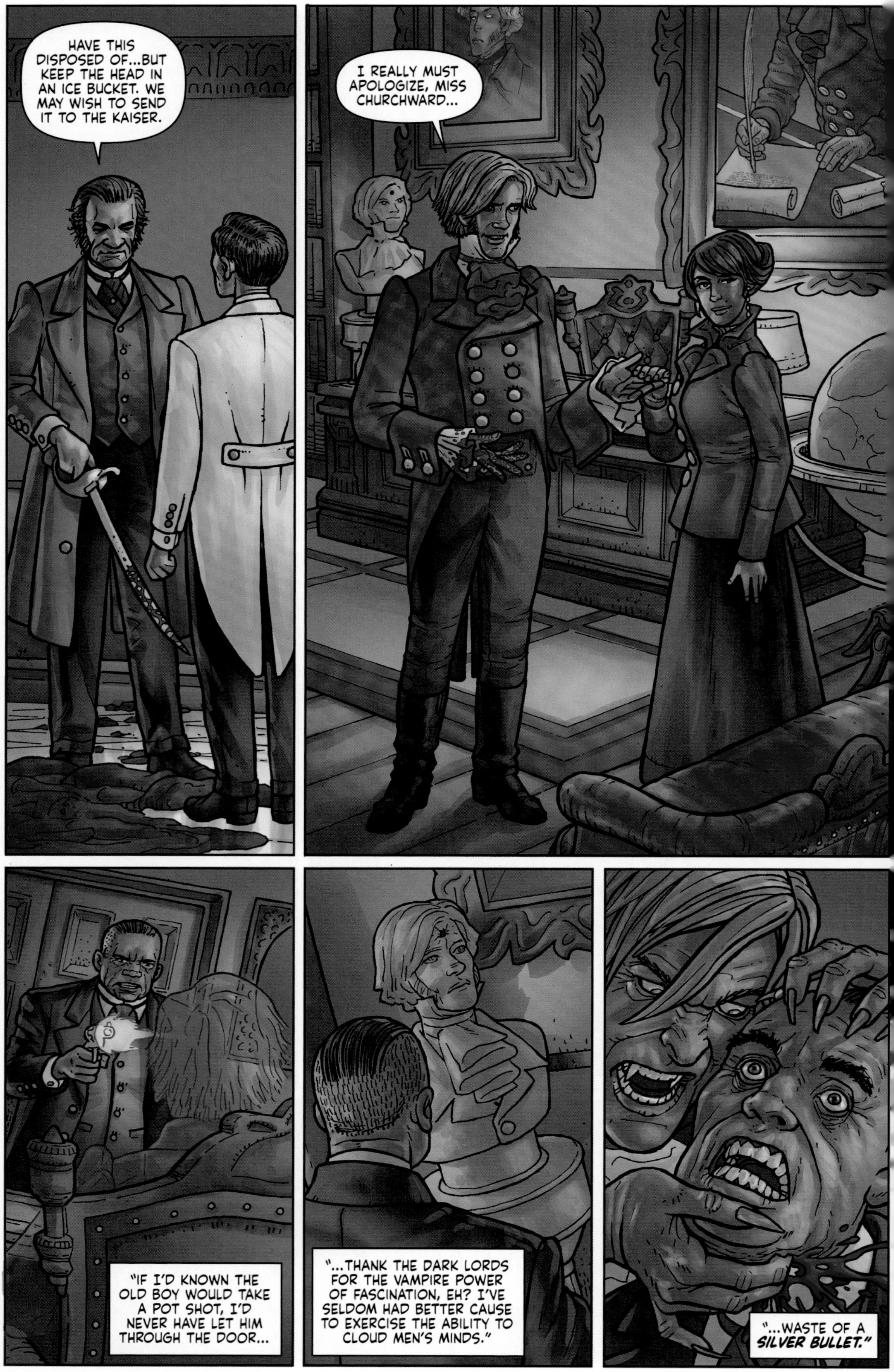
HAVE THIS DISPOSED OF...BUT KEEP THE HEAD IN AN ICE BUCKET. WE MAY WISH TO SEND IT TO THE KAISER.
I REALLY MUST APOLOGIZE, MISS CHURCHWARD...
"IF I'D KNOWN THE OLD BOY WOULD TAKE A POT SHOT, I'D NEVER HAVE LET HIM THROUGH THE DOOR...
"...THANK THE DARK LORDS FOR THE VAMPIRE POWER OF FASCINATION, EH? I'VE SELDOM HAD BETTER CAUSE TO EXERCISE THE ABILITY TO CLOUD MEN'S MINDS."
"...WASTE OF A *SILVER BULLET.*"

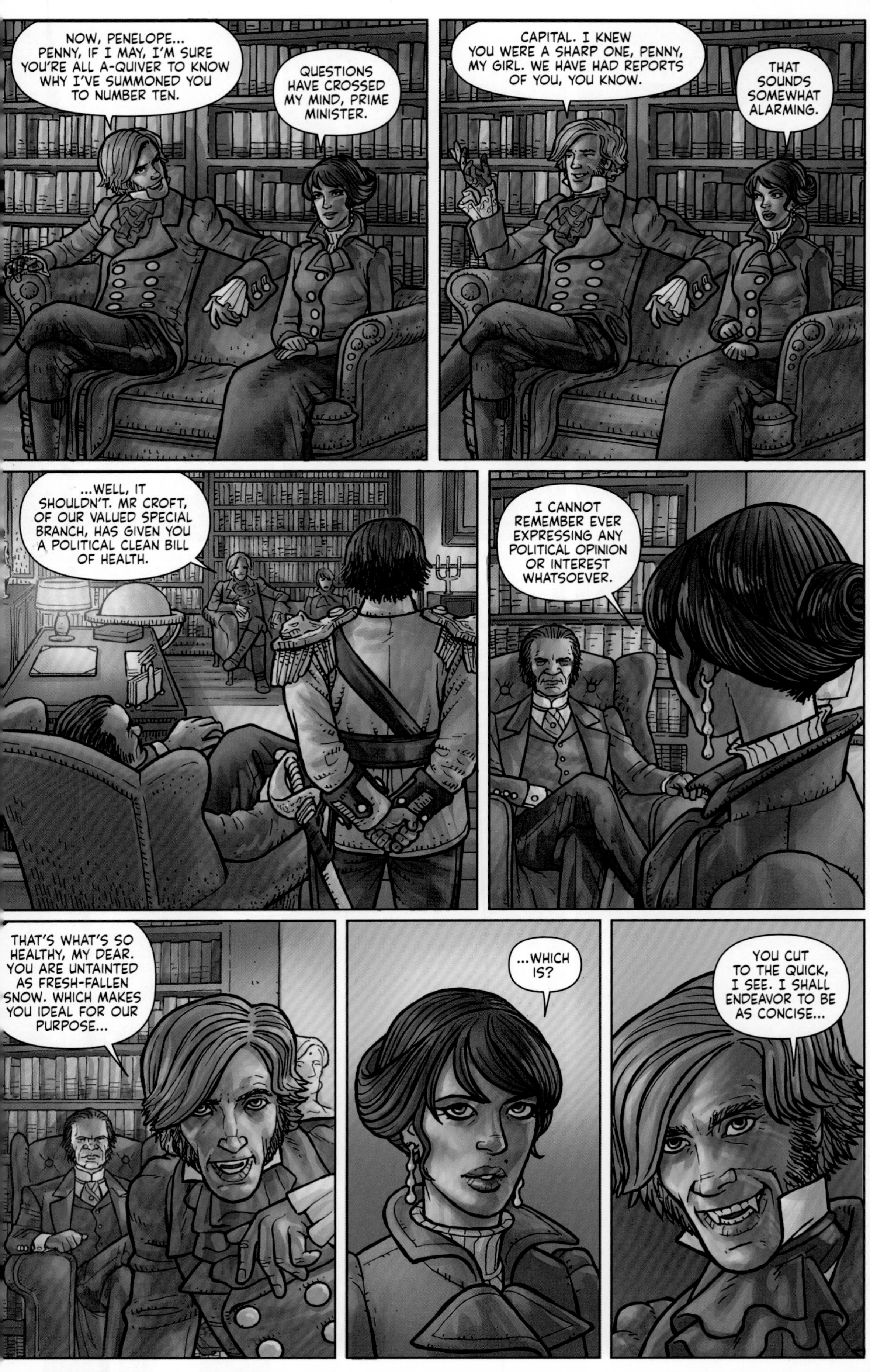
NOW, PENELOPE... PENNY, IF I MAY, I'M SURE YOU'RE ALL A-QUIVER TO KNOW WHY I'VE SUMMONED YOU TO NUMBER TEN.
QUESTIONS HAVE CROSSED MY MIND, PRIME MINISTER.
CAPITAL. I KNEW YOU WERE A SHARP ONE, PENNY, MY GIRL. WE HAVE HAD REPORTS OF YOU, YOU KNOW.
THAT SOUNDS SOMEWHAT ALARMING.
...WELL, IT SHOULDN'T. MR CROFT, OF OUR VALUED SPECIAL BRANCH, HAS GIVEN YOU A POLITICAL CLEAN BILL OF HEALTH.
I CANNOT REMEMBER EVER EXPRESSING ANY POLITICAL OPINION OR INTEREST WHATSOEVER.
THAT'S WHAT'S SO HEALTHY, MY DEAR. YOU ARE UNTAINTED AS FRESH-FALLEN SNOW. WHICH MAKES YOU IDEAL FOR OUR PURPOSE...
...WHICH IS?
YOU CUT TO THE QUICK, I SEE. I SHALL ENDEAVOR TO BE AS CONCISE...

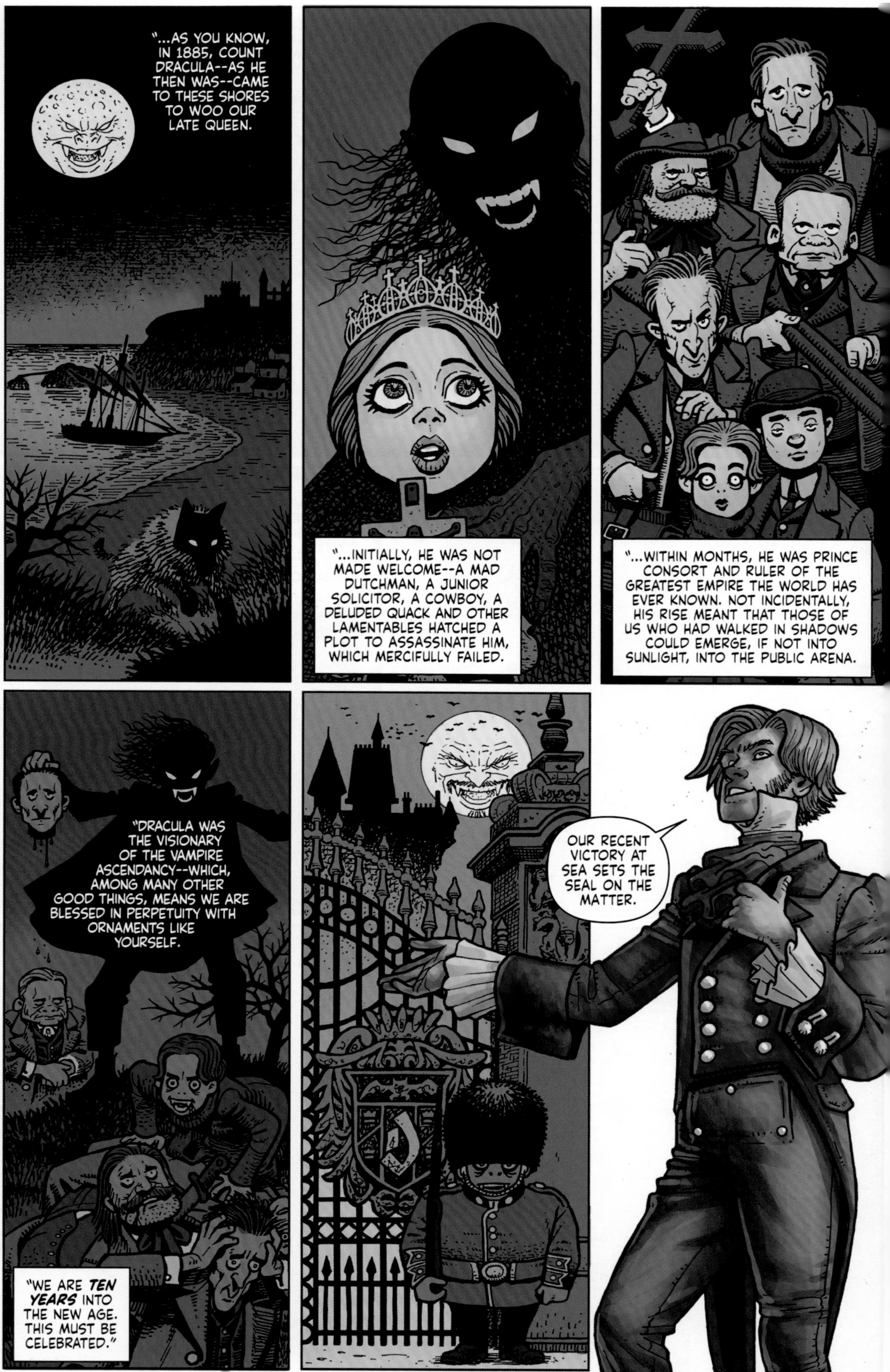
"...AS YOU KNOW, IN 1885, COUNT DRACULA--AS HE THEN WAS--CAME TO THESE SHORES TO WOO OUR LATE QUEEN.
"...INITIALLY, HE WAS NOT MADE WELCOME--A MAD DUTCHMAN, A JUNIOR SOLICITOR, A COWBOY, A DELUDED QUACK AND OTHER LAMENTABLES HATCHED A PLOT TO ASSASSINATE HIM, WHICH MERCIFULLY FAILED.
"...WITHIN MONTHS, HE WAS PRINCE CONSORT AND RULER OF THE GREATEST EMPIRE THE WORLD HAS EVER KNOWN. NOT INCIDENTALLY, HIS RISE MEANT THAT THOSE OF US WHO HAD WALKED IN SHADOWS COULD EMERGE, IF NOT INTO SUNLIGHT, INTO THE PUBLIC ARENA.
"DRACULA WAS THE VISIONARY OF THE VAMPIRE ASCENDANCY--WHICH, AMONG MANY OTHER GOOD THINGS, MEANS WE ARE BLESSED IN PERPETUITY WITH ORNAMENTS LIKE YOURSELF.
"WE ARE ***TEN YEARS*** INTO THE NEW AGE. THIS MUST BE CELEBRATED."
OUR RECENT VICTORY AT SEA SETS THE SEAL ON THE MATTER.

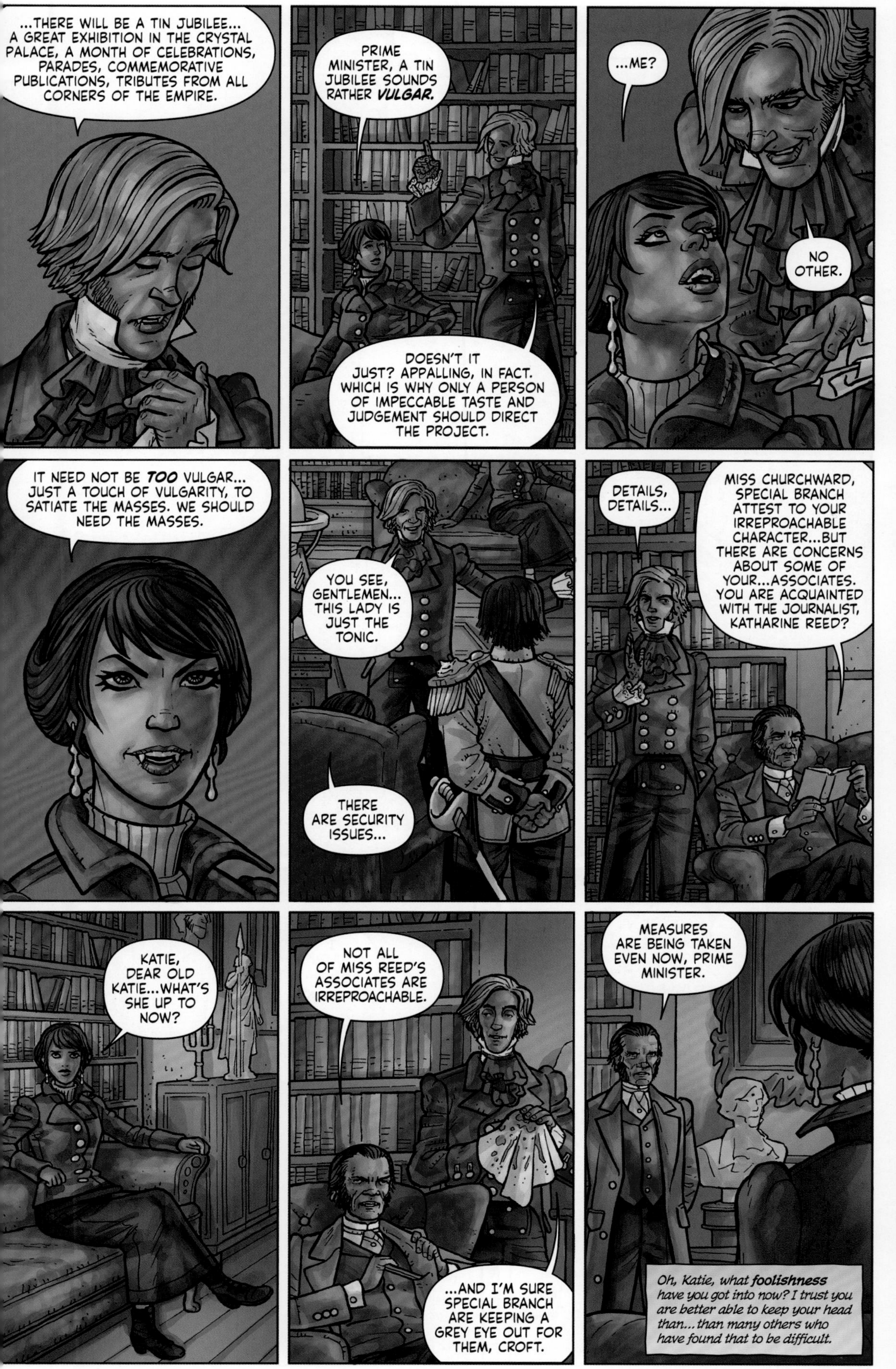
...THERE WILL BE A TIN JUBILEE... A GREAT EXHIBITION IN THE CRYSTAL PALACE, A MONTH OF CELEBRATIONS, PARADES, COMMEMORATIVE PUBLICATIONS, TRIBUTES FROM ALL CORNERS OF THE EMPIRE.
PRIME MINISTER, A TIN JUBILEE SOUNDS RATHER *VULGAR.*
DOESN'T IT JUST? APPALLING, IN FACT. WHICH IS WHY ONLY A PERSON OF IMPECCABLE TASTE AND JUDGEMENT SHOULD DIRECT THE PROJECT.
...ME?
NO OTHER.
IT NEED NOT BE *TOO* VULGAR... JUST A TOUCH OF VULGARITY, TO SATIATE THE MASSES. WE SHOULD NEED THE MASSES.
YOU SEE, GENTLEMEN... THIS LADY IS JUST THE TONIC.
THERE ARE SECURITY ISSUES...
DETAILS, DETAILS...
MISS CHURCHWARD, SPECIAL BRANCH ATTEST TO YOUR IRREPROACHABLE CHARACTER...BUT THERE ARE CONCERNS ABOUT SOME OF YOUR...ASSOCIATES. YOU ARE ACQUAINTED WITH THE JOURNALIST, KATHARINE REED?
KATIE, DEAR OLD KATIE...WHAT'S SHE UP TO NOW?
NOT ALL OF MISS REED'S ASSOCIATES ARE IRREPROACHABLE.
...AND I'M SURE SPECIAL BRANCH ARE KEEPING A GREY EYE OUT FOR THEM, CROFT.
MEASURES ARE BEING TAKEN EVEN NOW, PRIME MINISTER.
*Oh, Katie, what **foolishness** have you got into now? I trust you are better able to keep your head than... than many others who have found that to be difficult.*

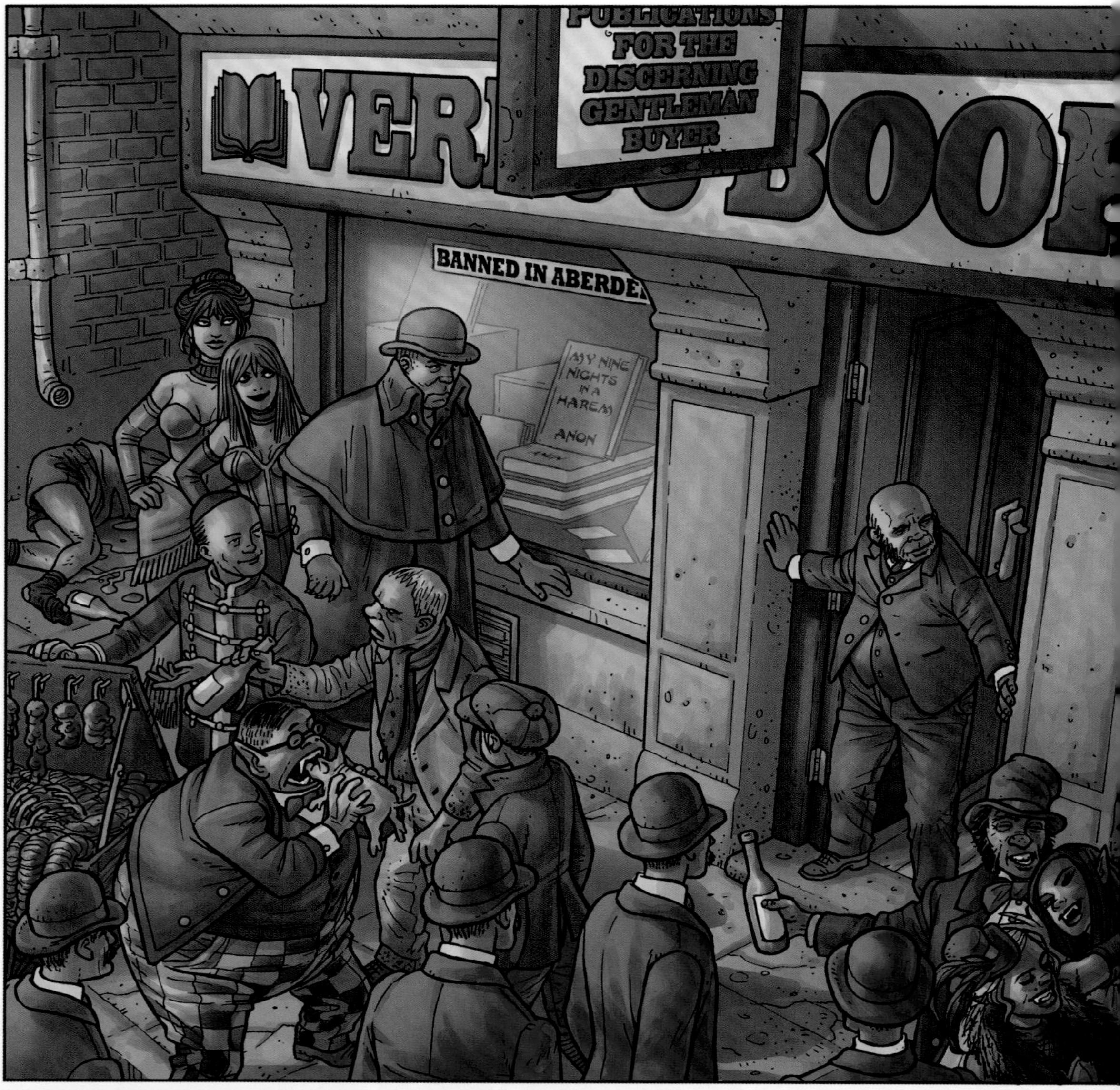
PUBLICATIONS FOR THE DISCERNING GENTLEMAN BUYER
VER
BOO
BANNED IN ABERDE
MY NINE NIGHTS IN A HAREM
ANON

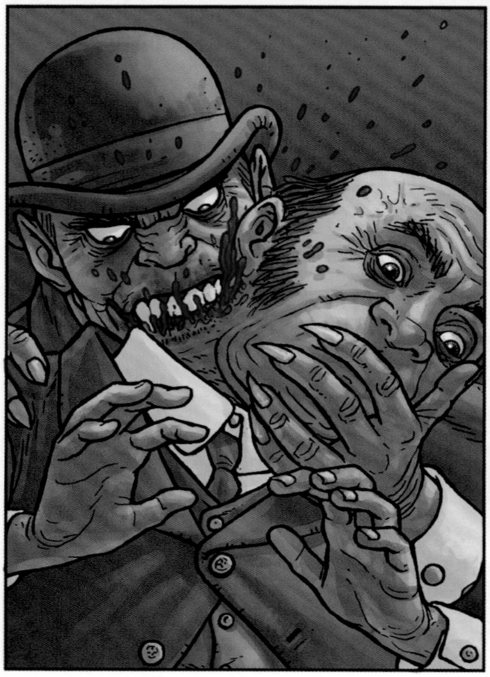

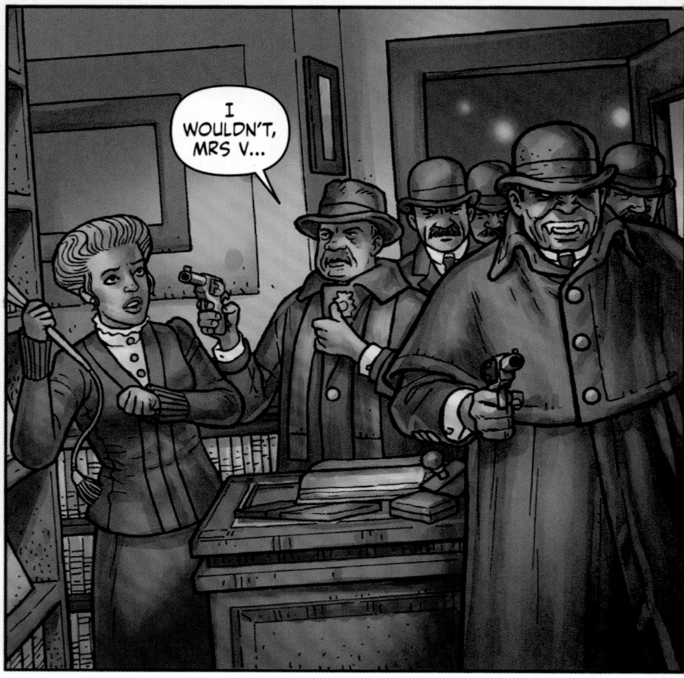
I WOULDN'T, MRS V...

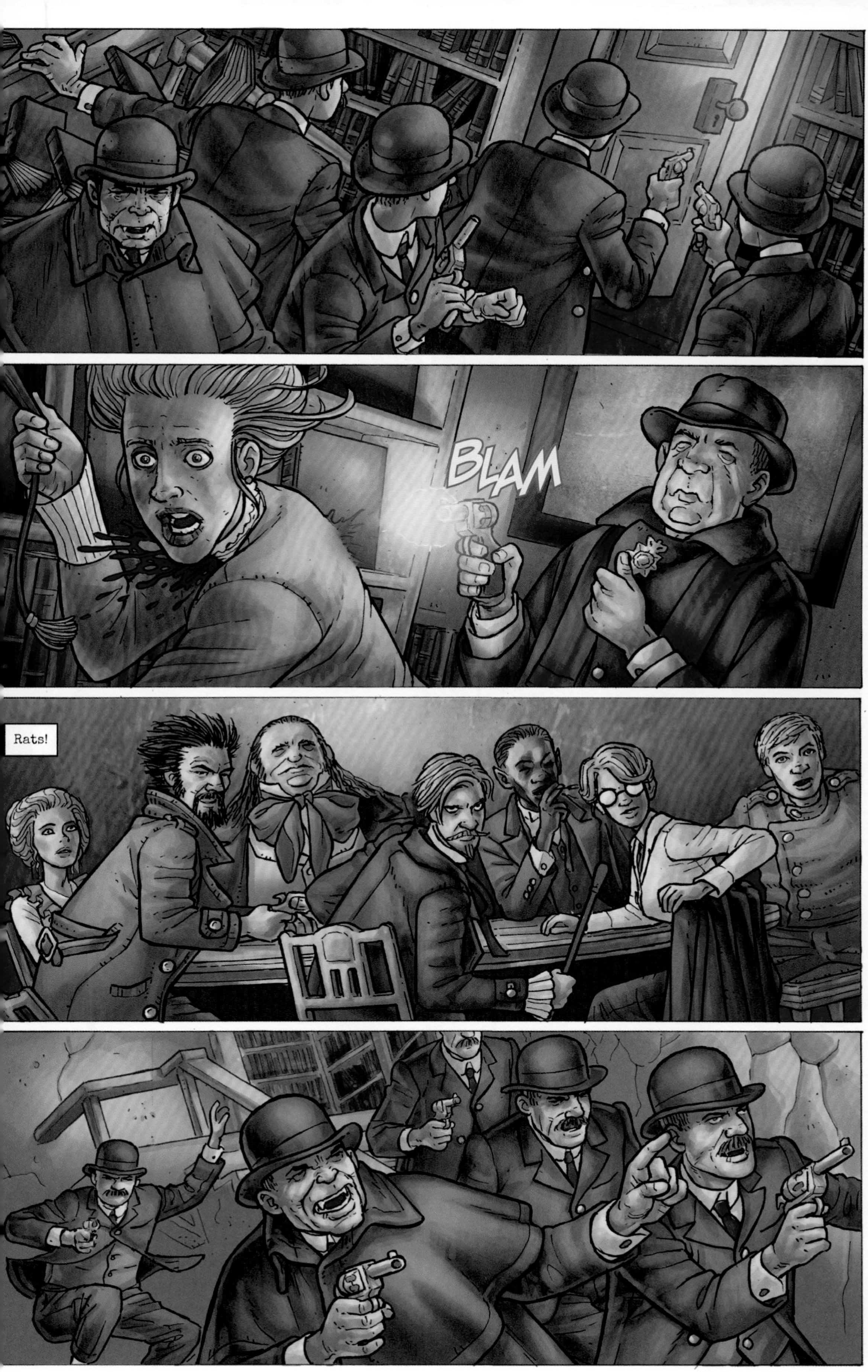
BLAM
Rats!

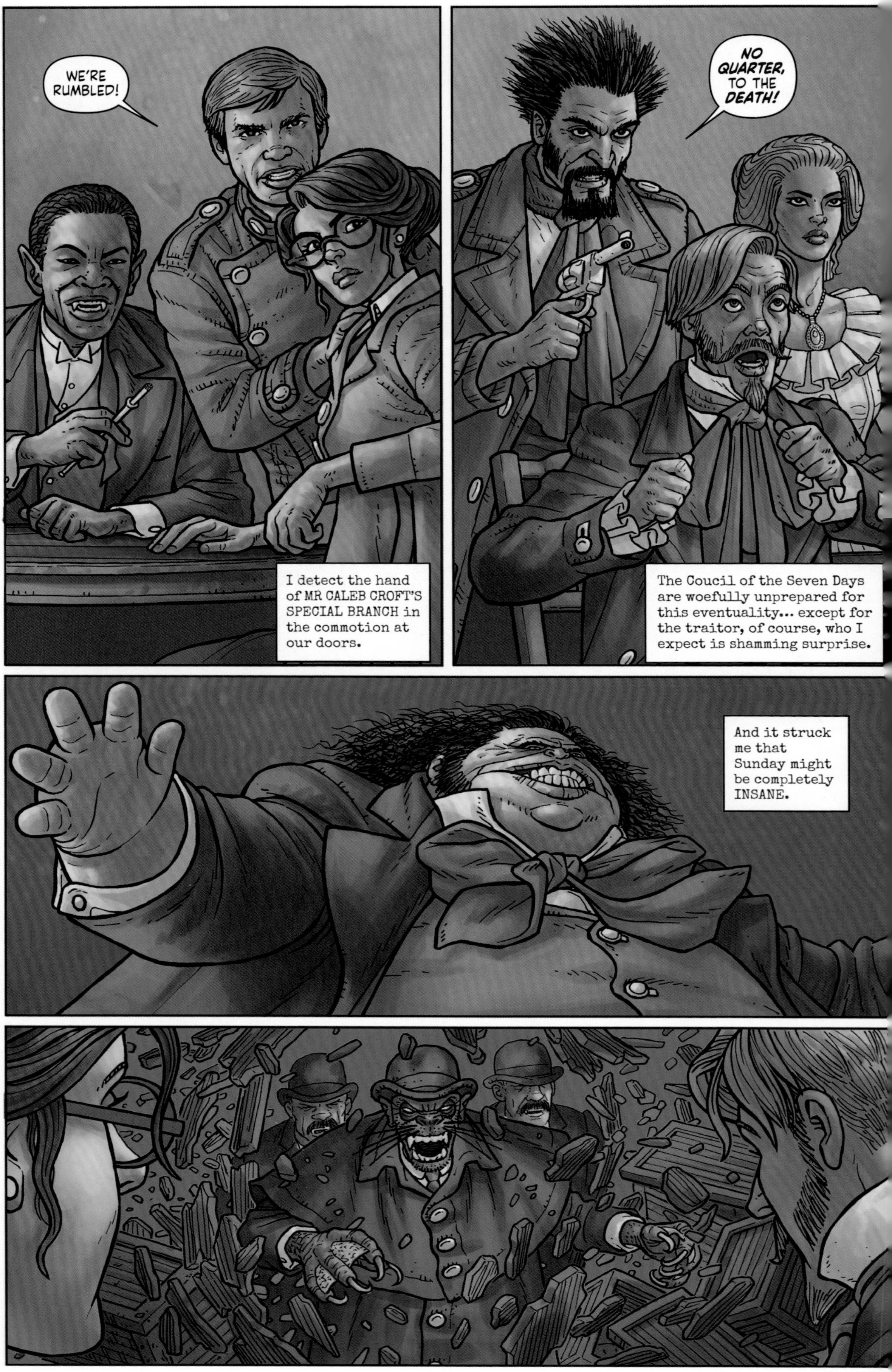
WE'RE RUMBLED!
I detect the hand of MR CALEB CROFT'S SPECIAL BRANCH in the commotion at our doors.
NO QUARTER, TO THE DEATH!
The Coucil of the Seven Days are woefully unprepared for this eventuality... except for the traitor, of course, who I expect is shamming surprise.
And it struck me that Sunday might be completely INSANE.

CHAPTER TWO

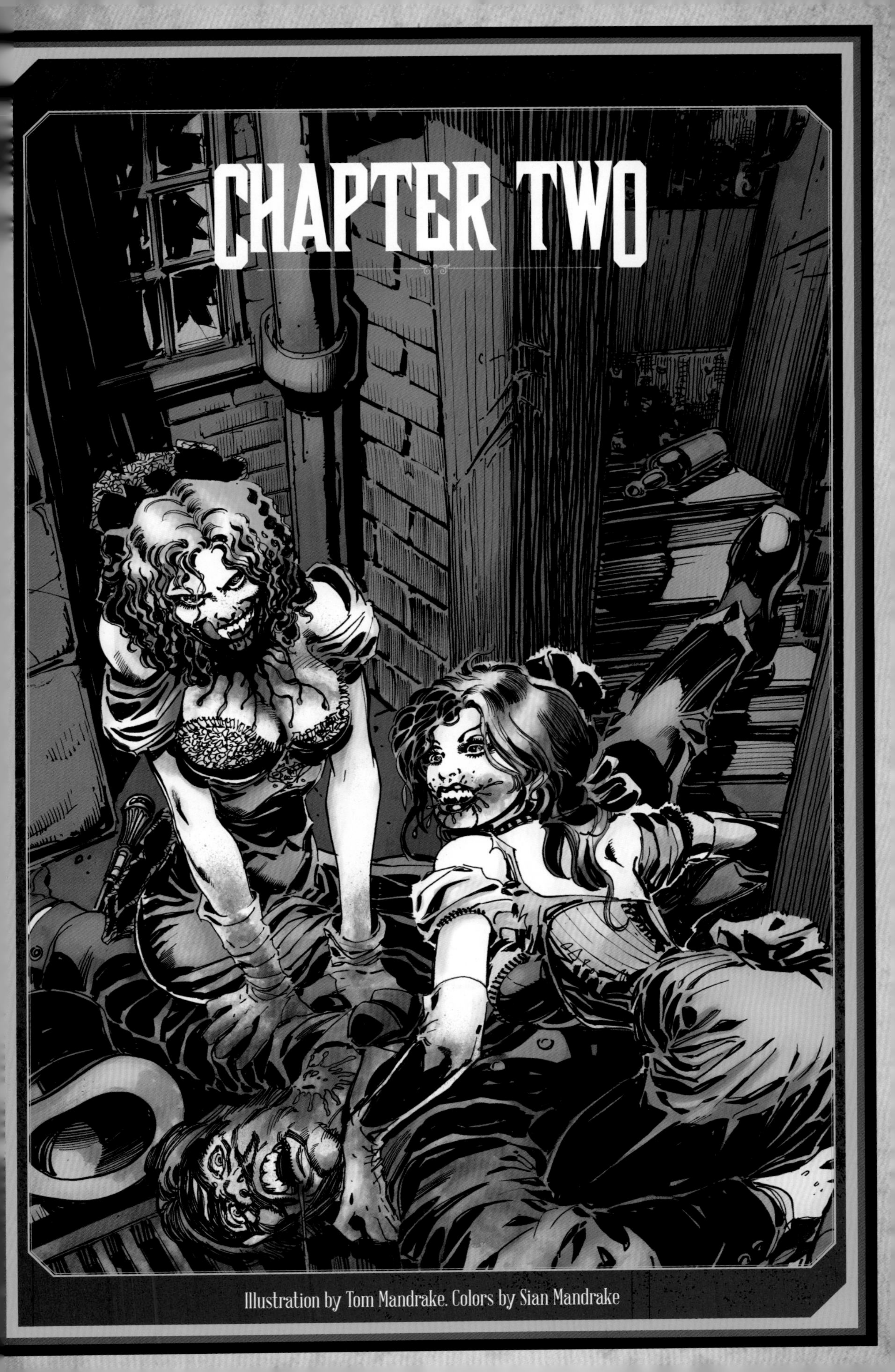

Illustration by Tom Mandrake. Colors by Sian Mandrake

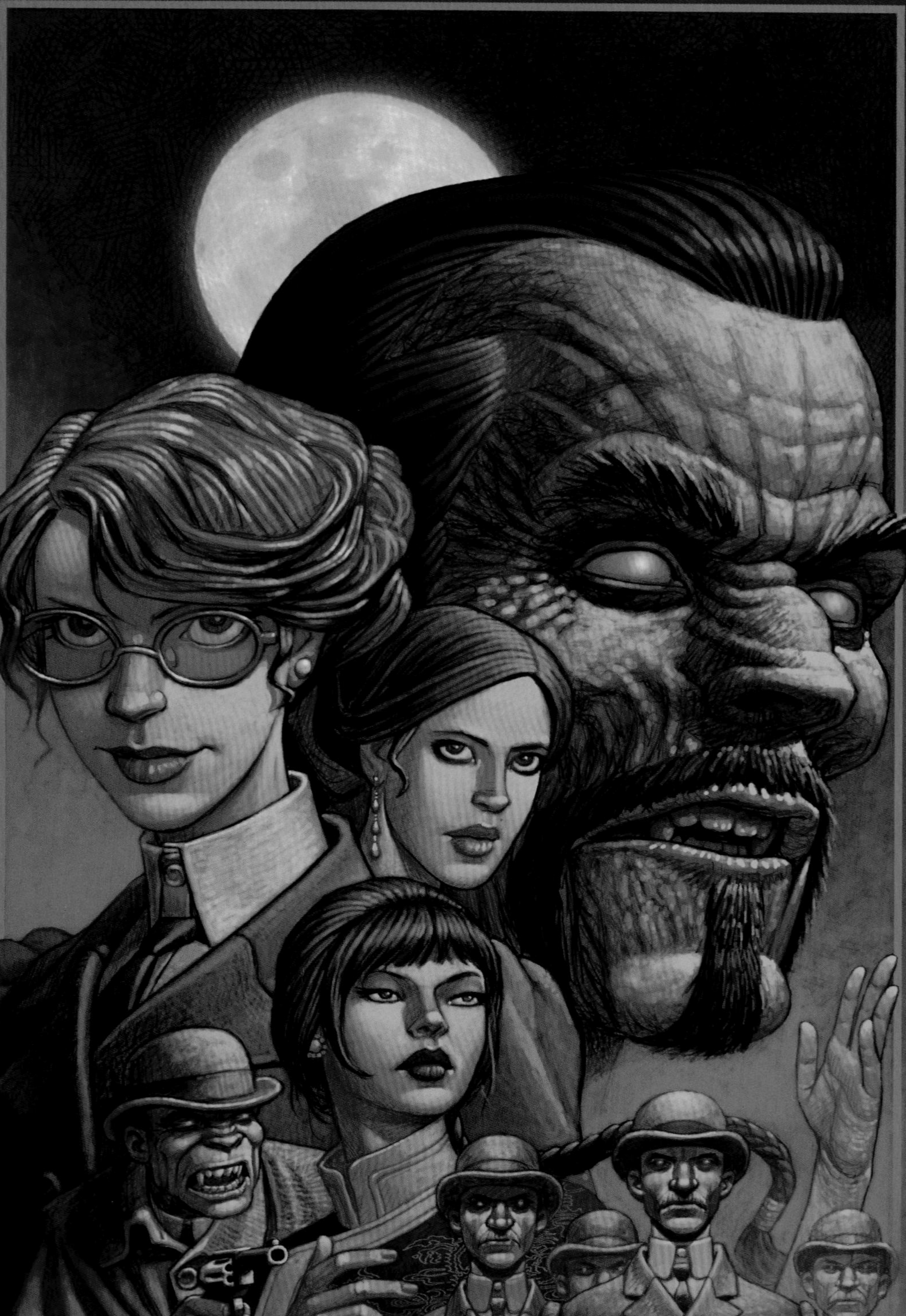

Illustration by Paul McCaffrey

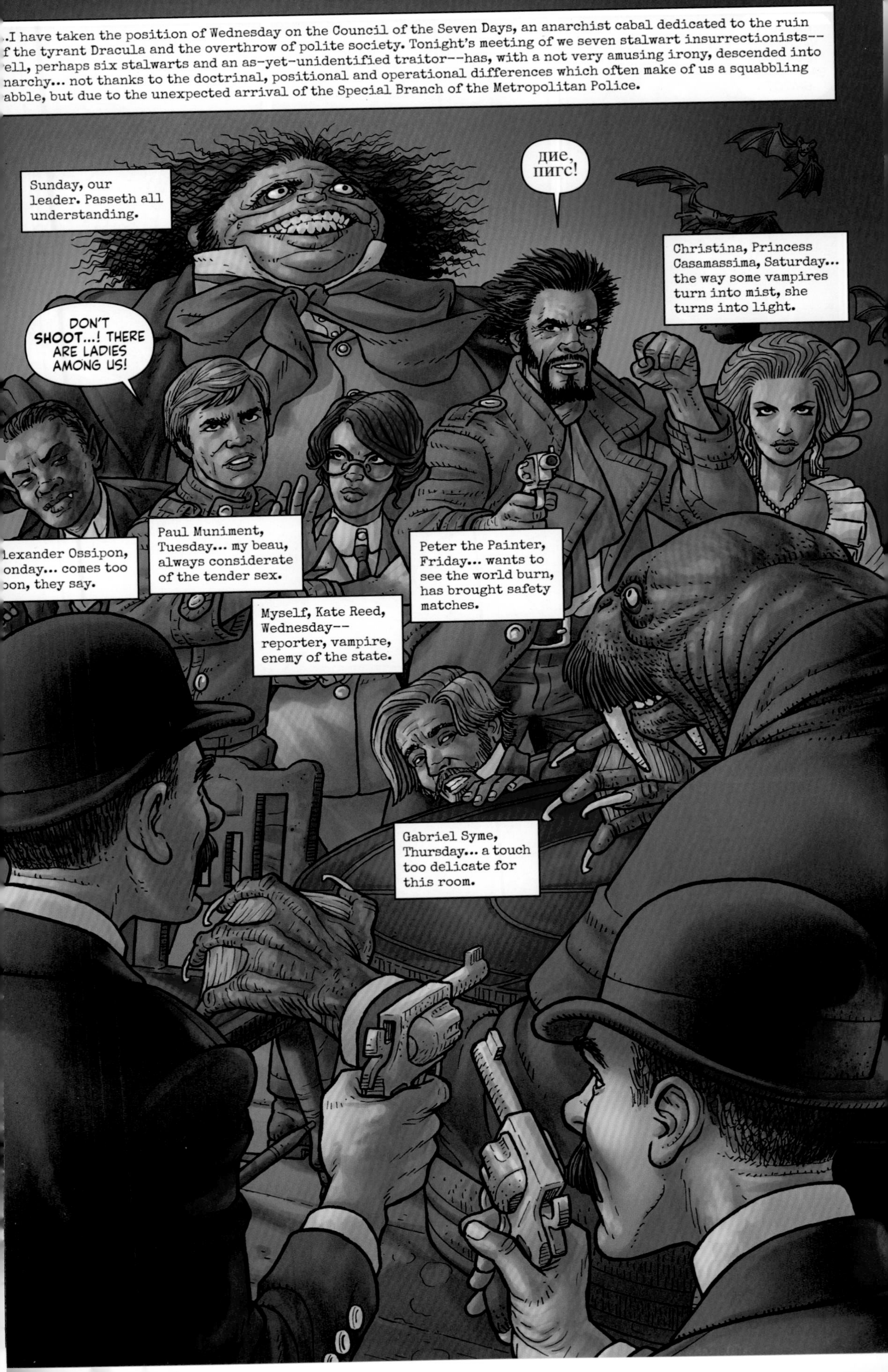
.I have taken the position of Wednesday on the Council of the Seven Days, an anarchist cabal dedicated to the ruin f the tyrant Dracula and the overthrow of polite society. Tonight's meeting of we seven stalwart insurrectionists--ell, perhaps six stalwarts and an as-yet-unidentified traitor--has, with a not very amusing irony, descended into narchy... not thanks to the doctrinal, positional and operational differences which often make of us a squabbling abble, but due to the unexpected arrival of the Special Branch of the Metropolitan Police.
Sunday, our leader. Passeth all understanding.
дие, пигс!
Christina, Princess Casamassima, Saturday... the way some vampires turn into mist, she turns into light.
DON'T SHOOT...! THERE ARE LADIES AMONG US!
lexander Ossipon, onday... comes too oon, they say.
Paul Muniment, Tuesday... my beau, always considerate of the tender sex.
Peter the Painter, Friday... wants to see the world burn, has brought safety matches.
Myself, Kate Reed, Wednesday--reporter, vampire, enemy of the state.
Gabriel Syme, Thursday... a touch too delicate for this room.

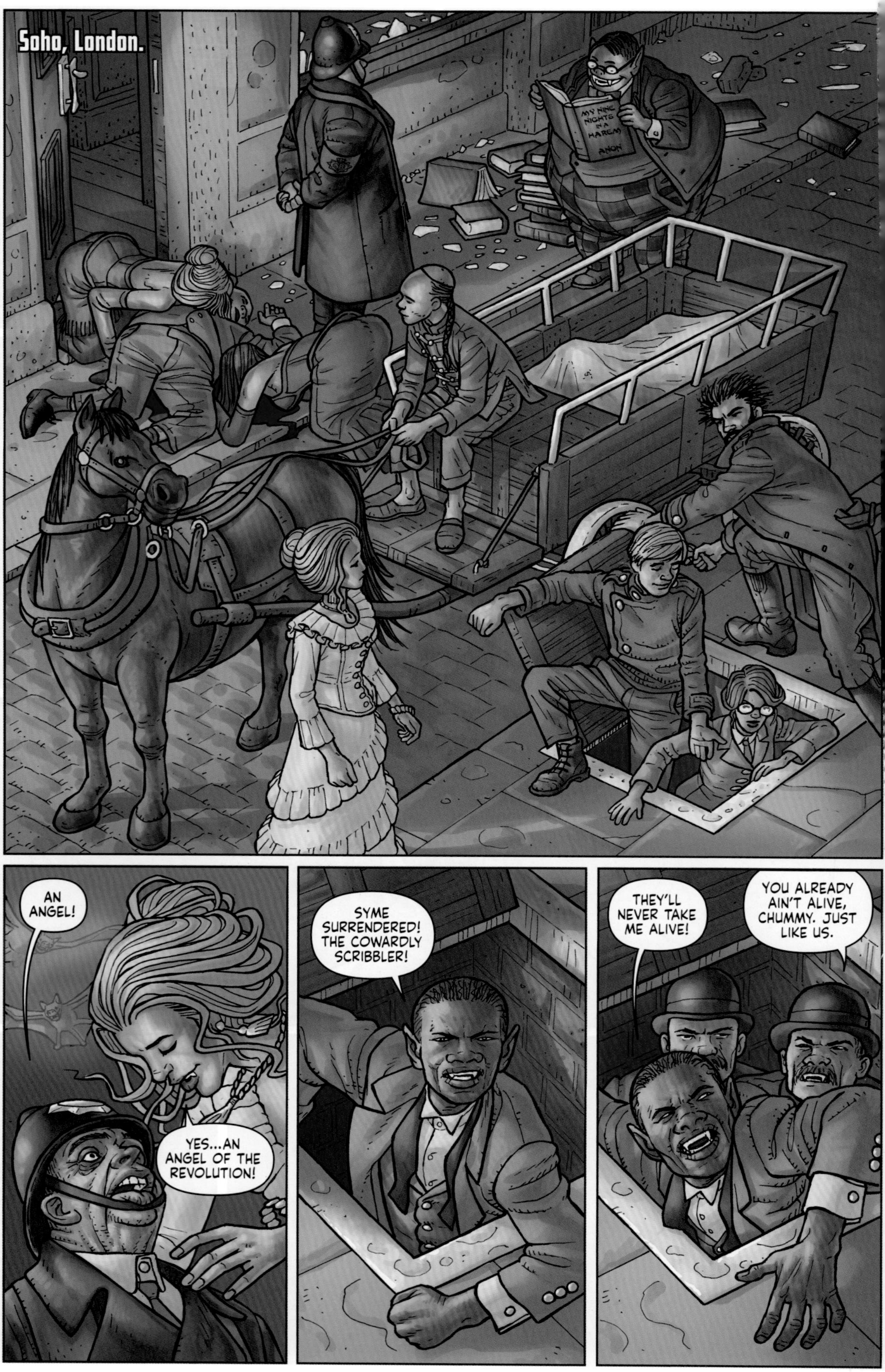
Soho, London.
MY NINE NIGHTS IN A HAREM
ANON
AN ANGEL!
YES...AN ANGEL OF THE REVOLUTION!
SYME SURRENDERED! THE COWARDLY SCRIBBLER!
THEY'LL NEVER TAKE ME ALIVE!
YOU ALREADY AIN'T ALIVE, CHUMMY. JUST LIKE US.

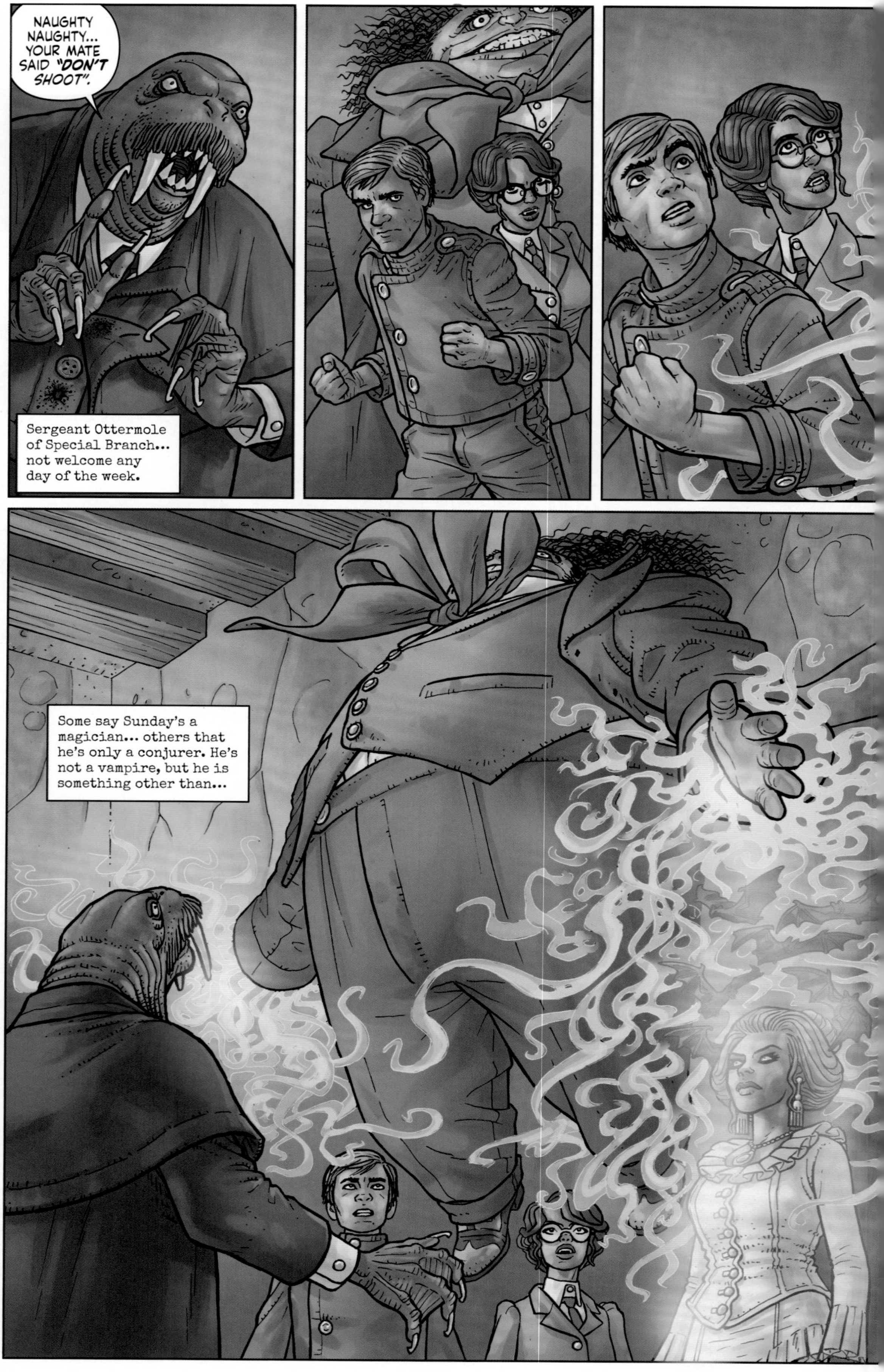
NAUGHTY NAUGHTY... YOUR MATE SAID "DON'T SHOOT".
Sergeant Ottermole of Special Branch... not welcome any day of the week.
Some say Sunday's a magician... others that he's only a conjurer. He's not a vampire, but he is something other than...

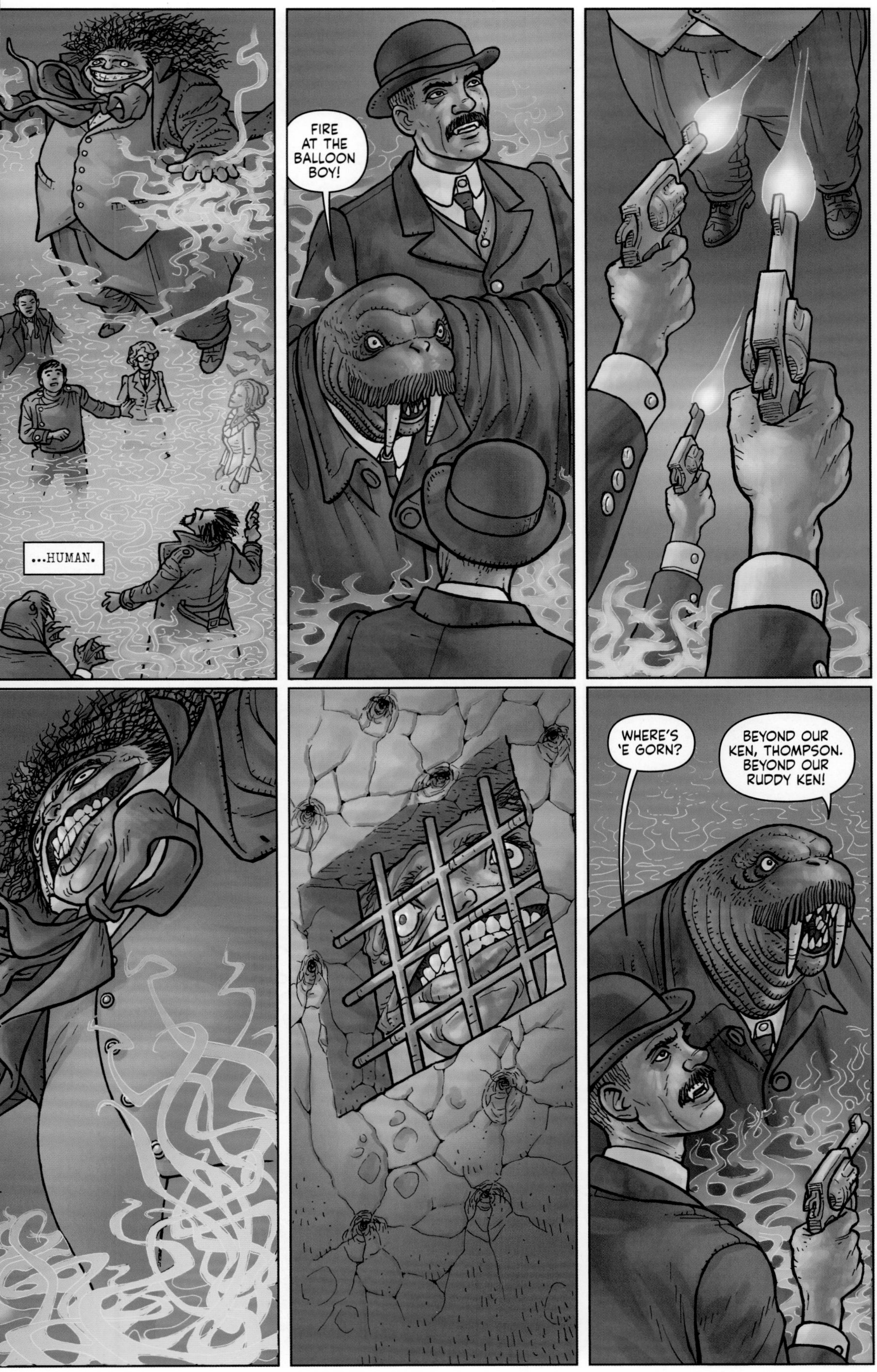
...HUMAN.
FIRE AT THE BALLOON BOY!
WHERE'S 'E GORN?
BEYOND OUR KEN, THOMPSON. BEYOND OUR RUDDY KEN!

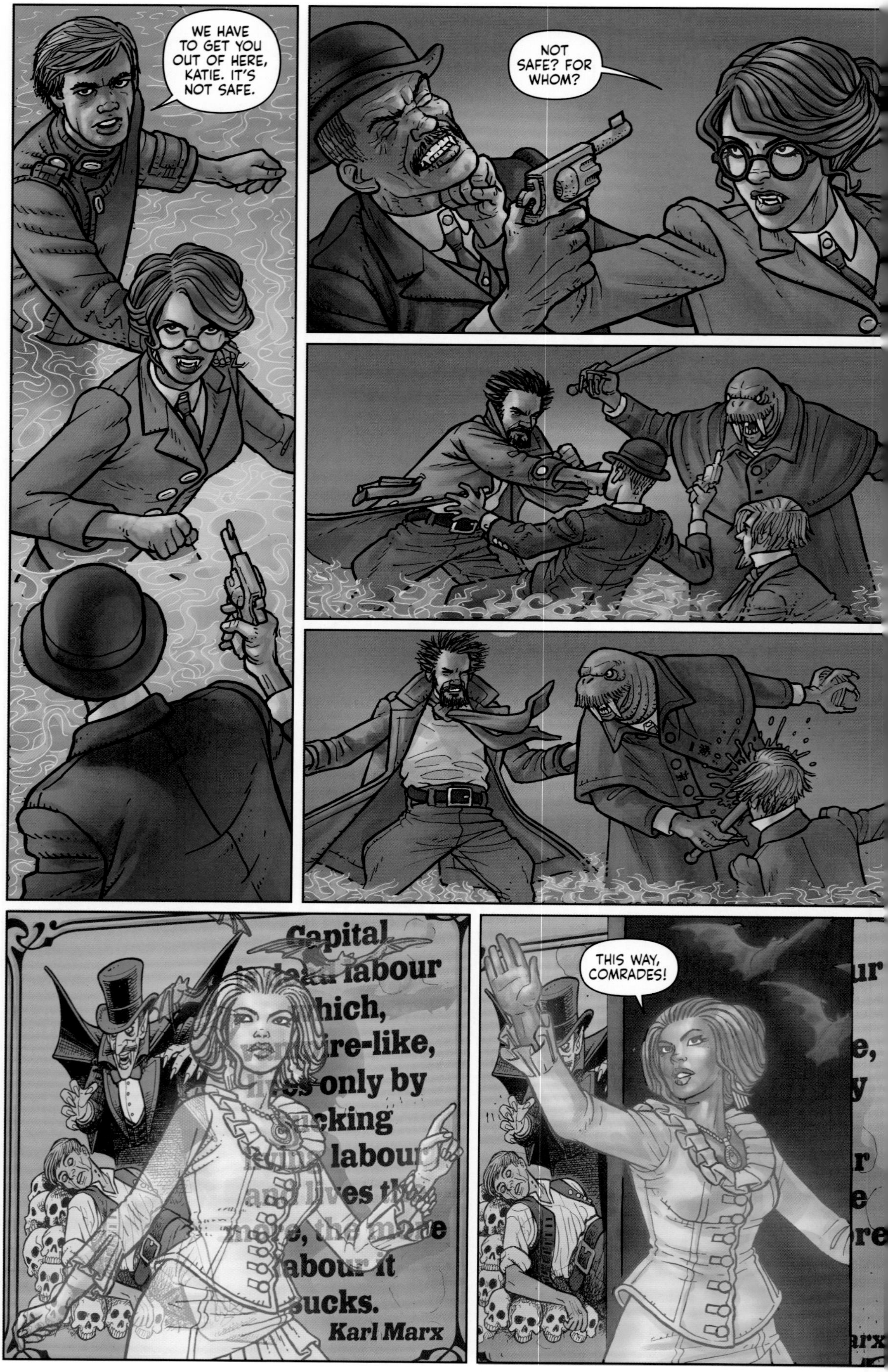
WE HAVE TO GET YOU OUT OF HERE, KATIE. IT'S NOT SAFE.
NOT SAFE? FOR WHOM?
Capital
labour
which,
ire-like,
only by
sucking
labour
lives th
more, the mo
abour it
sucks.
Karl Marx
THIS WAY, COMRADES!

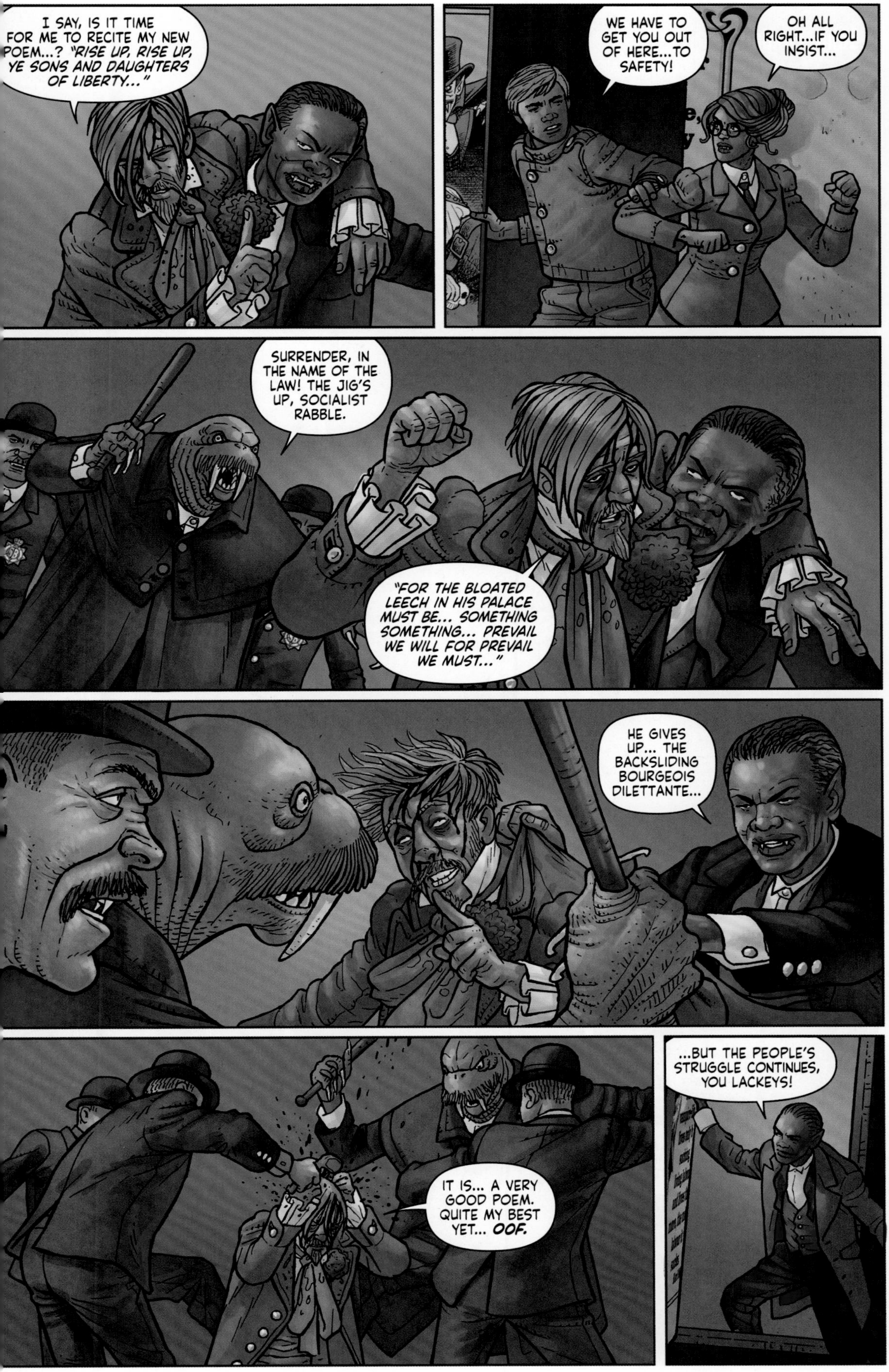
I SAY, IS IT TIME FOR ME TO RECITE MY NEW POEM...? "RISE UP, RISE UP, YE SONS AND DAUGHTERS OF LIBERTY..."
WE HAVE TO GET YOU OUT OF HERE...TO SAFETY!
OH ALL RIGHT...IF YOU INSIST...
SURRENDER, IN THE NAME OF THE LAW! THE JIG'S UP, SOCIALIST RABBLE.
"FOR THE BLOATED LEECH IN HIS PALACE MUST BE... SOMETHING SOMETHING... PREVAIL WE WILL FOR PREVAIL WE MUST..."
HE GIVES UP... THE BACKSLIDING BOURGEOIS DILETTANTE...
IT IS... A VERY GOOD POEM. QUITE MY BEST YET... OOF.
...BUT THE PEOPLE'S STRUGGLE CONTINUES, YOU LACKEYS!

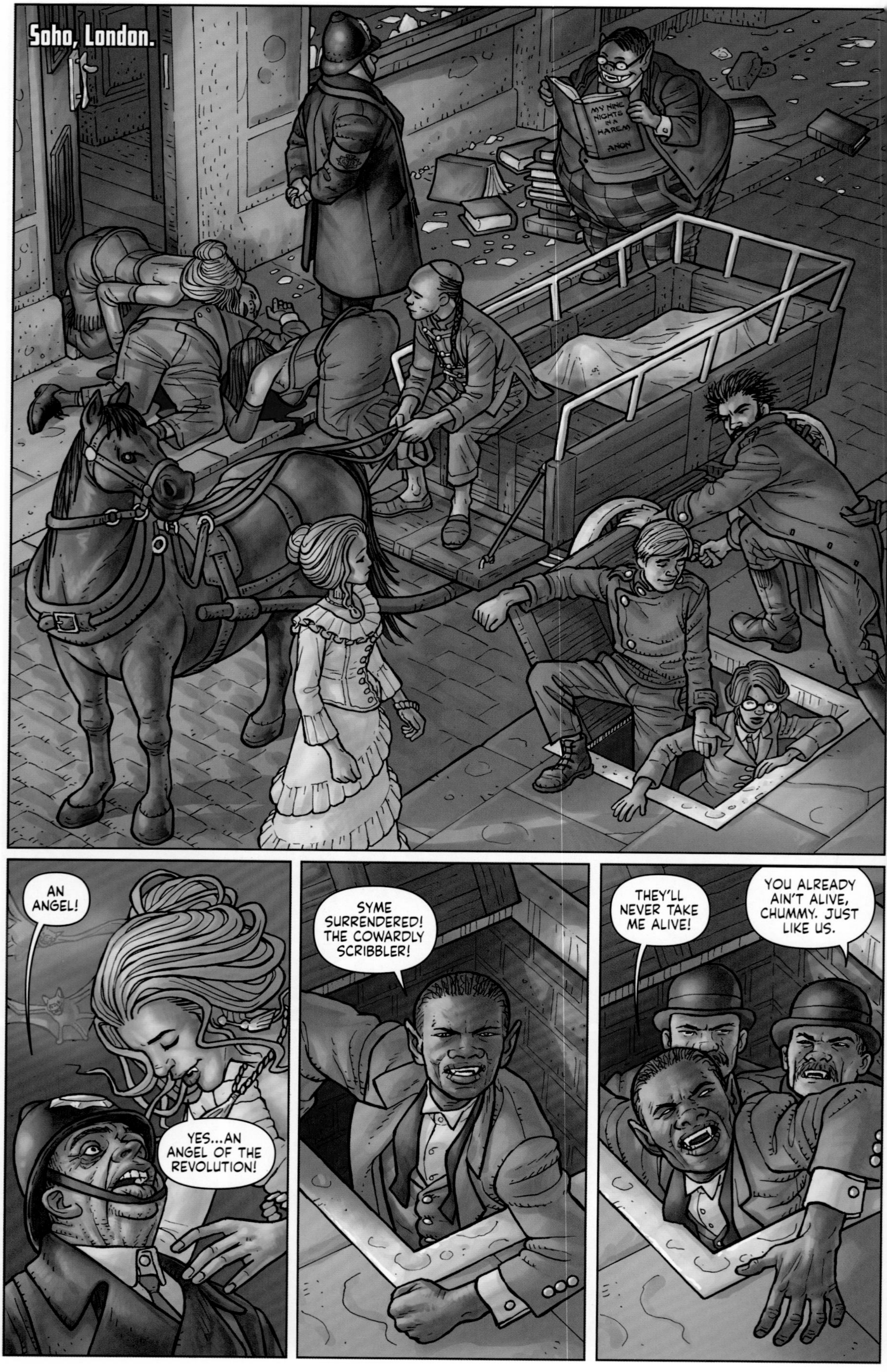
Soho, London.
MY NINE NIGHTS IN A HAREM ANON
AN ANGEL!
YES...AN ANGEL OF THE REVOLUTION!
SYME SURRENDERED! THE COWARDLY SCRIBBLER!
THEY'LL NEVER TAKE ME ALIVE!
YOU ALREADY AIN'T ALIVE, CHUMMY. JUST LIKE US.

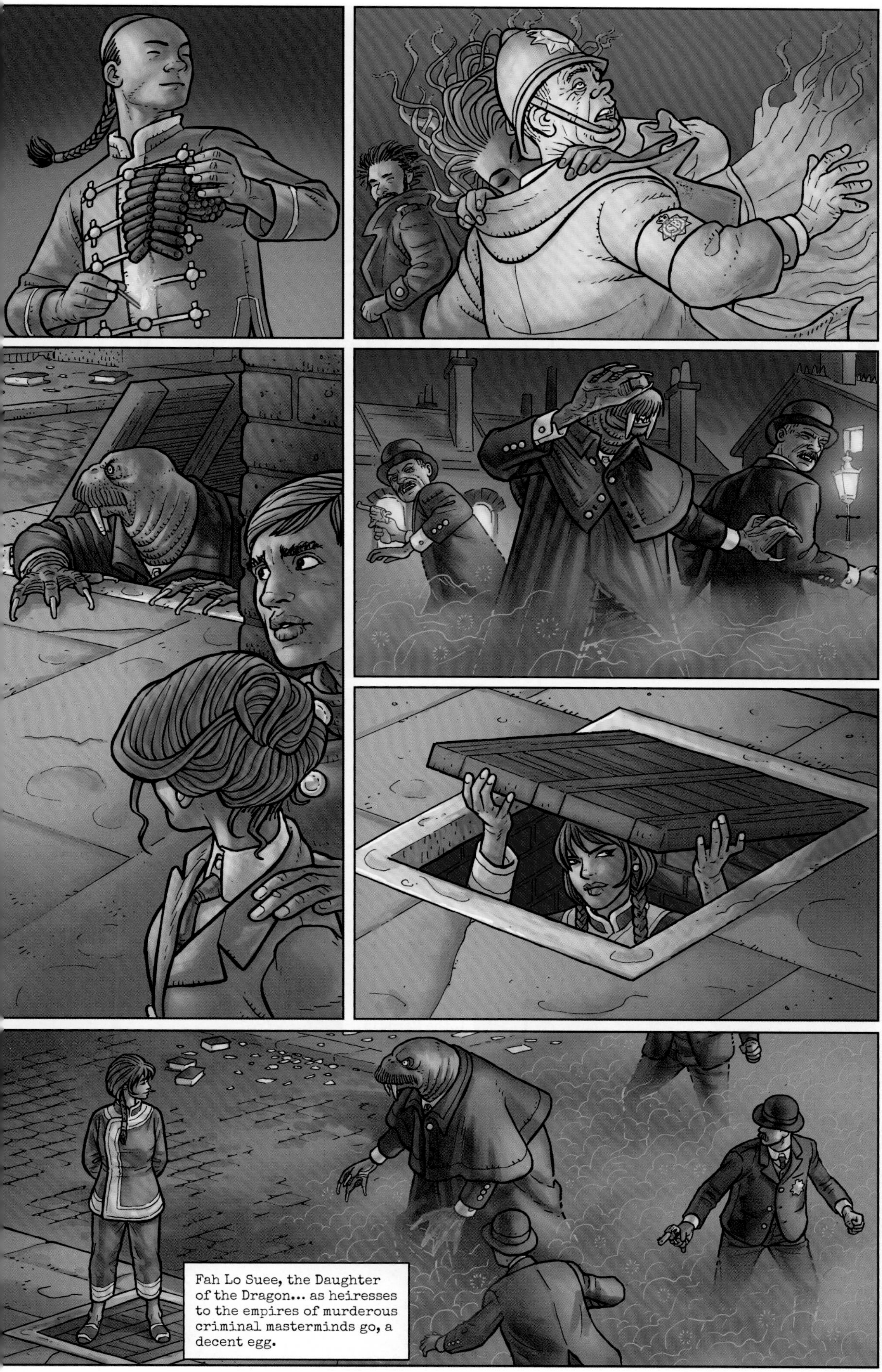
Fah Lo Suee, the Daughter of the Dragon... as heiresses to the empires of murderous criminal masterminds go, a decent egg.

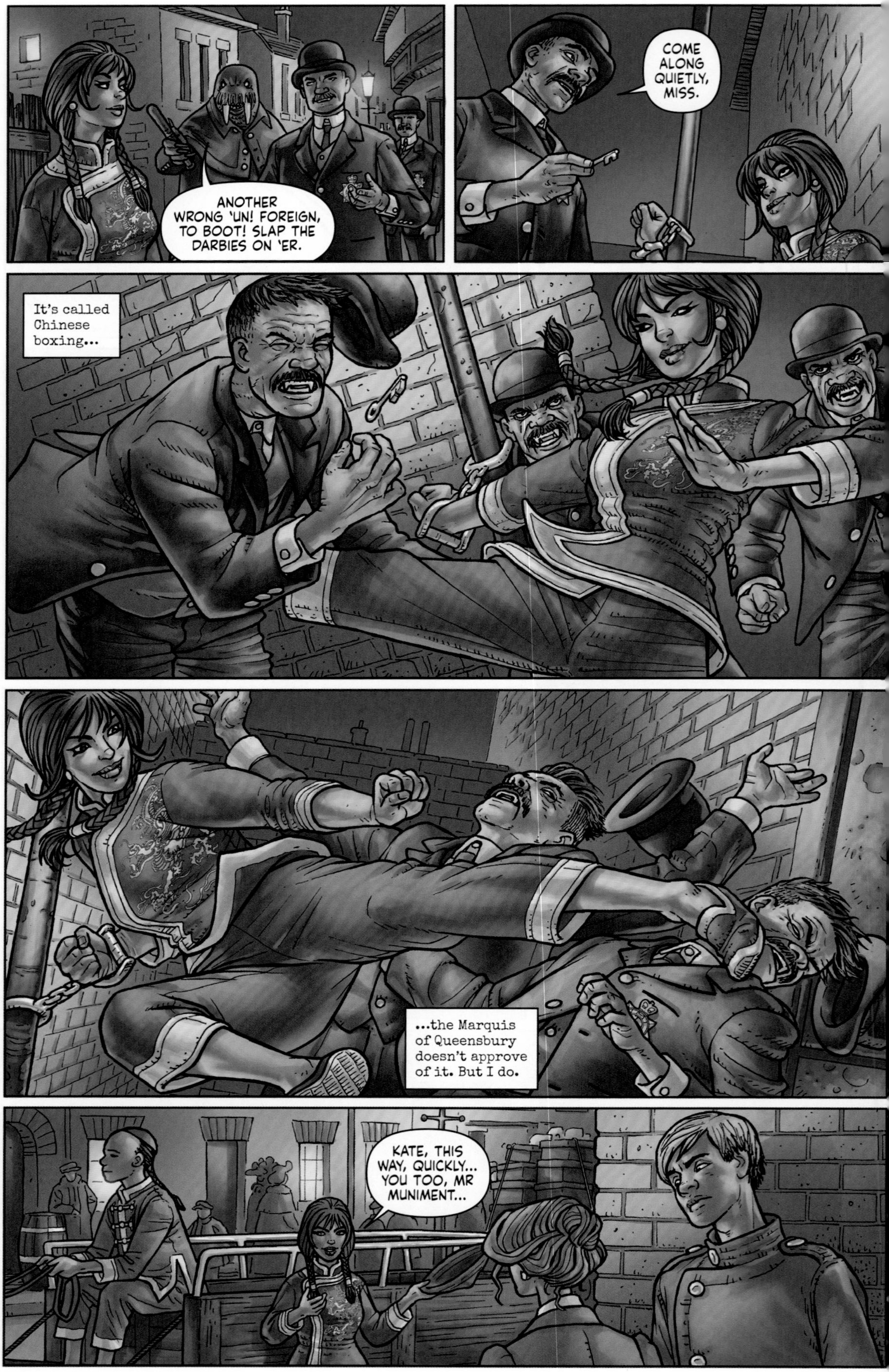
ANOTHER WRONG 'UN! FOREIGN, TO BOOT! SLAP THE DARBIES ON 'ER.
COME ALONG QUIETLY, MISS.
It's called Chinese boxing...
...the Marquis of Queensbury doesn't approve of it. But I do.
KATE, THIS WAY, QUICKLY... YOU TOO, MR MUNIMENT...

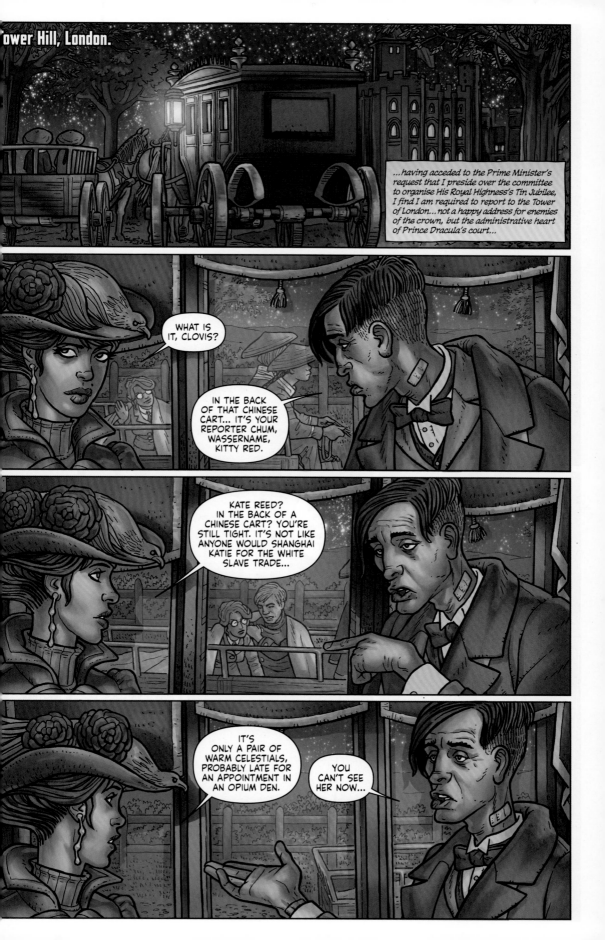

...having acceded to the Prime Minister's request that I preside over the committee to organise His Royal Highness's Tin Jubilee, I find I am required to report to the Tower of London...not a happy address for enemies of the crown, but the administrative heart of Prince Dracula's court...

WHAT IS IT, CLOVIS?

IN THE BACK OF THAT CHINESE CART... IT'S YOUR REPORTER CHUM, WASSERNAME, KITTY RED.

KATE REED? IN THE BACK OF A CHINESE CART? YOU'RE STILL TIGHT. IT'S NOT LIKE ANYONE WOULD SHANGHAI KATIE FOR THE WHITE SLAVE TRADE...

IT'S ONLY A PAIR OF WARM CELESTIALS, PROBABLY LATE FOR AN APPOINTMENT IN AN OPIUM DEN.

YOU CAN'T SEE HER NOW...

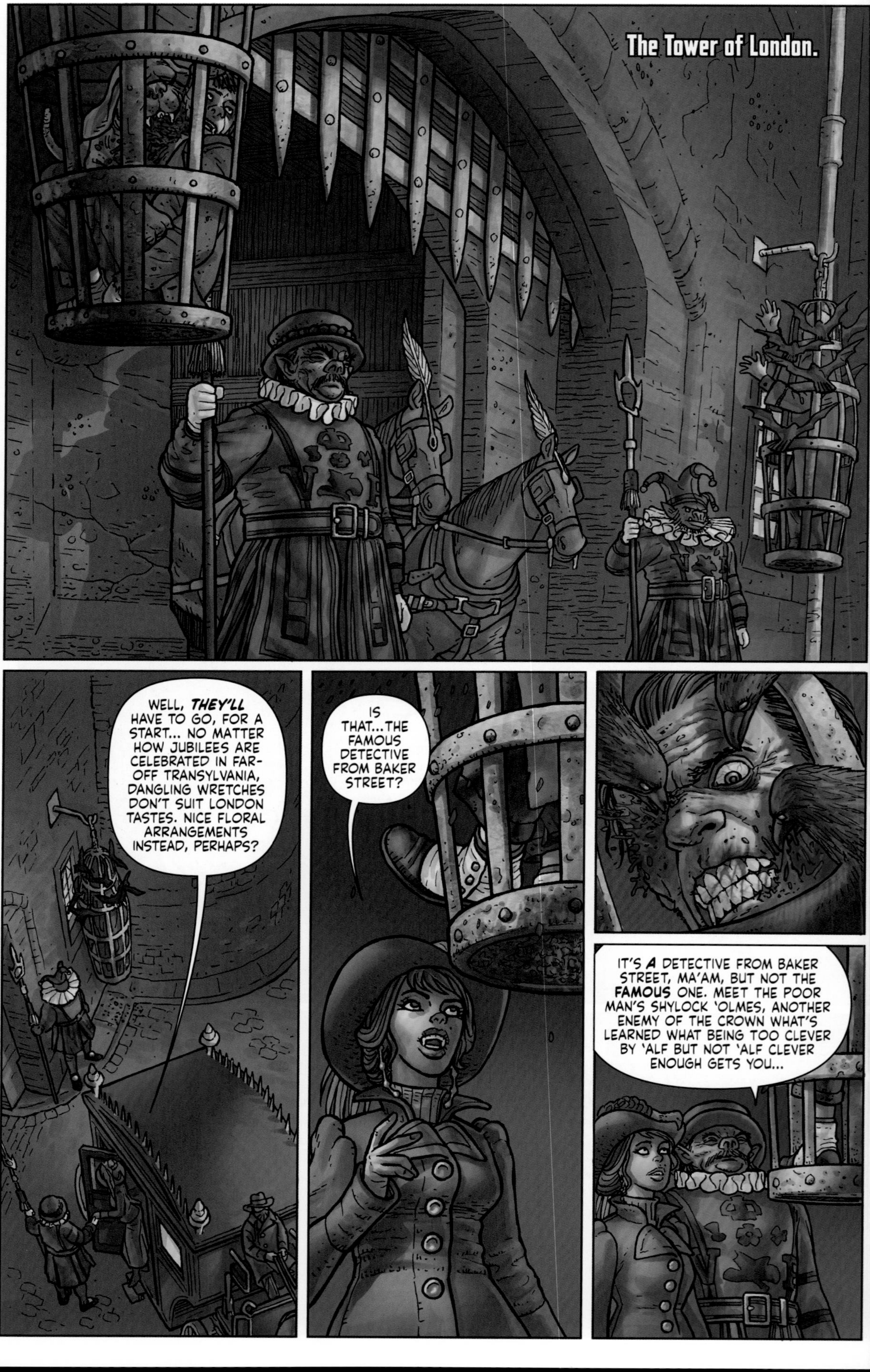
The Tower of London.
WELL, *THEY'LL* HAVE TO GO, FOR A START... NO MATTER HOW JUBILEES ARE CELEBRATED IN FAR-OFF TRANSYLVANIA, DANGLING WRETCHES DON'T SUIT LONDON TASTES. NICE FLORAL ARRANGEMENTS INSTEAD, PERHAPS?
IS THAT...THE FAMOUS DETECTIVE FROM BAKER STREET?
IT'S *A* DETECTIVE FROM BAKER STREET, MA'AM, BUT NOT THE **FAMOUS** ONE. MEET THE POOR MAN'S SHYLOCK 'OLMES, ANOTHER ENEMY OF THE CROWN WHAT'S LEARNED WHAT BEING TOO CLEVER BY 'ALF BUT NOT 'ALF CLEVER ENOUGH GETS YOU...

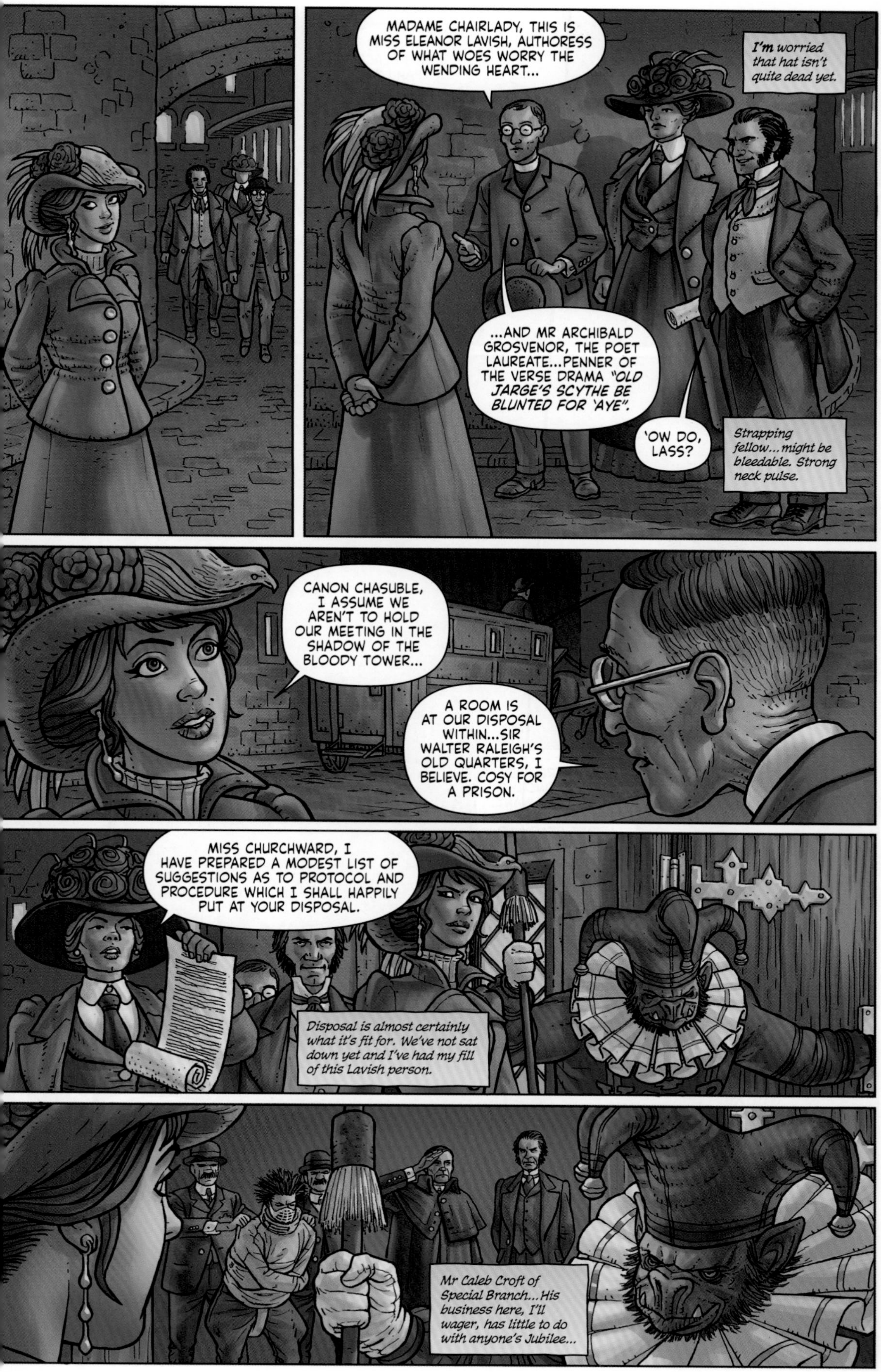
MADAME CHAIRLADY, THIS IS MISS ELEANOR LAVISH, AUTHORESS OF WHAT WOES WORRY THE WENDING HEART...
I'm worried that hat isn't quite dead yet.
...AND MR ARCHIBALD GROSVENOR, THE POET LAUREATE...PENNER OF THE VERSE DRAMA "OLD JARGE'S SCYTHE BE BLUNTED FOR 'AYE".
'OW DO, LASS?
Strapping fellow...might be bleedable. Strong neck pulse.
CANON CHASUBLE, I ASSUME WE AREN'T TO HOLD OUR MEETING IN THE SHADOW OF THE BLOODY TOWER...
A ROOM IS AT OUR DISPOSAL WITHIN...SIR WALTER RALEIGH'S OLD QUARTERS, I BELIEVE. COSY FOR A PRISON.
MISS CHURCHWARD, I HAVE PREPARED A MODEST LIST OF SUGGESTIONS AS TO PROTOCOL AND PROCEDURE WHICH I SHALL HAPPILY PUT AT YOUR DISPOSAL.
Disposal is almost certainly what it's fit for. We've not sat down yet and I've had my fill of this Lavish person.
Mr Caleb Croft of Special Branch...His business here, I'll wager, has little to do with anyone's Jubilee...

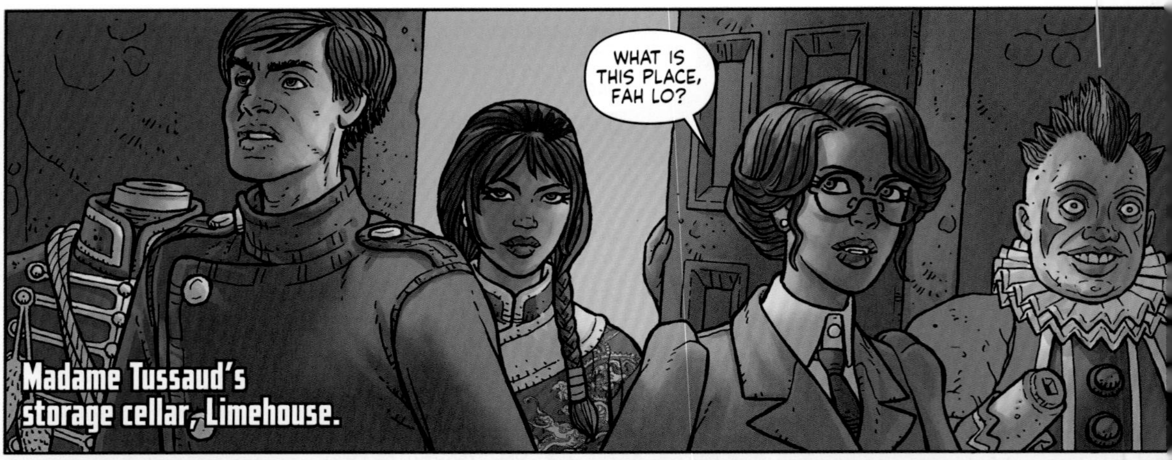
Madame Tussaud's storage cellar, Limehouse.
WHAT IS THIS PLACE, FAH LO?

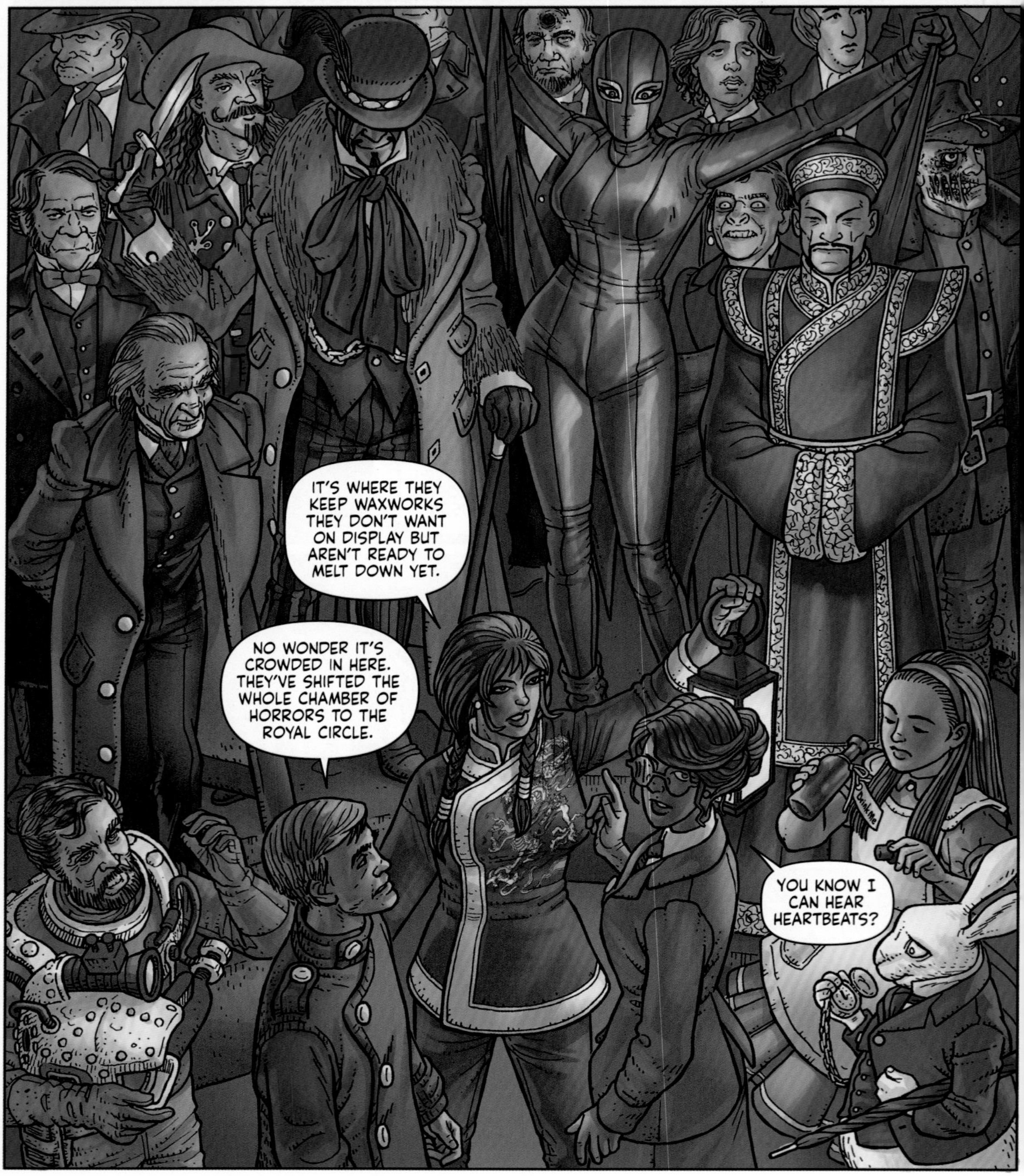
IT'S WHERE THEY KEEP WAXWORKS THEY DON'T WANT ON DISPLAY BUT AREN'T READY TO MELT DOWN YET.
NO WONDER IT'S CROWDED IN HERE. THEY'VE SHIFTED THE WHOLE CHAMBER OF HORRORS TO THE ROYAL CIRCLE.
YOU KNOW I CAN HEAR HEARTBEATS?

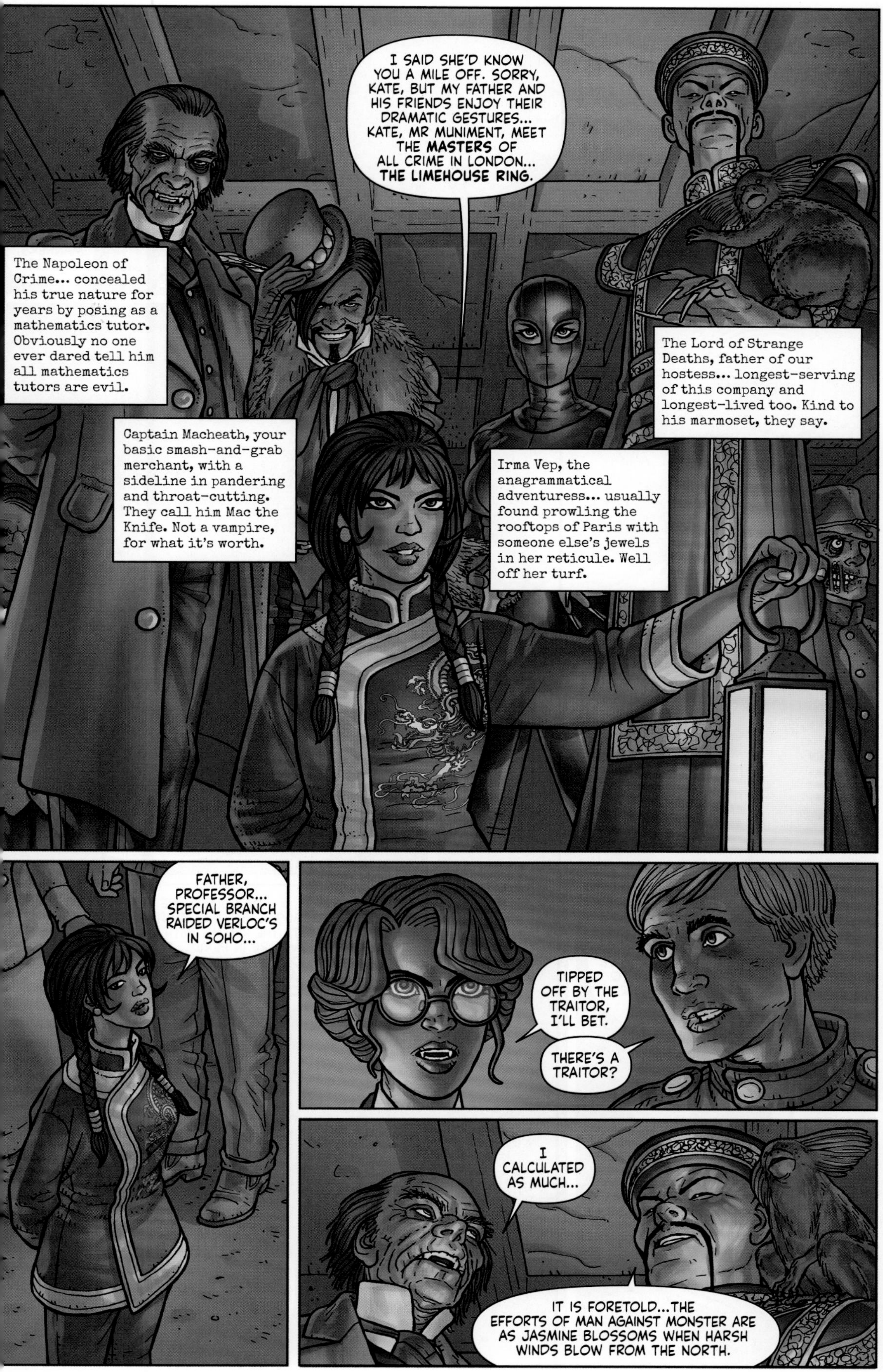
I SAID SHE'D KNOW YOU A MILE OFF. SORRY, KATE, BUT MY FATHER AND HIS FRIENDS ENJOY THEIR DRAMATIC GESTURES... KATE, MR MUNIMENT, MEET THE MASTERS OF ALL CRIME IN LONDON... THE LIMEHOUSE RING.
The Napoleon of Crime... concealed his true nature for years by posing as a mathematics tutor. Obviously no one ever dared tell him all mathematics tutors are evil.
Captain Macheath, your basic smash-and-grab merchant, with a sideline in pandering and throat-cutting. They call him Mac the Knife. Not a vampire, for what it's worth.
Irma Vep, the anagrammatical adventuress... usually found prowling the rooftops of Paris with someone else's jewels in her reticule. Well off her turf.
The Lord of Strange Deaths, father of our hostess... longest-serving of this company and longest-lived too. Kind to his marmoset, they say.
FATHER, PROFESSOR... SPECIAL BRANCH RAIDED VERLOC'S IN SOHO...
TIPPED OFF BY THE TRAITOR, I'LL BET.
THERE'S A TRAITOR?
I CALCULATED AS MUCH...
IT IS FORETOLD...THE EFFORTS OF MAN AGAINST MONSTER ARE AS JASMINE BLOSSOMS WHEN HARSH WINDS BLOW FROM THE NORTH.

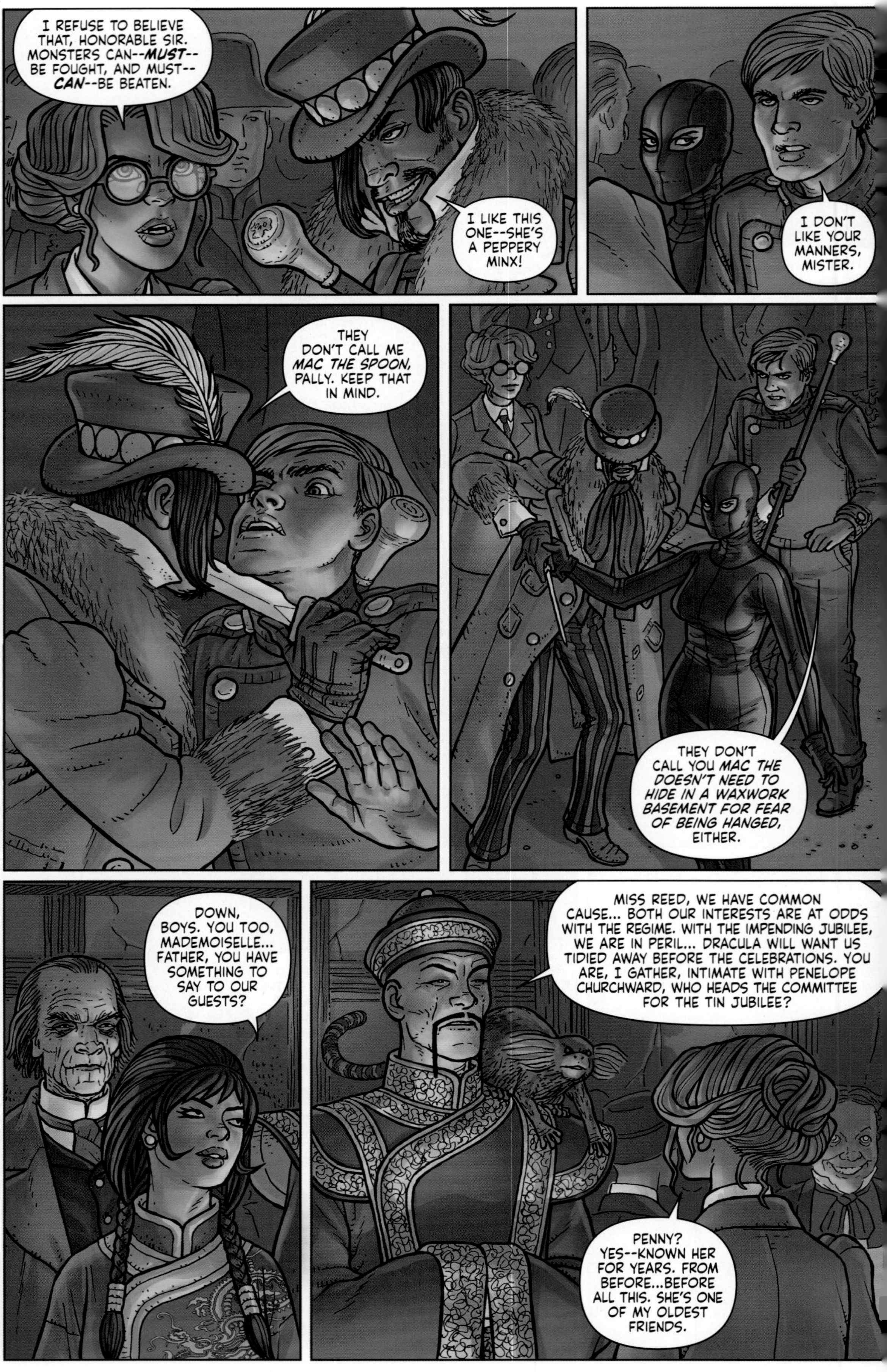
I REFUSE TO BELIEVE THAT, HONORABLE SIR. MONSTERS CAN--*MUST*--BE FOUGHT, AND MUST--*CAN*--BE BEATEN.
I LIKE THIS ONE--SHE'S A PEPPERY MINX!
I DON'T LIKE YOUR MANNERS, MISTER.
THEY DON'T CALL ME *MAC THE SPOON,* PALLY. KEEP THAT IN MIND.
THEY DON'T CALL YOU *MAC THE DOESN'T NEED TO HIDE IN A WAXWORK BASEMENT FOR FEAR OF BEING HANGED,* EITHER.
DOWN, BOYS. YOU TOO, MADEMOISELLE... FATHER, YOU HAVE SOMETHING TO SAY TO OUR GUESTS?
MISS REED, WE HAVE COMMON CAUSE... BOTH OUR INTERESTS ARE AT ODDS WITH THE REGIME. WITH THE IMPENDING JUBILEE, WE ARE IN PERIL... DRACULA WILL WANT US TIDIED AWAY BEFORE THE CELEBRATIONS. YOU ARE, I GATHER, INTIMATE WITH PENELOPE CHURCHWARD, WHO HEADS THE COMMITTEE FOR THE TIN JUBILEE?
PENNY? YES--KNOWN HER FOR YEARS. FROM BEFORE...BEFORE ALL THIS. SHE'S ONE OF MY OLDEST FRIENDS.

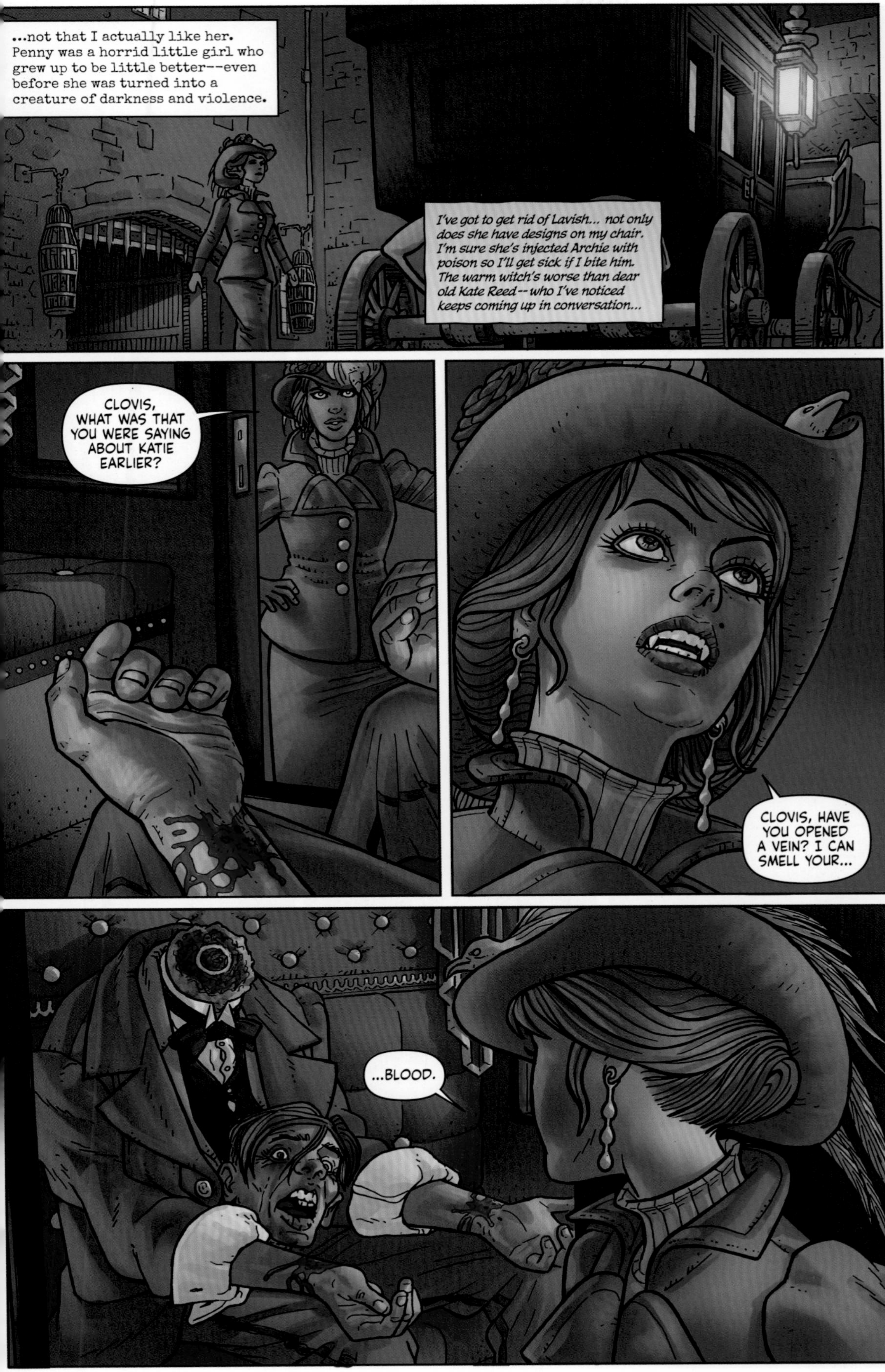
...not that I actually like her. Penny was a horrid little girl who grew up to be little better--even before she was turned into a creature of darkness and violence.
I've got to get rid of Lavish... not only does she have designs on my chair. I'm sure she's injected Archie with poison so I'll get sick if I bite him. The warm witch's worse than dear old Kate Reed--who I've noticed keeps coming up in conversation...
CLOVIS, WHAT WAS THAT YOU WERE SAYING ABOUT KATIE EARLIER?
CLOVIS, HAVE YOU OPENED A VEIN? I CAN SMELL YOUR...
...BLOOD.

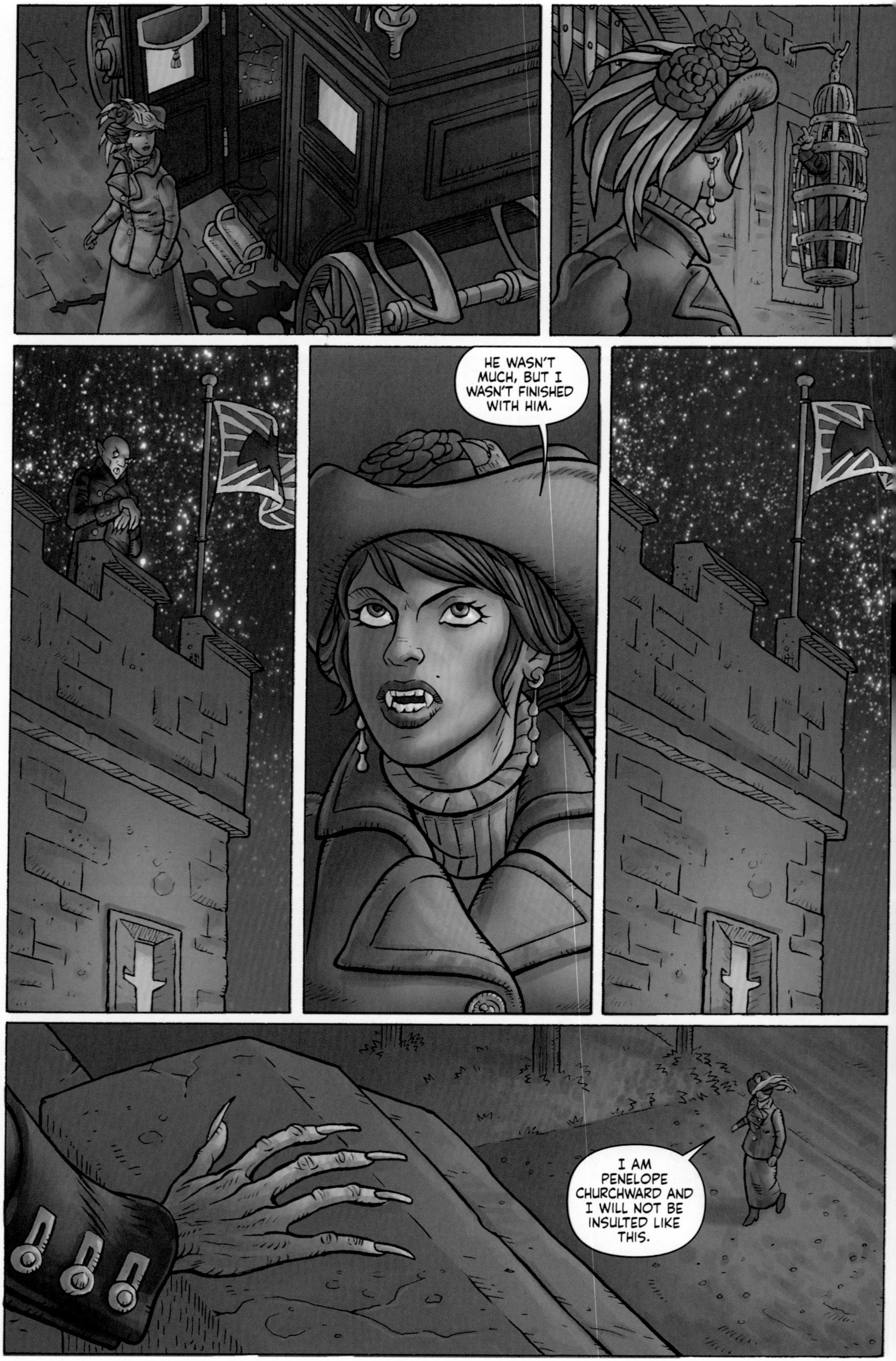

HE WASN'T MUCH, BUT I WASN'T FINISHED WITH HIM.
I AM PENELOPE CHURCHWARD AND I WILL NOT BE INSULTED LIKE THIS.

HO THERE, BEEFEATERS... STAUNCH GUARDIANS AND DEFENDERS OF THE CROWN, I'VE A BONE TO PICK...

...WHERE WAS THE GUARDING AND DEFENDING WHEN CLOVIS WAS BLED AND BEHEADED, EH? IS THIS THE SERVICE WE EXPECT?

OSSIPON, PERHAPS YOU HAVEN'T HEARD THE QUESTION PROPERLY. YOUR EARS ARE BLEEDING.

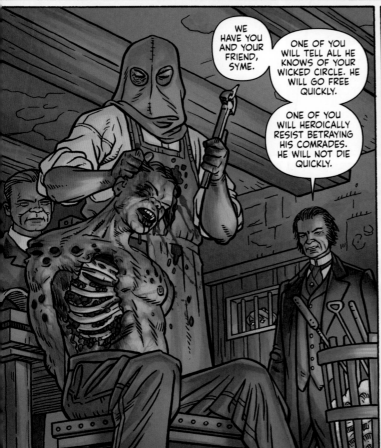

WE HAVE YOU AND YOUR FRIEND, SYME.

ONE OF YOU WILL TELL ALL HE KNOWS OF YOUR WICKED CIRCLE. HE WILL GO FREE QUICKLY.

ONE OF YOU WILL HEROICALLY RESIST BETRAYING HIS COMRADES. HE WILL NOT DIE QUICKLY.

SO, WHICH OF YOU WILL TALK FIRST?

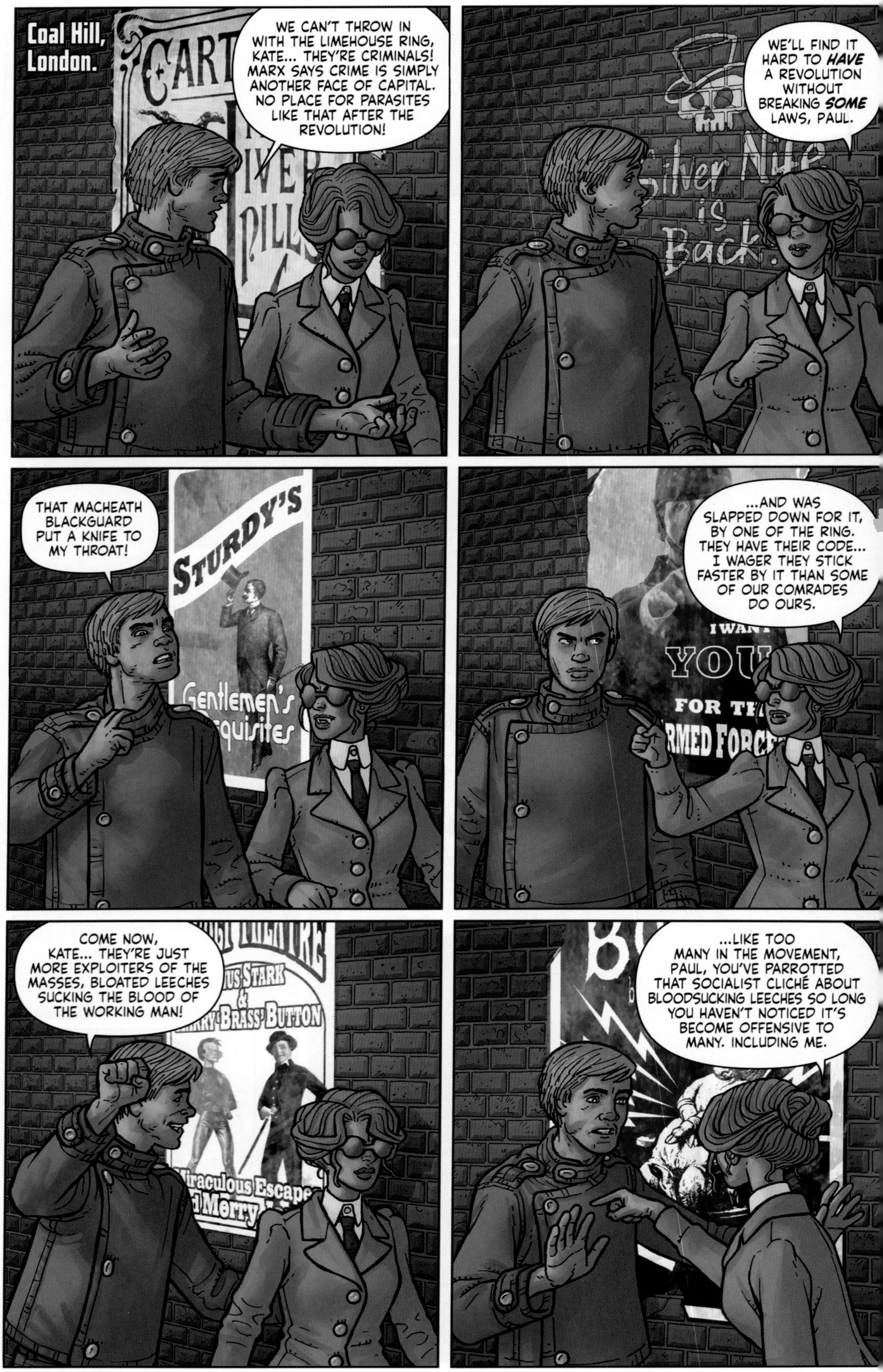
Coal Hill, London.
WE CAN'T THROW IN WITH THE LIMEHOUSE RING, KATE... THEY'RE CRIMINALS! MARX SAYS CRIME IS SIMPLY ANOTHER FACE OF CAPITAL. NO PLACE FOR PARASITES LIKE THAT AFTER THE REVOLUTION!
Silver Nite is Back.
WE'LL FIND IT HARD TO *HAVE* A REVOLUTION WITHOUT BREAKING *SOME* LAWS, PAUL.
STURDY'S
Gentlemen's
THAT MACHEATH BLACKGUARD PUT A KNIFE TO MY THROAT!
YOU
...AND WAS SLAPPED DOWN FOR IT, BY ONE OF THE RING. THEY HAVE THEIR CODE... I WAGER THEY STICK FASTER BY IT THAN SOME OF OUR COMRADES DO OURS.
COME NOW, KATE... THEY'RE JUST MORE EXPLOITERS OF THE MASSES, BLOATED LEECHES SUCKING THE BLOOD OF THE WORKING MAN!
...LIKE TOO MANY IN THE MOVEMENT, PAUL, YOU'VE PARROTTED THAT SOCIALIST CLICHÉ ABOUT BLOODSUCKING LEECHES SO LONG YOU HAVEN'T NOTICED IT'S BECOME OFFENSIVE TO MANY. INCLUDING ME.

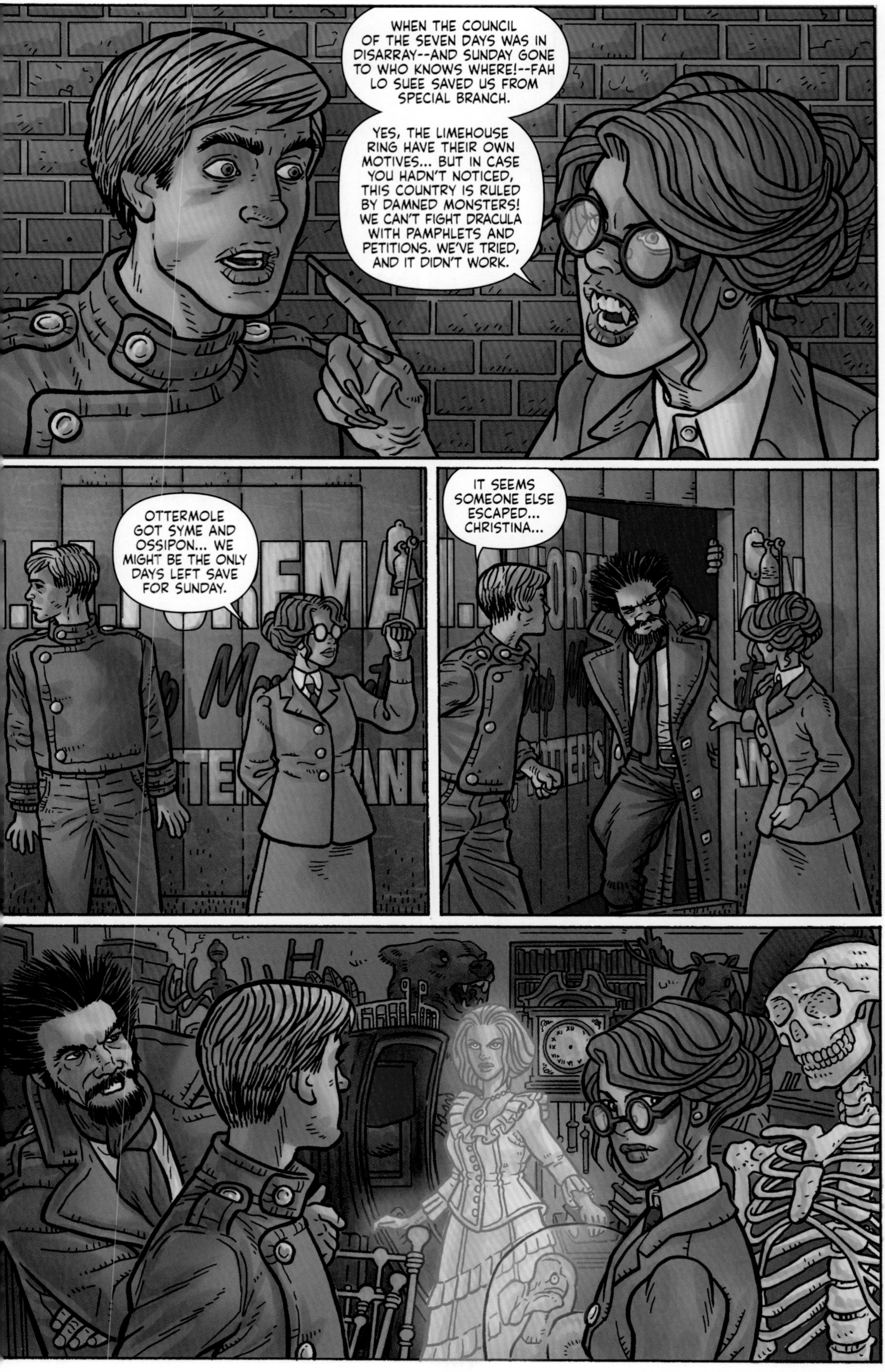
WHEN THE COUNCIL OF THE SEVEN DAYS WAS IN DISARRAY--AND SUNDAY GONE TO WHO KNOWS WHERE!--FAH LO SUEE SAVED US FROM SPECIAL BRANCH.
YES, THE LIMEHOUSE RING HAVE THEIR OWN MOTIVES... BUT IN CASE YOU HADN'T NOTICED, THIS COUNTRY IS RULED BY DAMNED MONSTERS! WE CAN'T FIGHT DRACULA WITH PAMPHLETS AND PETITIONS. WE'VE TRIED, AND IT DIDN'T WORK.
OTTERMOLE GOT SYME AND OSSIPON... WE MIGHT BE THE ONLY DAYS LEFT SAVE FOR SUNDAY.
IT SEEMS SOMEONE ELSE ESCAPED... CHRISTINA...

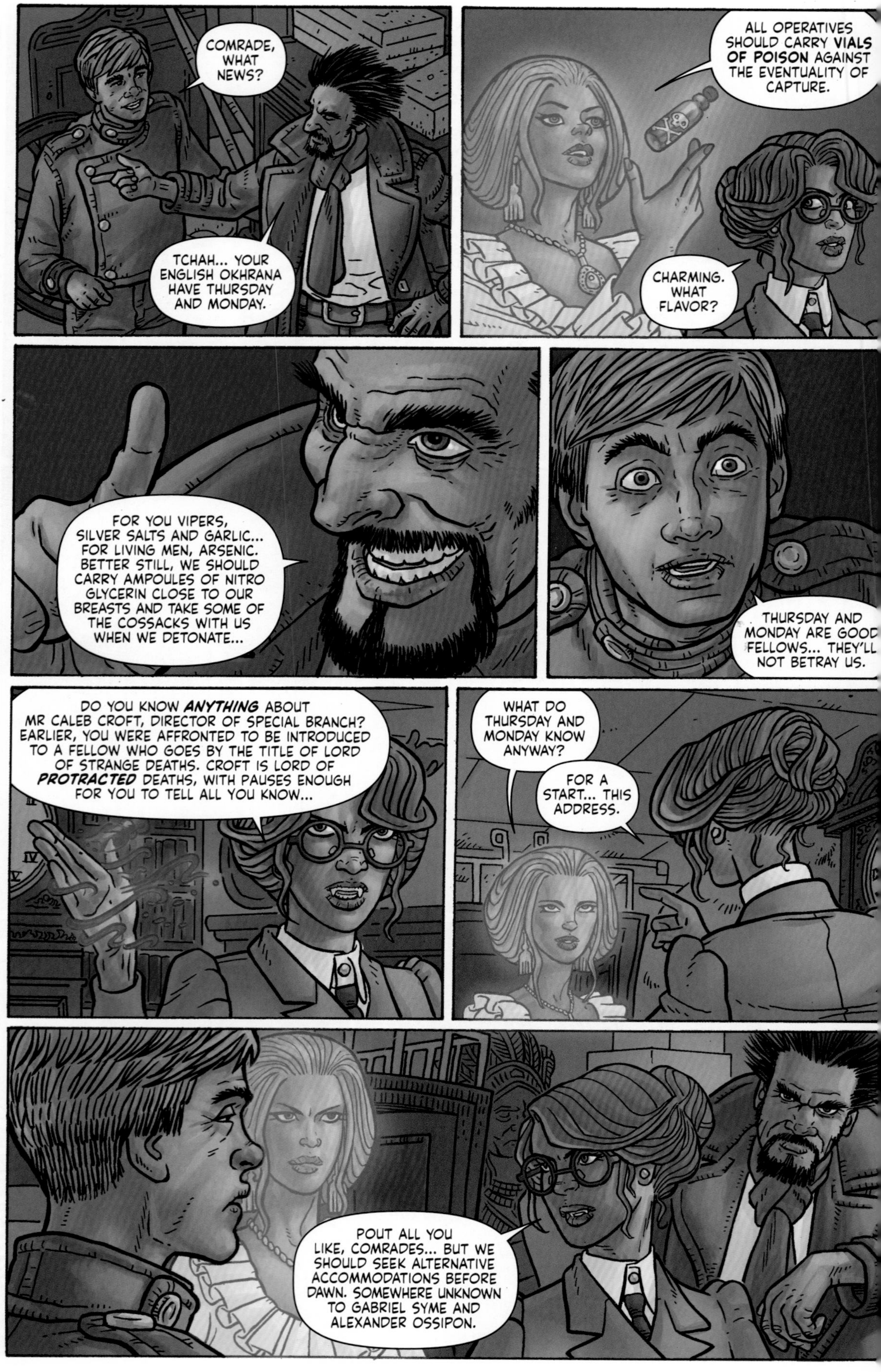
COMRADE, WHAT NEWS?
TCHAH... YOUR ENGLISH OKHRANA HAVE THURSDAY AND MONDAY.
ALL OPERATIVES SHOULD CARRY **VIALS OF POISON** AGAINST THE EVENTUALITY OF CAPTURE.
CHARMING. WHAT FLAVOR?
FOR YOU VIPERS, SILVER SALTS AND GARLIC... FOR LIVING MEN, ARSENIC. BETTER STILL, WE SHOULD CARRY AMPOULES OF NITRO GLYCERIN CLOSE TO OUR BREASTS AND TAKE SOME OF THE COSSACKS WITH US WHEN WE DETONATE...
THURSDAY AND MONDAY ARE GOOD FELLOWS... THEY'LL NOT BETRAY US.
DO YOU KNOW ***ANYTHING*** ABOUT MR CALEB CROFT, DIRECTOR OF SPECIAL BRANCH? EARLIER, YOU WERE AFFRONTED TO BE INTRODUCED TO A FELLOW WHO GOES BY THE TITLE OF LORD OF STRANGE DEATHS. CROFT IS LORD OF ***PROTRACTED*** DEATHS, WITH PAUSES ENOUGH FOR YOU TO TELL ALL YOU KNOW...
WHAT DO THURSDAY AND MONDAY KNOW ANYWAY?
FOR A START... THIS ADDRESS.
POUT ALL YOU LIKE, COMRADES... BUT WE SHOULD SEEK ALTERNATIVE ACCOMMODATIONS BEFORE DAWN. SOMEWHERE UNKNOWN TO GABRIEL SYME AND ALEXANDER OSSIPON.

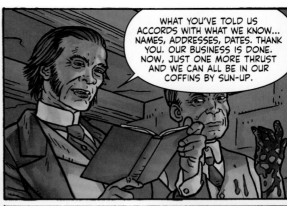

WHAT YOU'VE TOLD US ACCORDS WITH WHAT WE KNOW... NAMES, ADDRESSES, DATES. THANK YOU. OUR BUSINESS IS DONE. NOW, JUST ONE MORE THRUST AND WE CAN ALL BE IN OUR COFFINS BY SUN-UP.

...BUT I AM *NOT* AN ANARCHIST, I AM AN *AGENT PROVOCATEUR*... SENT AMONG THEM TO SMOKE OUT THE INSURRECTIONISTS. I AM *STRIGOI*, LIKE YOU! I AM *NO TRAITOR*.

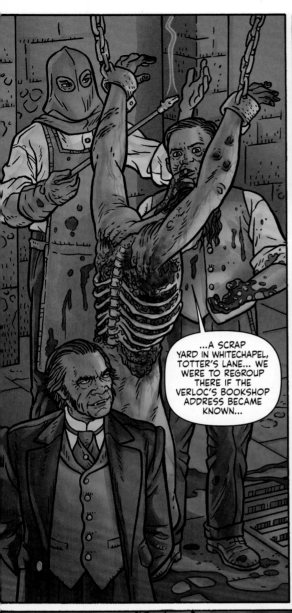

...A SCRAP YARD IN WHITECHAPEL, TOTTER'S LANE... WE WERE TO REGROUP THERE IF THE VERLOC'S BOOKSHOP ADDRESS BECAME KNOWN...

OH YES YOU ARE... AND SO AM I.

NEATLY DONE, CONSTABLE SYME. THERE'S A PROMOTION IN THIS FOR YOU.

Scarcely pleasant... but Mr Croft and associates have been far too busy in the last hours to have served poor Clovis so abominably... someone else is behind that pretty piece of work.

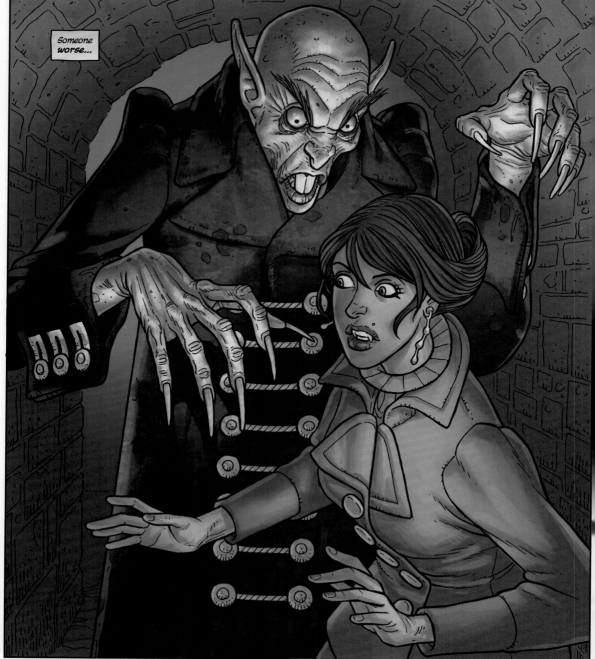

Someone *worse...*

CHAPTER THREE

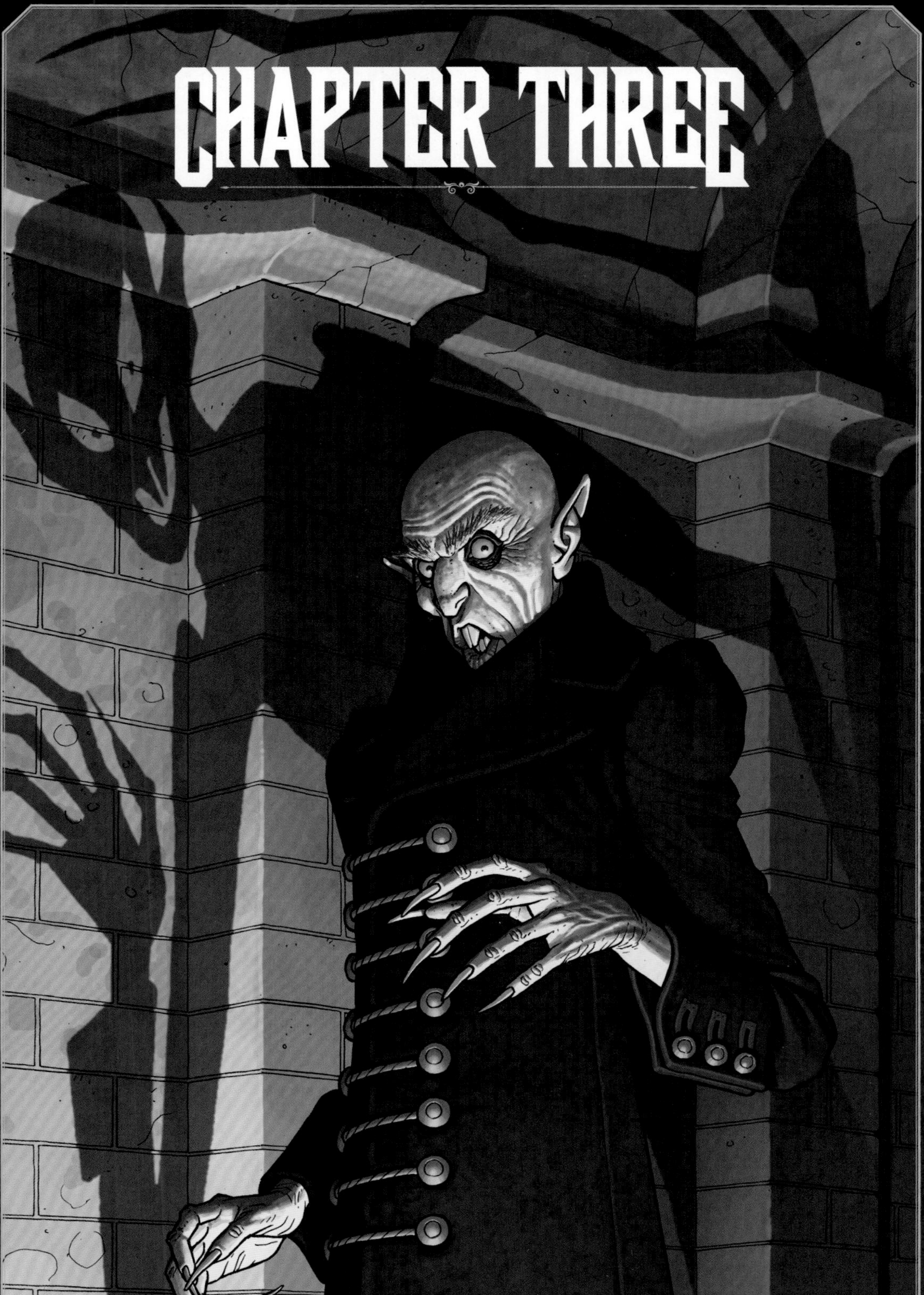

Illustration by Paul McCaffrey

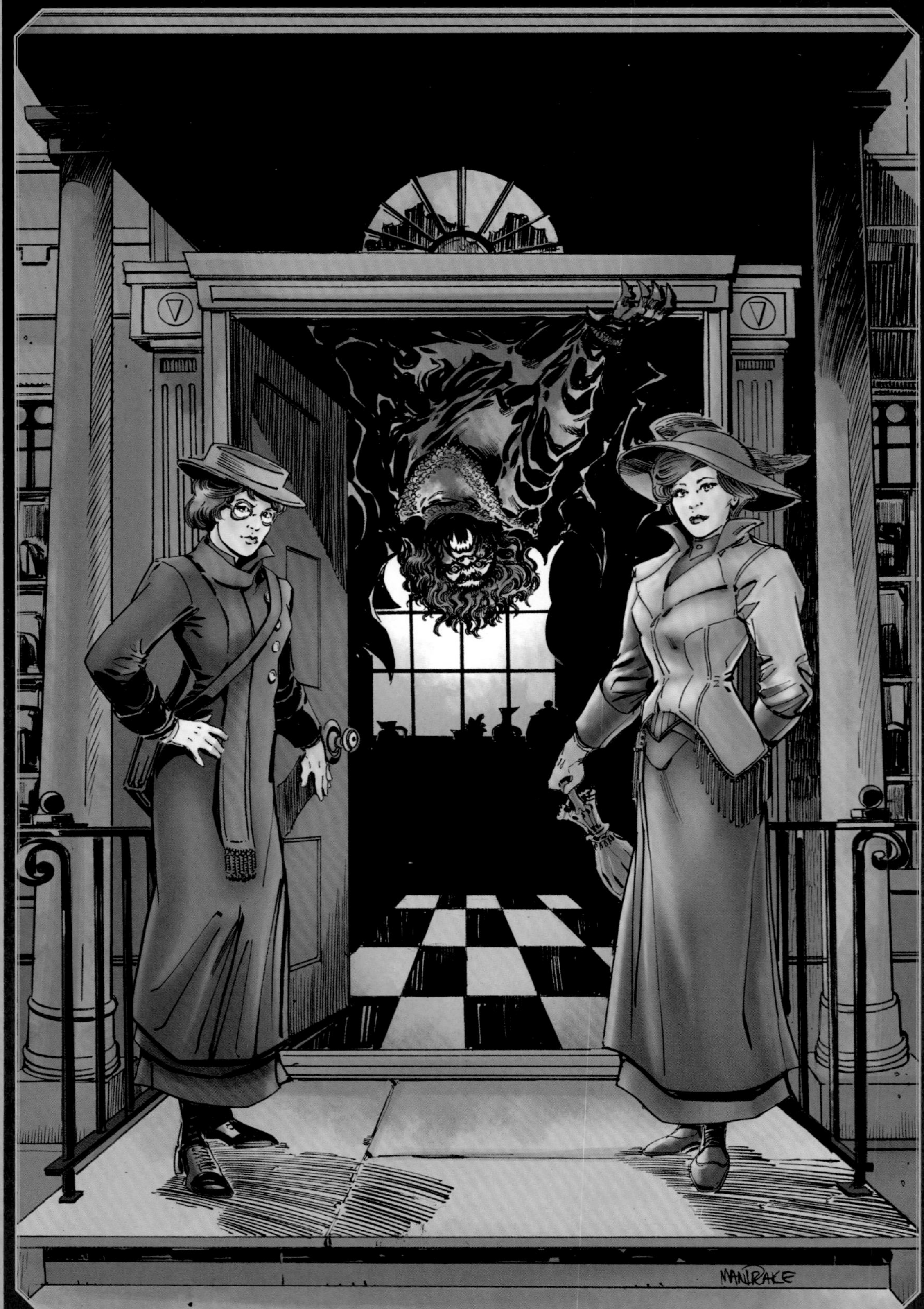
MANDRAKE

Illustration by Tom Mandrake. Colors by Sian Mandrake

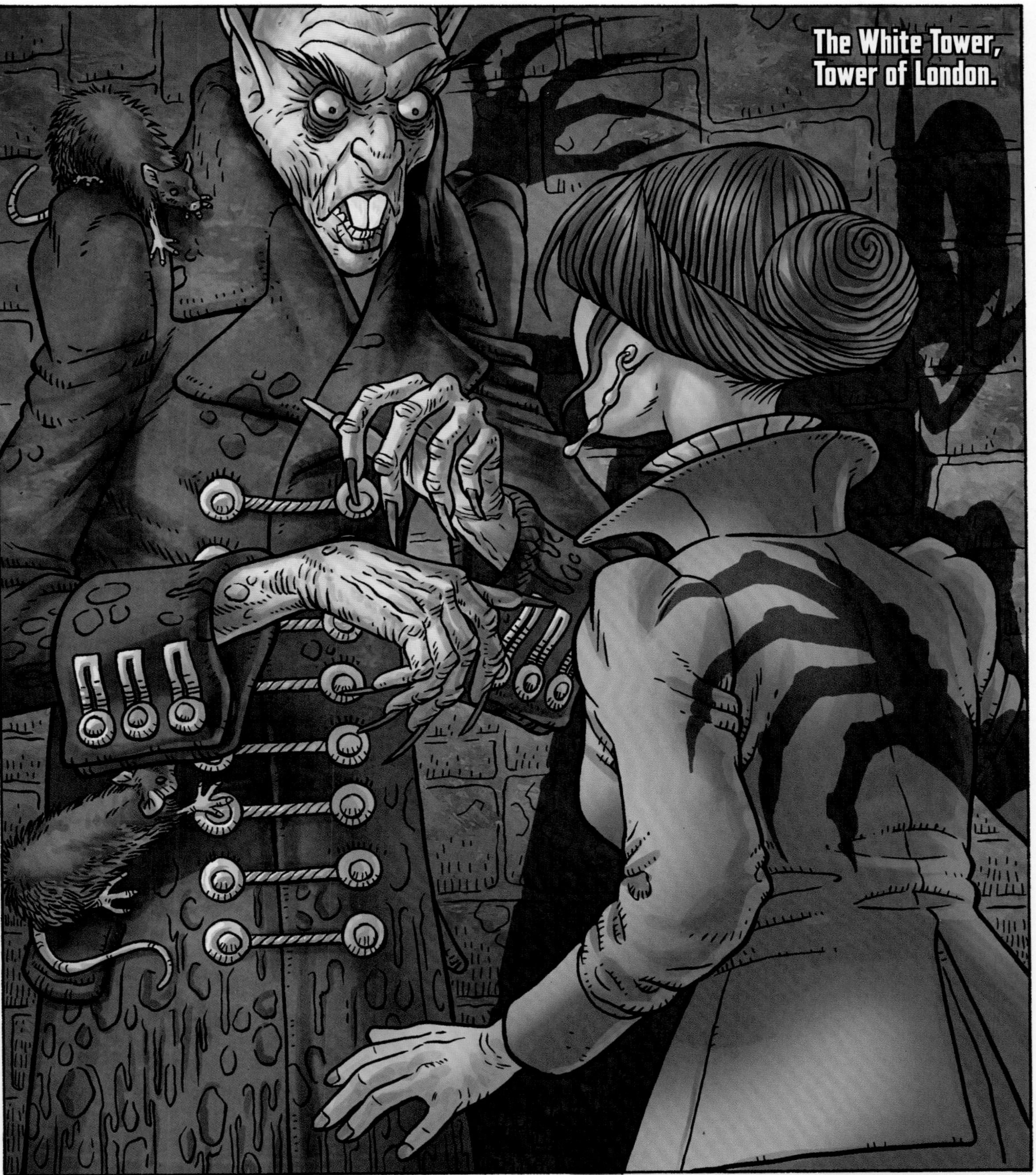
The White Tower,
Tower of London.

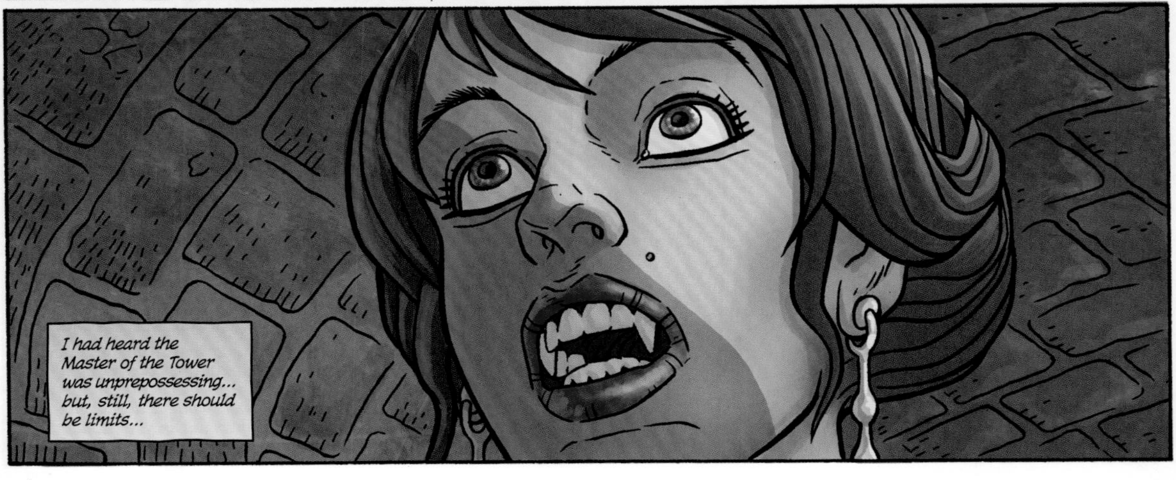
I had heard the
Master of the Tower
was unprepossessing...
but, still, there should
be limits...

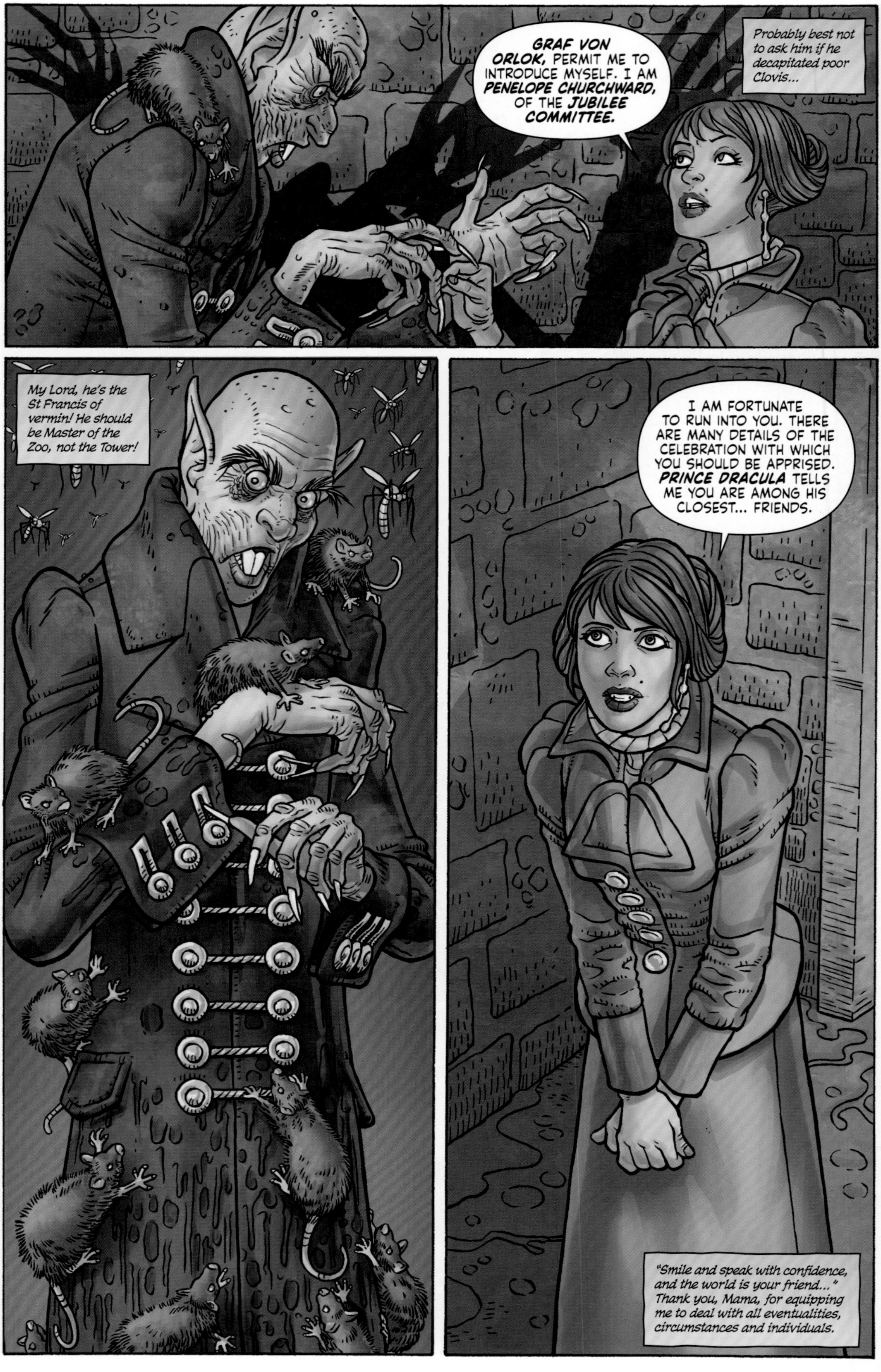
GRAF VON ORLOK, PERMIT ME TO INTRODUCE MYSELF. I AM PENELOPE CHURCHWARD, OF THE JUBILEE COMMITTEE.
Probably best not to ask him if he decapitated poor Clovis...
My Lord, he's the St Francis of vermin! He should be Master of the Zoo, not the Tower!
I AM FORTUNATE TO RUN INTO YOU. THERE ARE MANY DETAILS OF THE CELEBRATION WITH WHICH YOU SHOULD BE APPRISED. PRINCE DRACULA TELLS ME YOU ARE AMONG HIS CLOSEST... FRIENDS.
"Smile and speak with confidence, and the world is your friend..." Thank you, Mama, for equipping me to deal with all eventualities, circumstances and individuals.

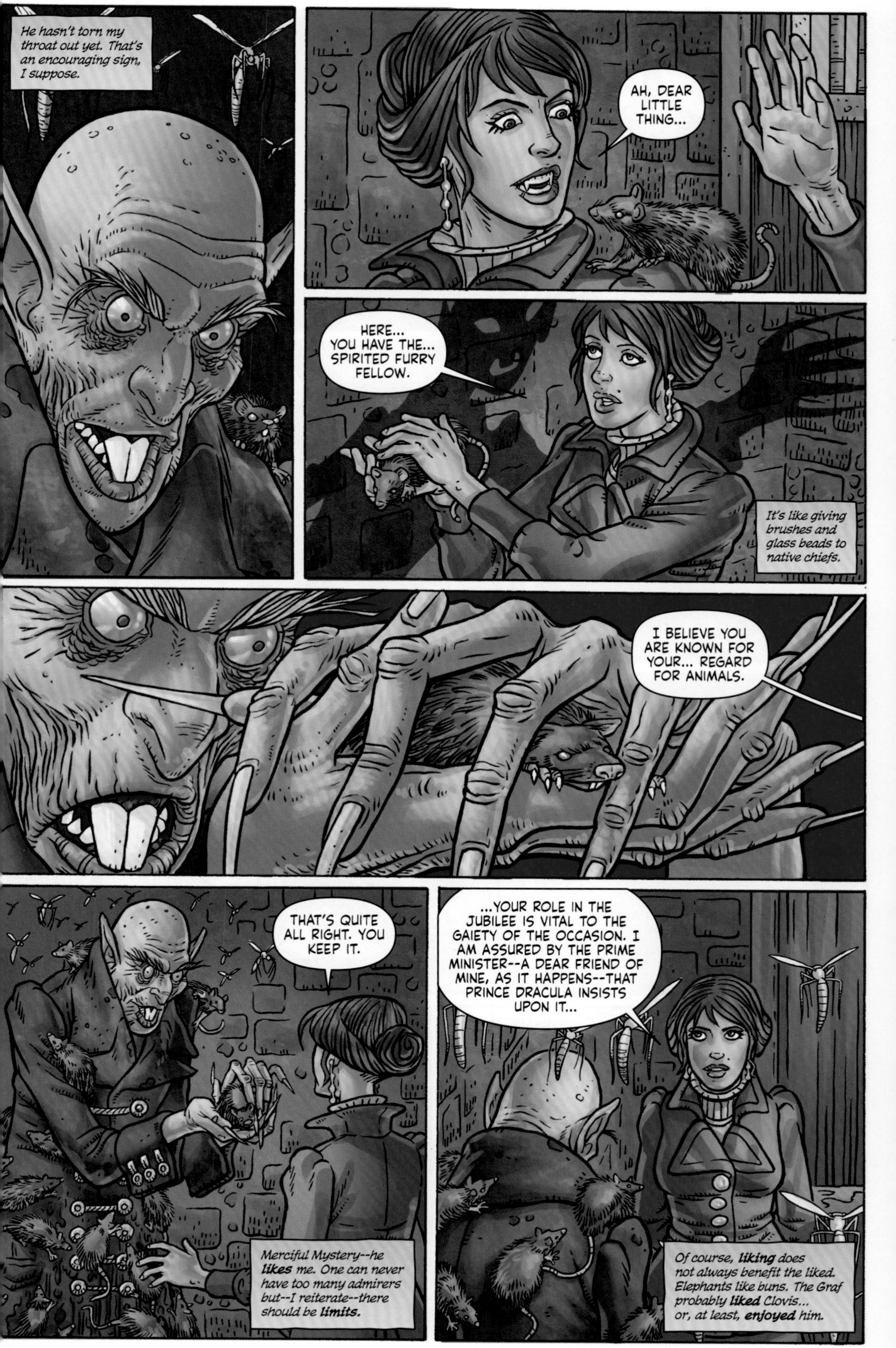
He hasn't torn my throat out yet. That's an encouraging sign, I suppose.
AH, DEAR LITTLE THING...
HERE... YOU HAVE THE... SPIRITED FURRY FELLOW.
It's like giving brushes and glass beads to native chiefs.
I BELIEVE YOU ARE KNOWN FOR YOUR... REGARD FOR ANIMALS.
THAT'S QUITE ALL RIGHT. YOU KEEP IT.
Merciful Mystery--he **likes** me. One can never have too many admirers but--I reiterate--there should be **limits.**
...YOUR ROLE IN THE JUBILEE IS VITAL TO THE GAIETY OF THE OCCASION. I AM ASSURED BY THE PRIME MINISTER--A DEAR FRIEND OF MINE, AS IT HAPPENS--THAT PRINCE DRACULA INSISTS UPON IT...
Of course, **liking** does not always benefit the liked. Elephants like buns. The Graf probably **liked** Clovis... or, at least, **enjoyed** him.

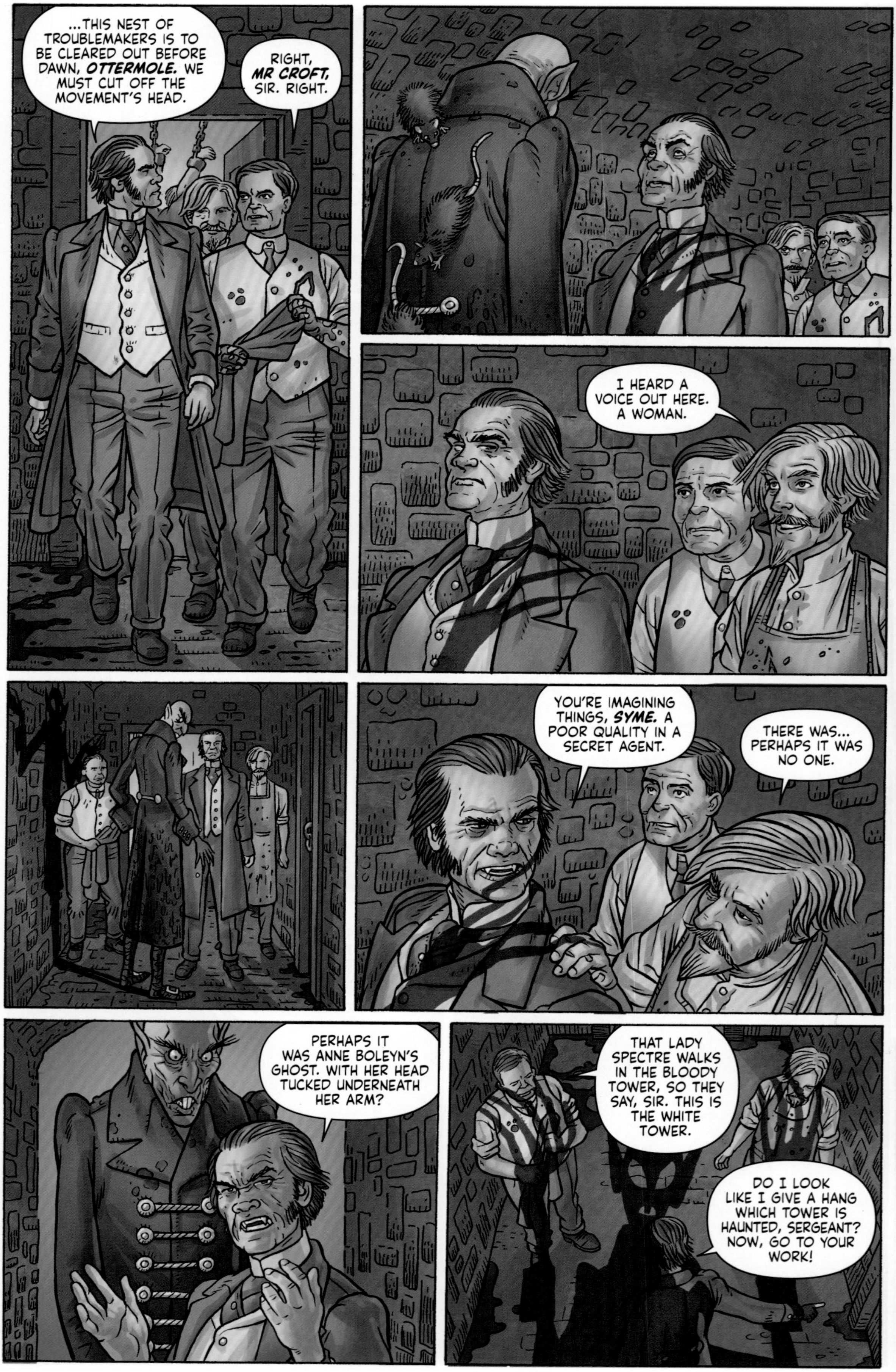
...THIS NEST OF TROUBLEMAKERS IS TO BE CLEARED OUT BEFORE DAWN, ***OTTERMOLE.*** WE MUST CUT OFF THE MOVEMENT'S HEAD.
RIGHT, ***MR CROFT,*** SIR. RIGHT.
I HEARD A VOICE OUT HERE. A WOMAN.
YOU'RE IMAGINING THINGS, ***SYME.*** A POOR QUALITY IN A SECRET AGENT.
THERE WAS... PERHAPS IT WAS NO ONE.
PERHAPS IT WAS ANNE BOLEYN'S GHOST. WITH HER HEAD TUCKED UNDERNEATH HER ARM?
THAT LADY SPECTRE WALKS IN THE BLOODY TOWER, SO THEY SAY, SIR. THIS IS THE WHITE TOWER.
DO I LOOK LIKE I GIVE A HANG WHICH TOWER IS HAUNTED, SERGEANT? NOW, GO TO YOUR WORK!

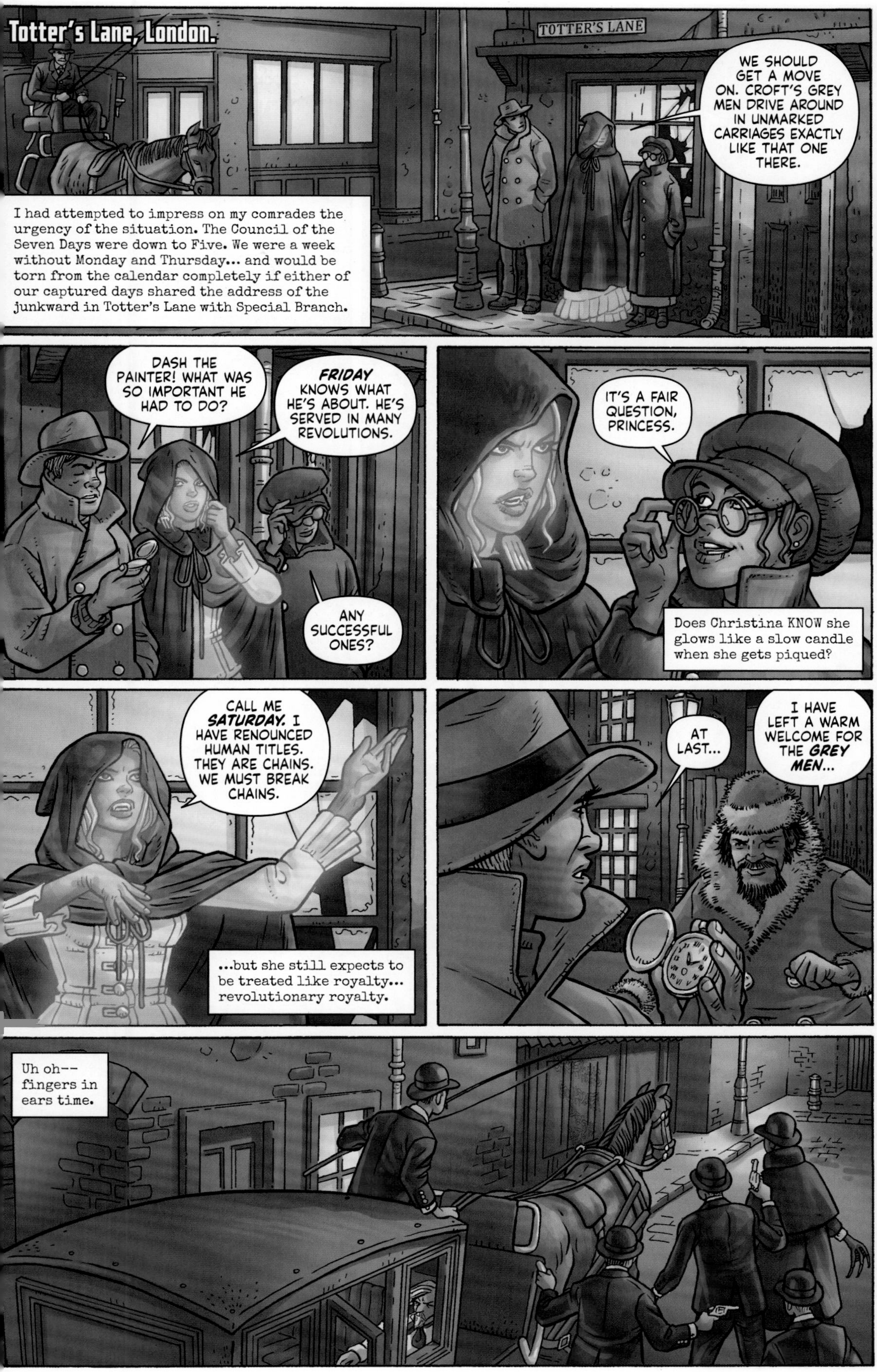

Totter's Lane, London.
TOTTER'S LANE
WE SHOULD GET A MOVE ON. CROFT'S GREY MEN DRIVE AROUND IN UNMARKED CARRIAGES EXACTLY LIKE THAT ONE THERE.
I had attempted to impress on my comrades the urgency of the situation. The Council of the Seven Days were down to Five. We were a week without Monday and Thursday... and would be torn from the calendar completely if either of our captured days shared the address of the junkward in Totter's Lane with Special Branch.
DASH THE PAINTER! WHAT WAS SO IMPORTANT HE HAD TO DO?
FRIDAY KNOWS WHAT HE'S ABOUT. HE'S SERVED IN MANY REVOLUTIONS.
ANY SUCCESSFUL ONES?
IT'S A FAIR QUESTION, PRINCESS.
Does Christina KNOW she glows like a slow candle when she gets piqued?
CALL ME SATURDAY. I HAVE RENOUNCED HUMAN TITLES. THEY ARE CHAINS. WE MUST BREAK CHAINS.
...but she still expects to be treated like royalty... revolutionary royalty.
AT LAST...
I HAVE LEFT A WARM WELCOME FOR THE GREY MEN...
Uh oh-- fingers in ears time.

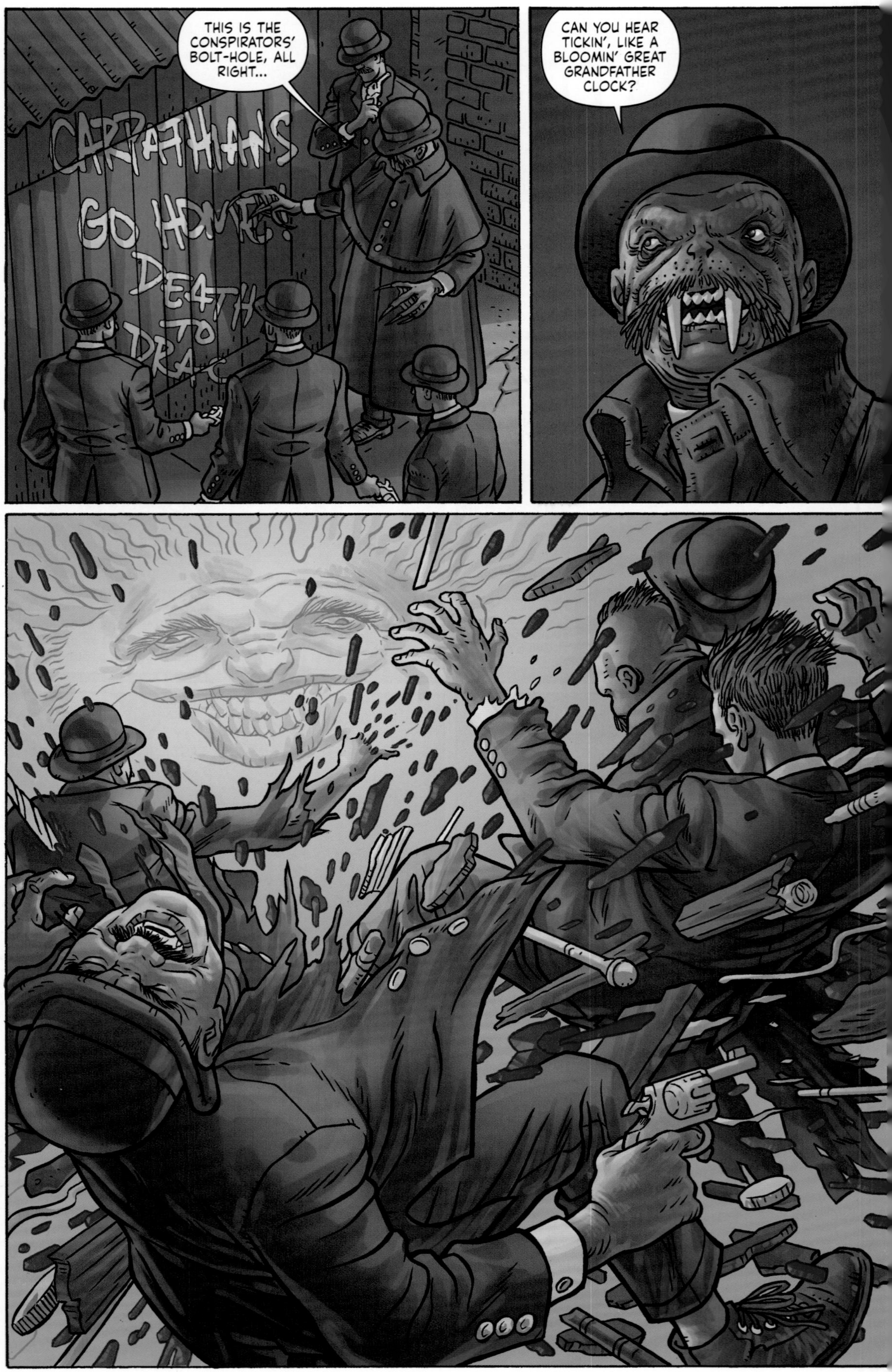

THIS IS THE CONSPIRATORS' BOLT-HOLE, ALL RIGHT...
CARPATHIANS GO HOME! DEATH TO DRAC
CAN YOU HEAR TICKIN', LIKE A BLOOMIN' GREAT GRANDFATHER CLOCK?

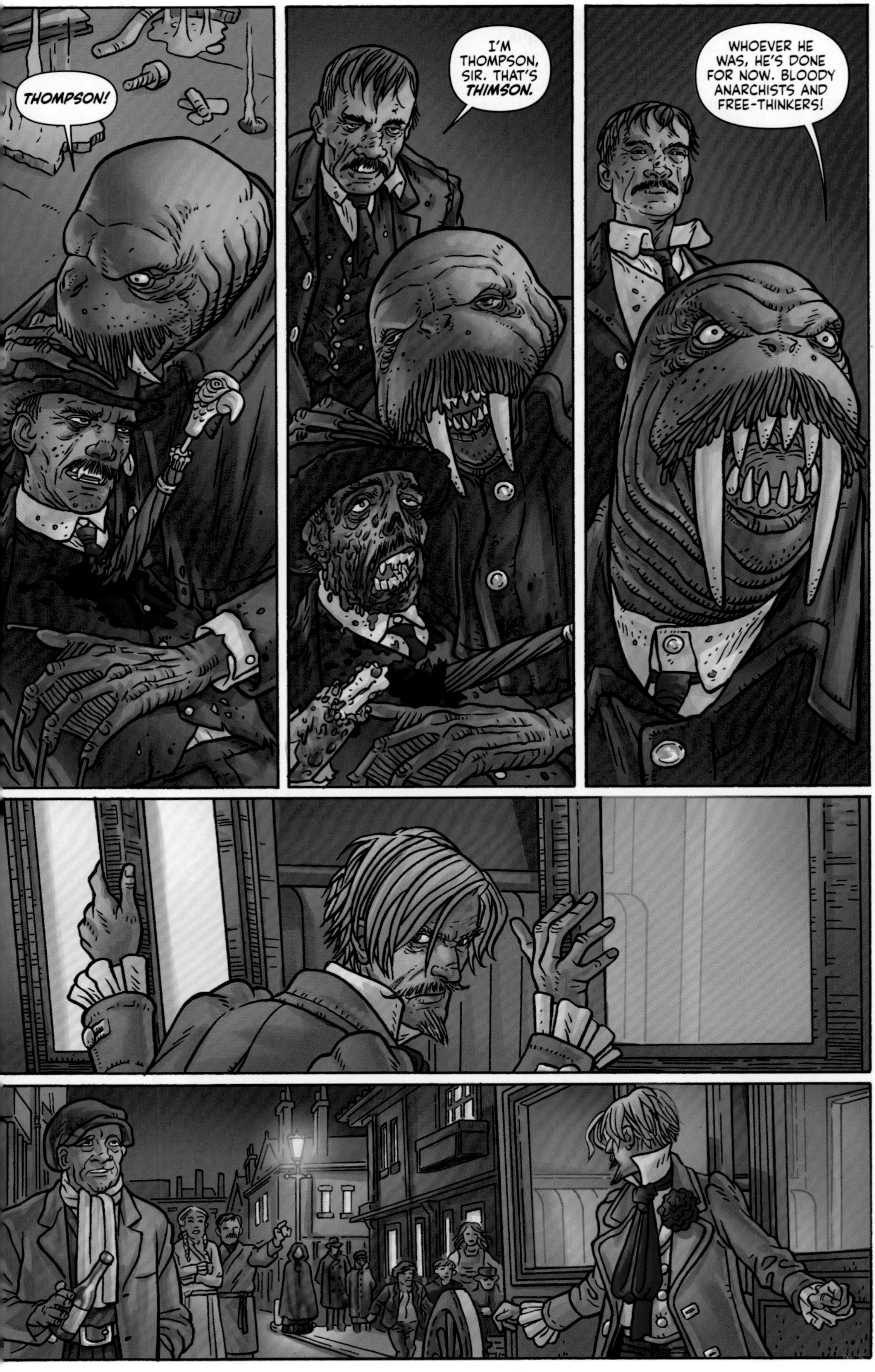
THOMPSON!
I'M THOMPSON, SIR. THAT'S *THIMSON.*
WHOEVER HE WAS, HE'S DONE FOR NOW. BLOODY ANARCHISTS AND FREE-THINKERS!

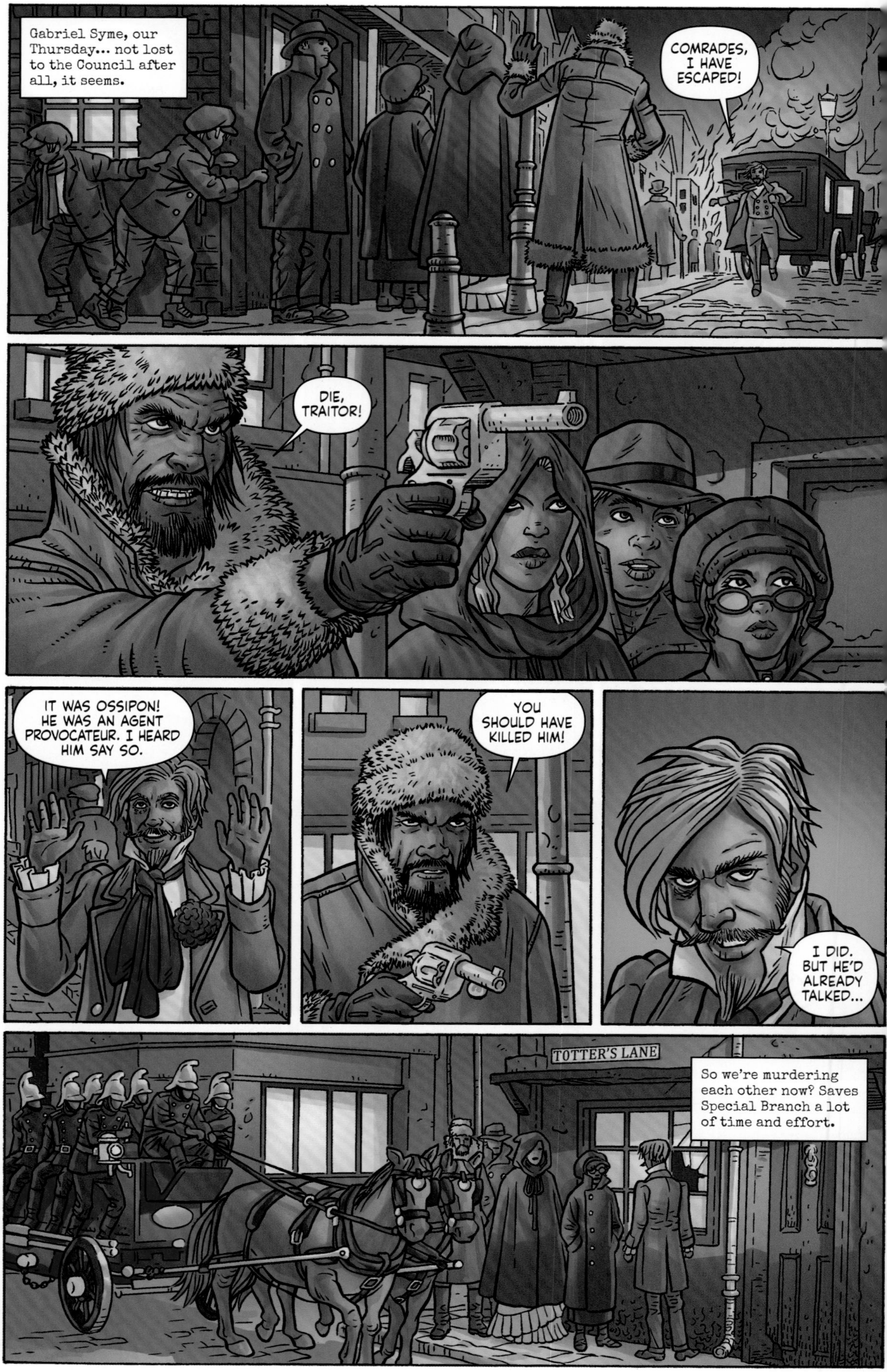
Gabriel Syme, our Thursday... not lost to the Council after all, it seems.
COMRADES, I HAVE ESCAPED!
DIE, TRAITOR!
IT WAS OSSIPON! HE WAS AN AGENT PROVOCATEUR. I HEARD HIM SAY SO.
YOU SHOULD HAVE KILLED HIM!
I DID. BUT HE'D ALREADY TALKED...
TOTTER'S LANE
So we're murdering each other now? Saves Special Branch a lot of time and effort.

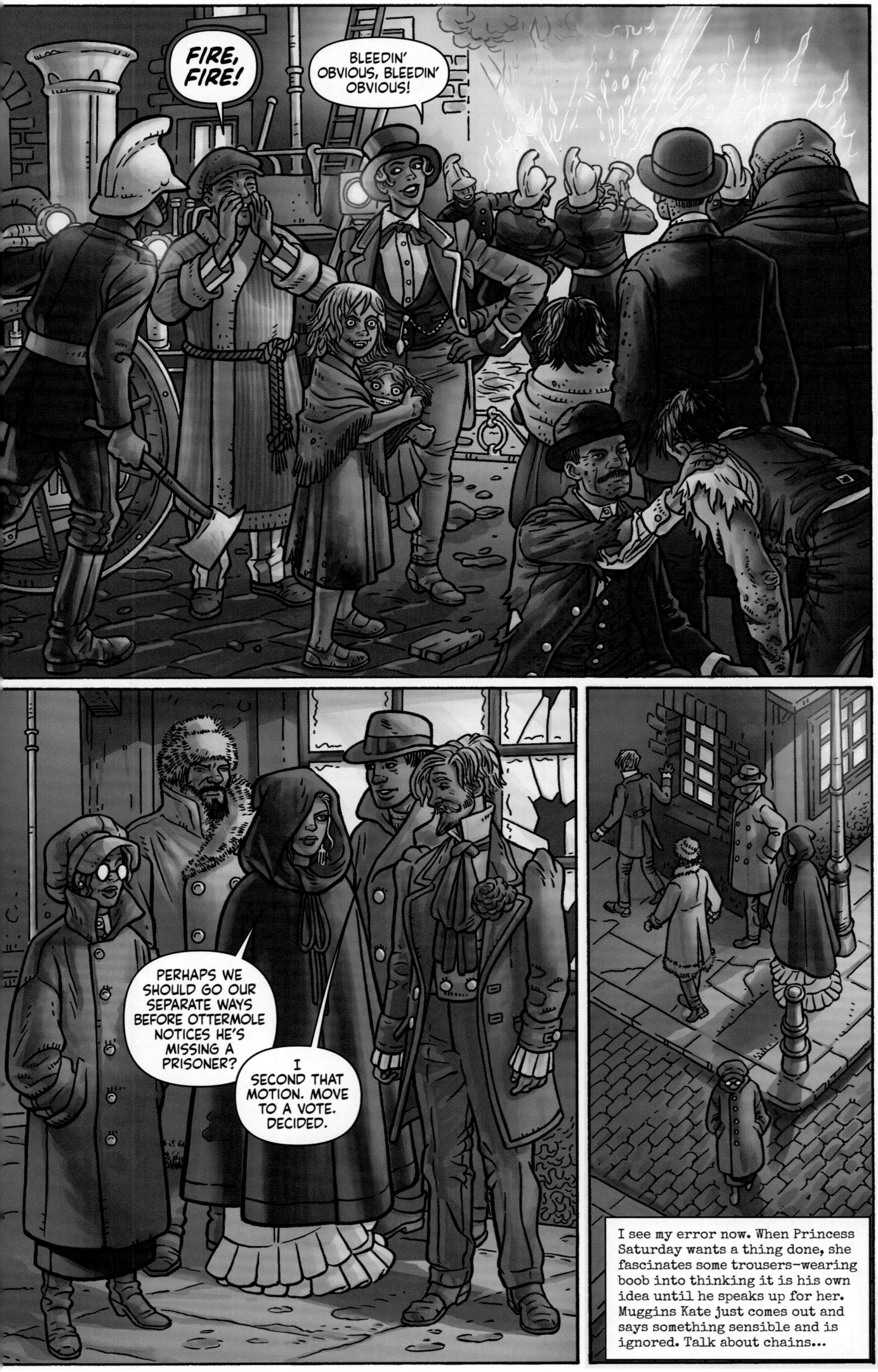
FIRE, FIRE!
BLEEDIN' OBVIOUS, BLEEDIN' OBVIOUS!
PERHAPS WE SHOULD GO OUR SEPARATE WAYS BEFORE OTTERMOLE NOTICES HE'S MISSING A PRISONER?
I SECOND THAT MOTION. MOVE TO A VOTE. DECIDED.
I see my error now. When Princess Saturday wants a thing done, she fascinates some trousers-wearing boob into thinking it is his own idea until he speaks up for her. Muggins Kate just comes out and says something sensible and is ignored. Talk about chains...

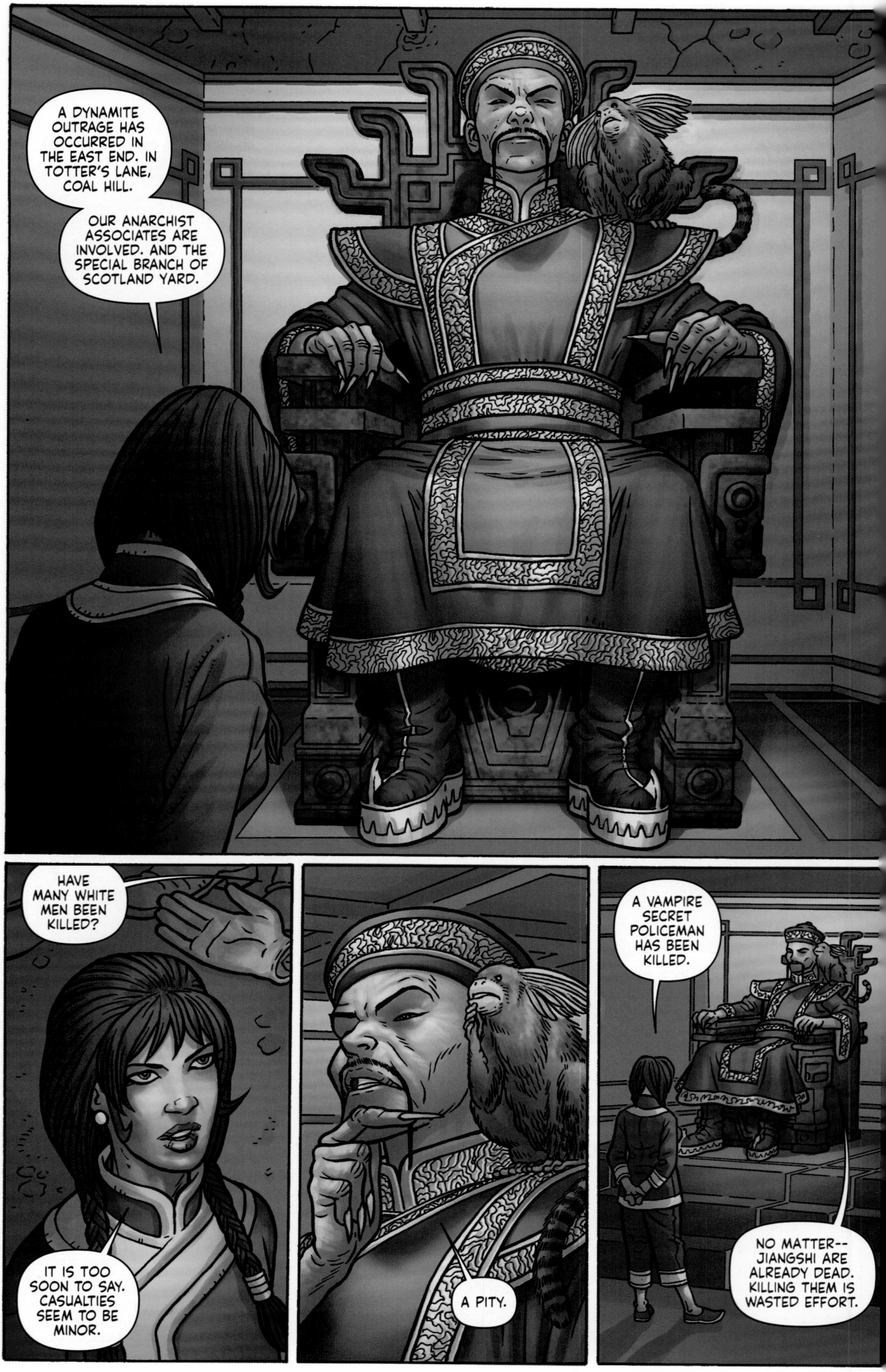
A DYNAMITE OUTRAGE HAS OCCURRED IN THE EAST END. IN TOTTER'S LANE, COAL HILL.
OUR ANARCHIST ASSOCIATES ARE INVOLVED. AND THE SPECIAL BRANCH OF SCOTLAND YARD.
HAVE MANY WHITE MEN BEEN KILLED?
IT IS TOO SOON TO SAY. CASUALTIES SEEM TO BE MINOR.
A PITY.
A VAMPIRE SECRET POLICEMAN HAS BEEN KILLED.
NO MATTER-- JIANGSHI ARE ALREADY DEAD. KILLING THEM IS WASTED EFFORT.

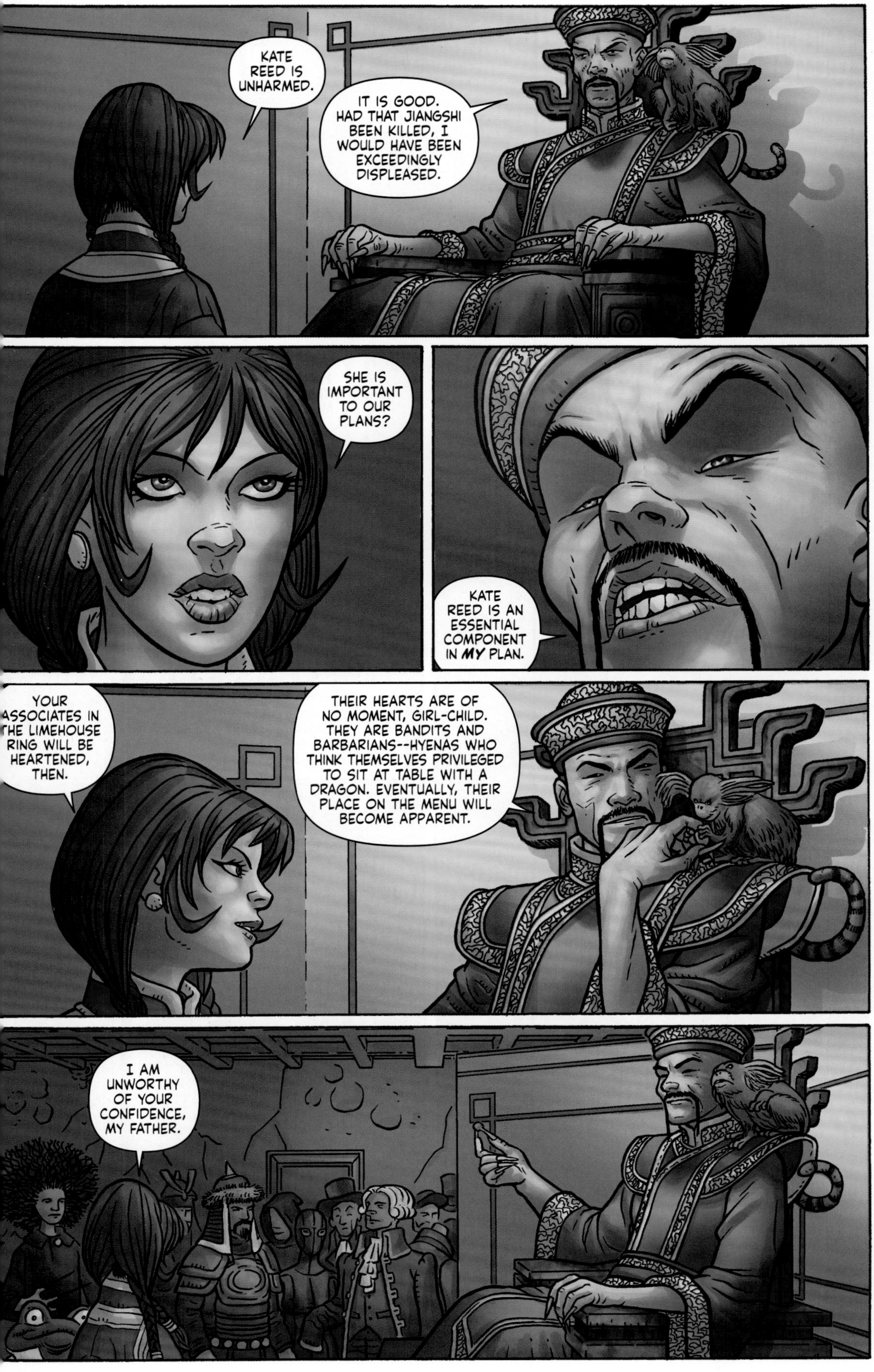
KATE REED IS UNHARMED.
IT IS GOOD. HAD THAT JIANGSHI BEEN KILLED, I WOULD HAVE BEEN EXCEEDINGLY DISPLEASED.
SHE IS IMPORTANT TO OUR PLANS?
KATE REED IS AN ESSENTIAL COMPONENT IN *MY* PLAN.
YOUR ASSOCIATES IN THE LIMEHOUSE RING WILL BE HEARTENED, THEN.
THEIR HEARTS ARE OF NO MOMENT, GIRL-CHILD. THEY ARE BANDITS AND BARBARIANS--HYENAS WHO THINK THEMSELVES PRIVILEGED TO SIT AT TABLE WITH A DRAGON. EVENTUALLY, THEIR PLACE ON THE MENU WILL BECOME APPARENT.
I AM UNWORTHY OF YOUR CONFIDENCE, MY FATHER.

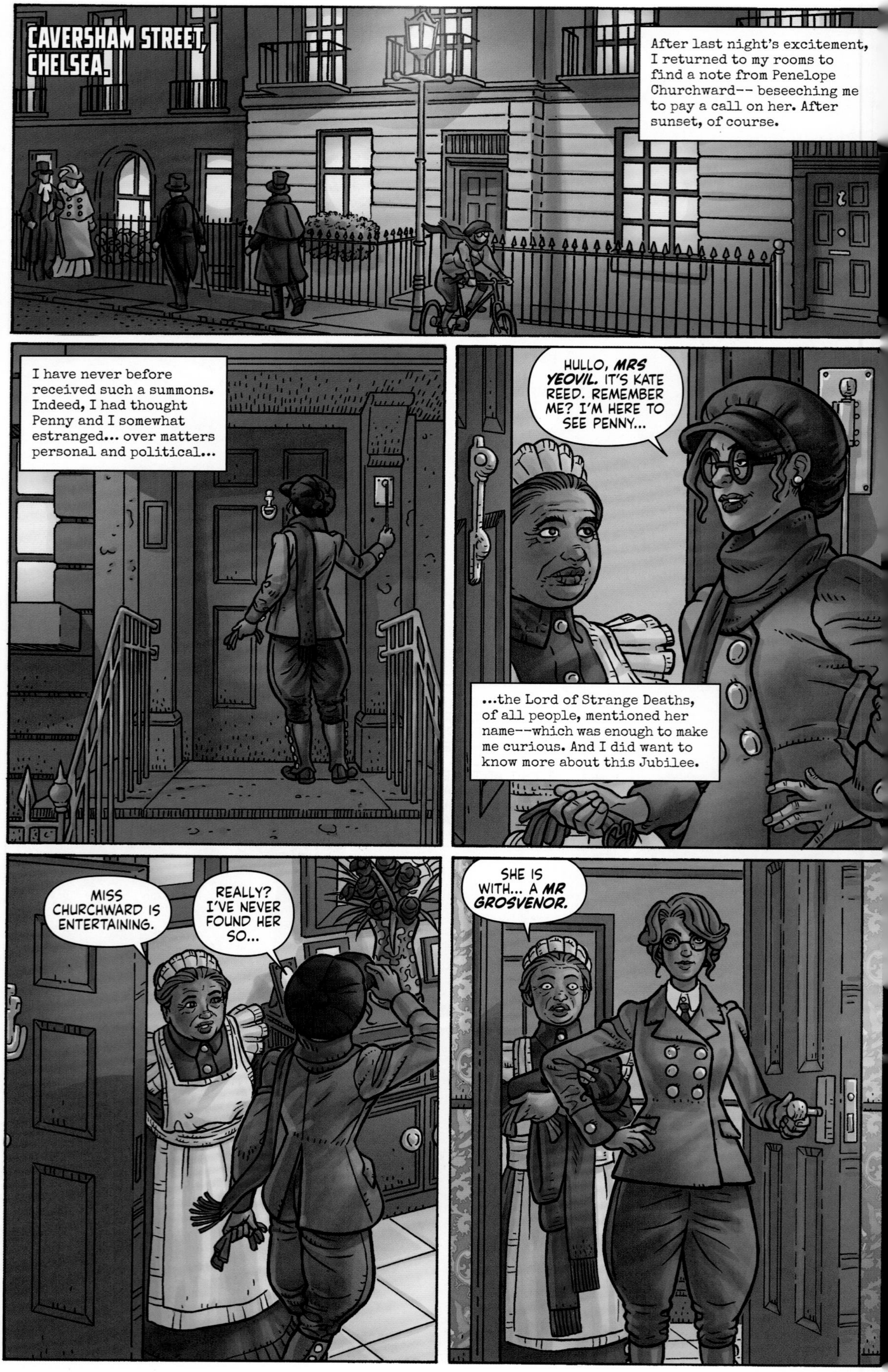
CAVERSHAM STREET, CHELSEA.
After last night's excitement, I returned to my rooms to find a note from Penelope Churchward-- beseeching me to pay a call on her. After sunset, of course.
I have never before received such a summons. Indeed, I had thought Penny and I somewhat estranged... over matters personal and political...
HULLO, MRS YEOVIL. IT'S KATE REED. REMEMBER ME? I'M HERE TO SEE PENNY...
...the Lord of Strange Deaths, of all people, mentioned her name--which was enough to make me curious. And I did want to know more about this Jubilee.
MISS CHURCHWARD IS ENTERTAINING.
REALLY? I'VE NEVER FOUND HER SO...
SHE IS WITH... A MR GROSVENOR.

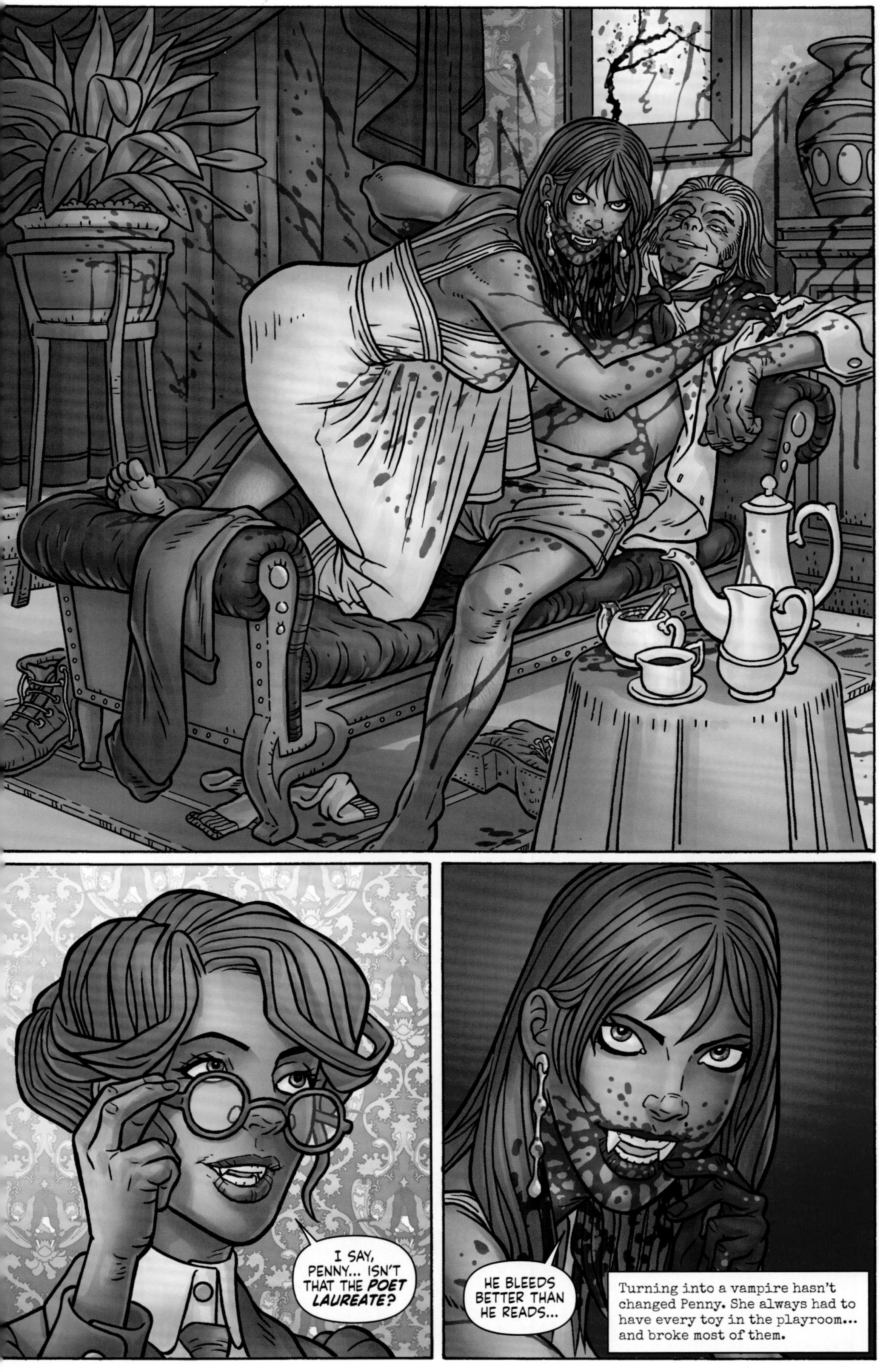
I SAY, PENNY... ISN'T THAT THE *POET LAUREATE?*
HE BLEEDS BETTER THAN HE READS...
Turning into a vampire hasn't changed Penny. She always had to have every toy in the playroom... and broke most of them.

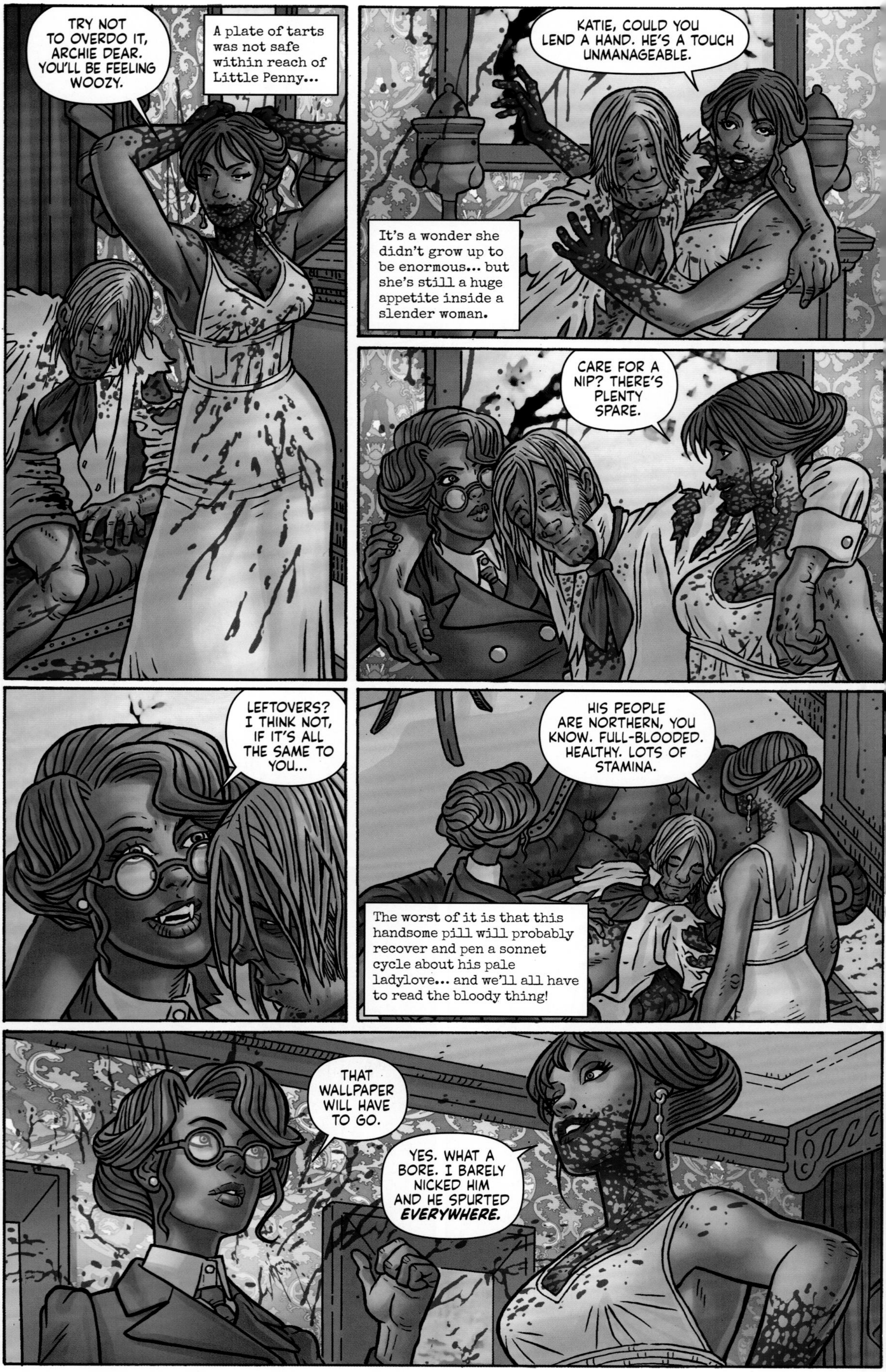
TRY NOT TO OVERDO IT, ARCHIE DEAR. YOU'LL BE FEELING WOOZY.
A plate of tarts was not safe within reach of Little Penny...
KATIE, COULD YOU LEND A HAND. HE'S A TOUCH UNMANAGEABLE.
It's a wonder she didn't grow up to be enormous... but she's still a huge appetite inside a slender woman.
CARE FOR A NIP? THERE'S PLENTY SPARE.
LEFTOVERS? I THINK NOT, IF IT'S ALL THE SAME TO YOU...
HIS PEOPLE ARE NORTHERN, YOU KNOW. FULL-BLOODED. HEALTHY. LOTS OF STAMINA.
The worst of it is that this handsome pill will probably recover and pen a sonnet cycle about his pale ladylove... and we'll all have to read the bloody thing!
THAT WALLPAPER WILL HAVE TO GO.
YES. WHAT A BORE. I BARELY NICKED HIM AND HE SPURTED *EVERYWHERE.*

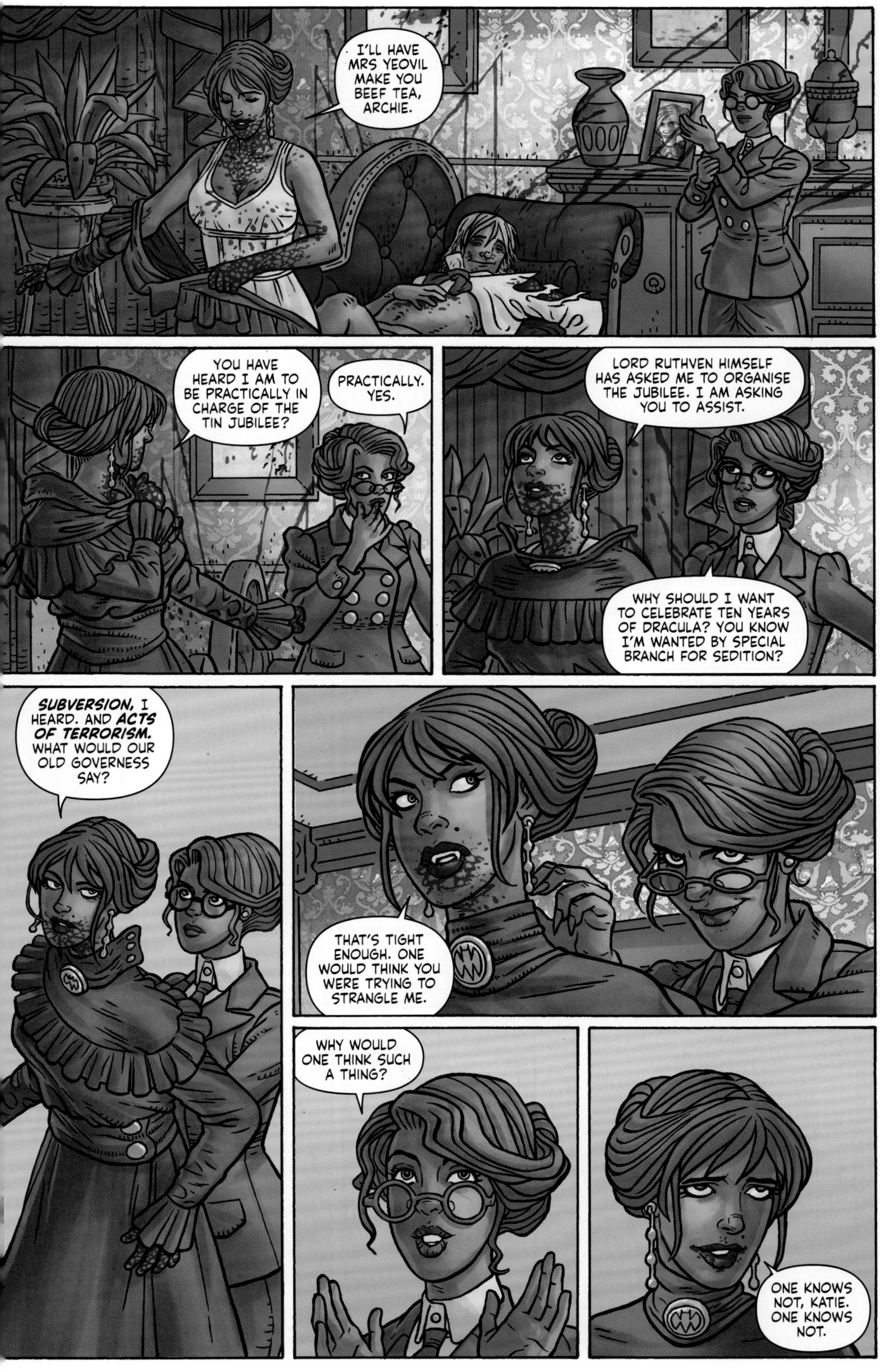
I'LL HAVE MRS YEOVIL MAKE YOU BEEF TEA, ARCHIE.
YOU HAVE HEARD I AM TO BE PRACTICALLY IN CHARGE OF THE TIN JUBILEE?
PRACTICALLY. YES.
LORD RUTHVEN HIMSELF HAS ASKED ME TO ORGANISE THE JUBILEE. I AM ASKING YOU TO ASSIST.
WHY SHOULD I WANT TO CELEBRATE TEN YEARS OF DRACULA? YOU KNOW I'M WANTED BY SPECIAL BRANCH FOR SEDITION?
SUBVERSION, I HEARD. AND *ACTS OF TERRORISM.* WHAT WOULD OUR OLD GOVERNESS SAY?
THAT'S TIGHT ENOUGH. ONE WOULD THINK YOU WERE TRYING TO STRANGLE ME.
WHY WOULD ONE THINK SUCH A THING?
ONE KNOWS NOT, KATIE. ONE KNOWS NOT.

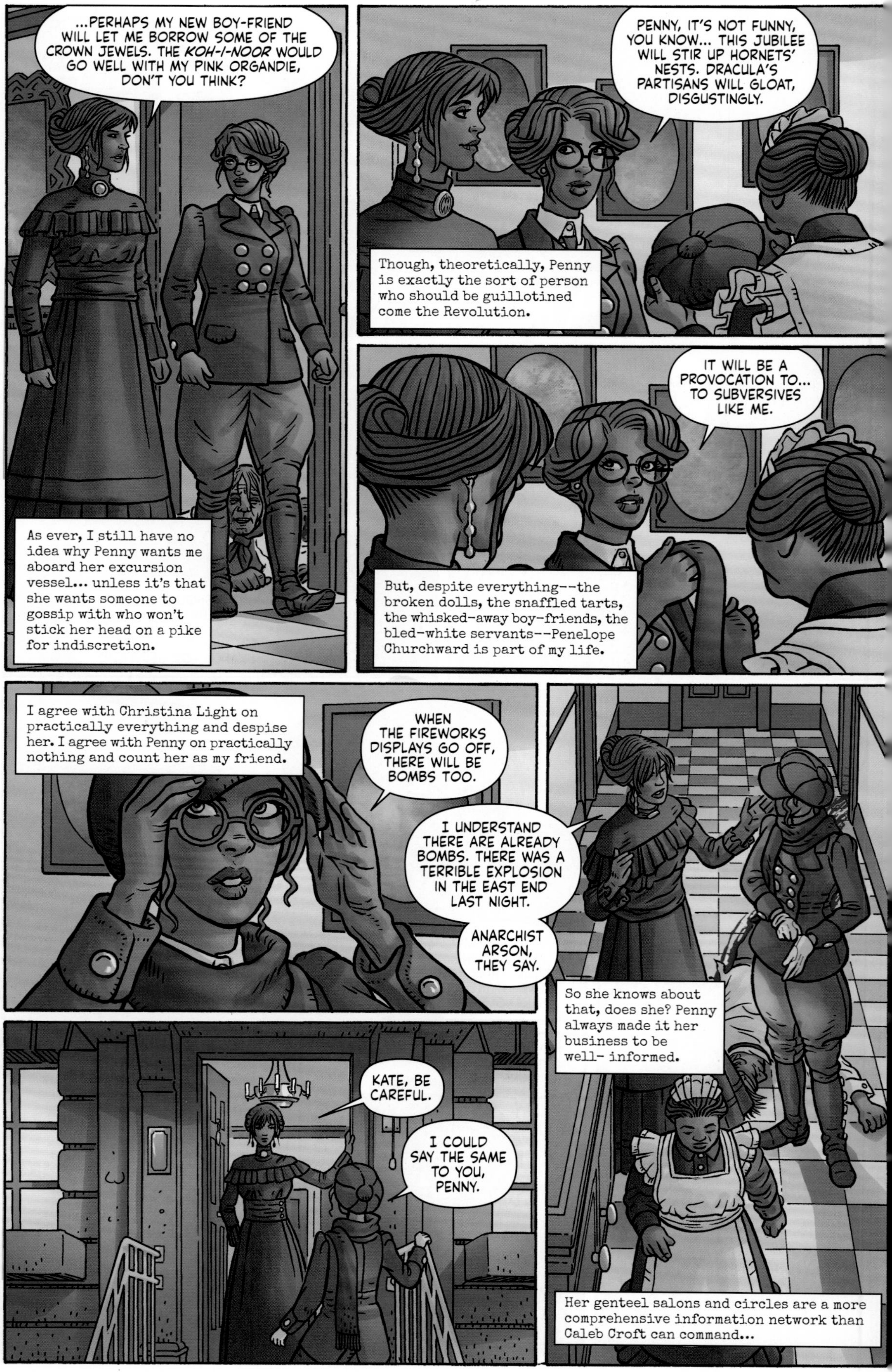

...PERHAPS MY NEW BOY-FRIEND WILL LET ME BORROW SOME OF THE CROWN JEWELS. THE *KOH-I-NOOR* WOULD GO WELL WITH MY PINK ORGANDIE, DON'T YOU THINK?
As ever, I still have no idea why Penny wants me aboard her excursion vessel... unless it's that she wants someone to gossip with who won't stick her head on a pike for indiscretion.
PENNY, IT'S NOT FUNNY, YOU KNOW... THIS JUBILEE WILL STIR UP HORNETS' NESTS. DRACULA'S PARTISANS WILL GLOAT, DISGUSTINGLY.
Though, theoretically, Penny is exactly the sort of person who should be guillotined come the Revolution.
IT WILL BE A PROVOCATION TO... TO SUBVERSIVES LIKE ME.
But, despite everything--the broken dolls, the snaffled tarts, the whisked-away boy-friends, the bled-white servants--Penelope Churchward is part of my life.
I agree with Christina Light on practically everything and despise her. I agree with Penny on practically nothing and count her as my friend.
WHEN THE FIREWORKS DISPLAYS GO OFF, THERE WILL BE BOMBS TOO.
I UNDERSTAND THERE ARE ALREADY BOMBS. THERE WAS A TERRIBLE EXPLOSION IN THE EAST END LAST NIGHT.
ANARCHIST ARSON, THEY SAY.
So she knows about that, does she? Penny always made it her business to be well- informed.
KATE, BE CAREFUL.
I COULD SAY THE SAME TO YOU, PENNY.
Her genteel salons and circles are a more comprehensive information network than Caleb Croft can command...

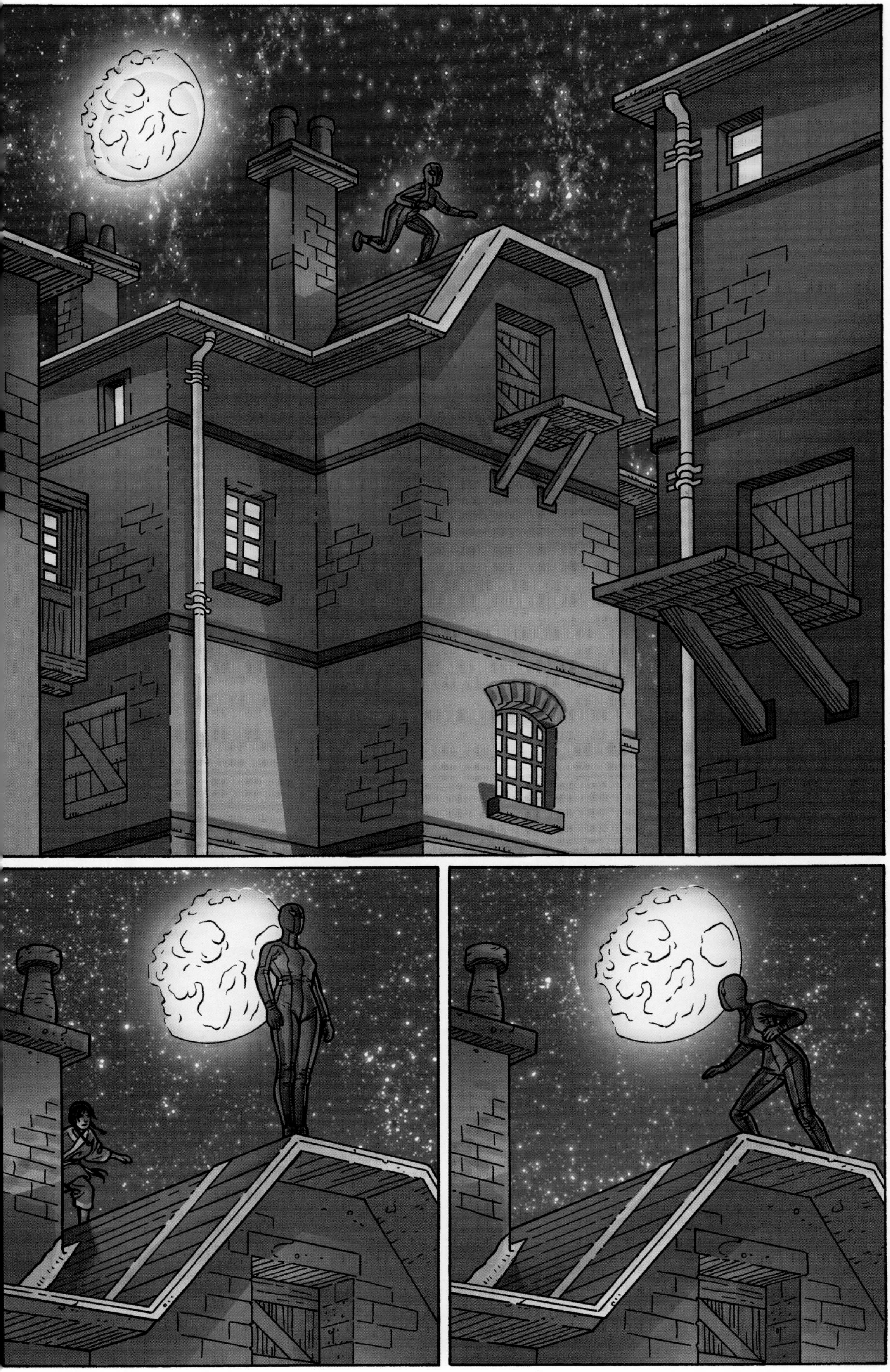

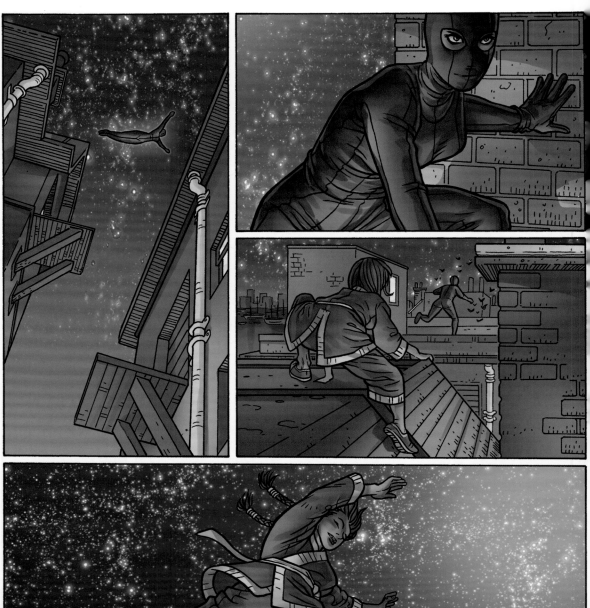

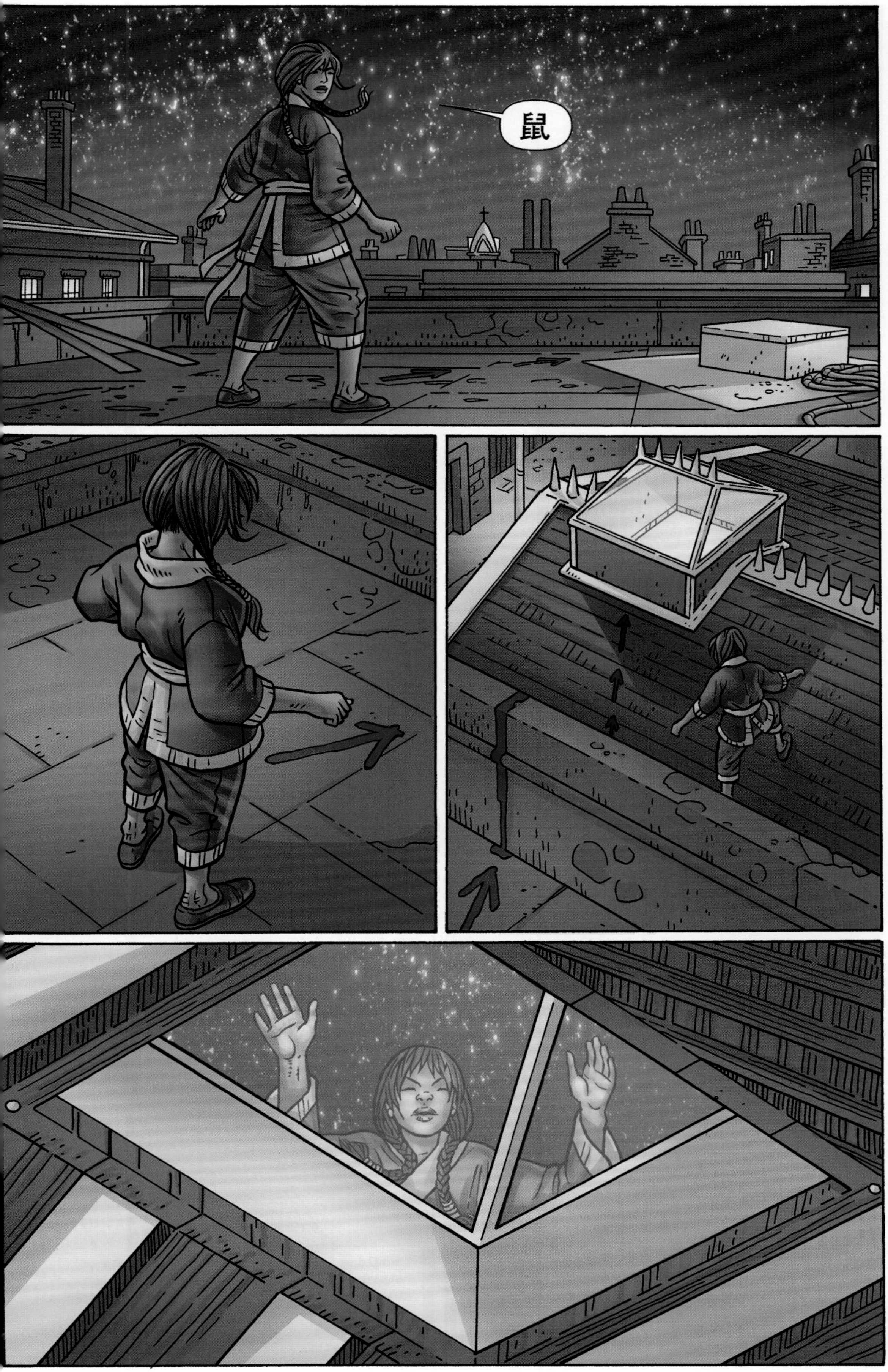
鼠

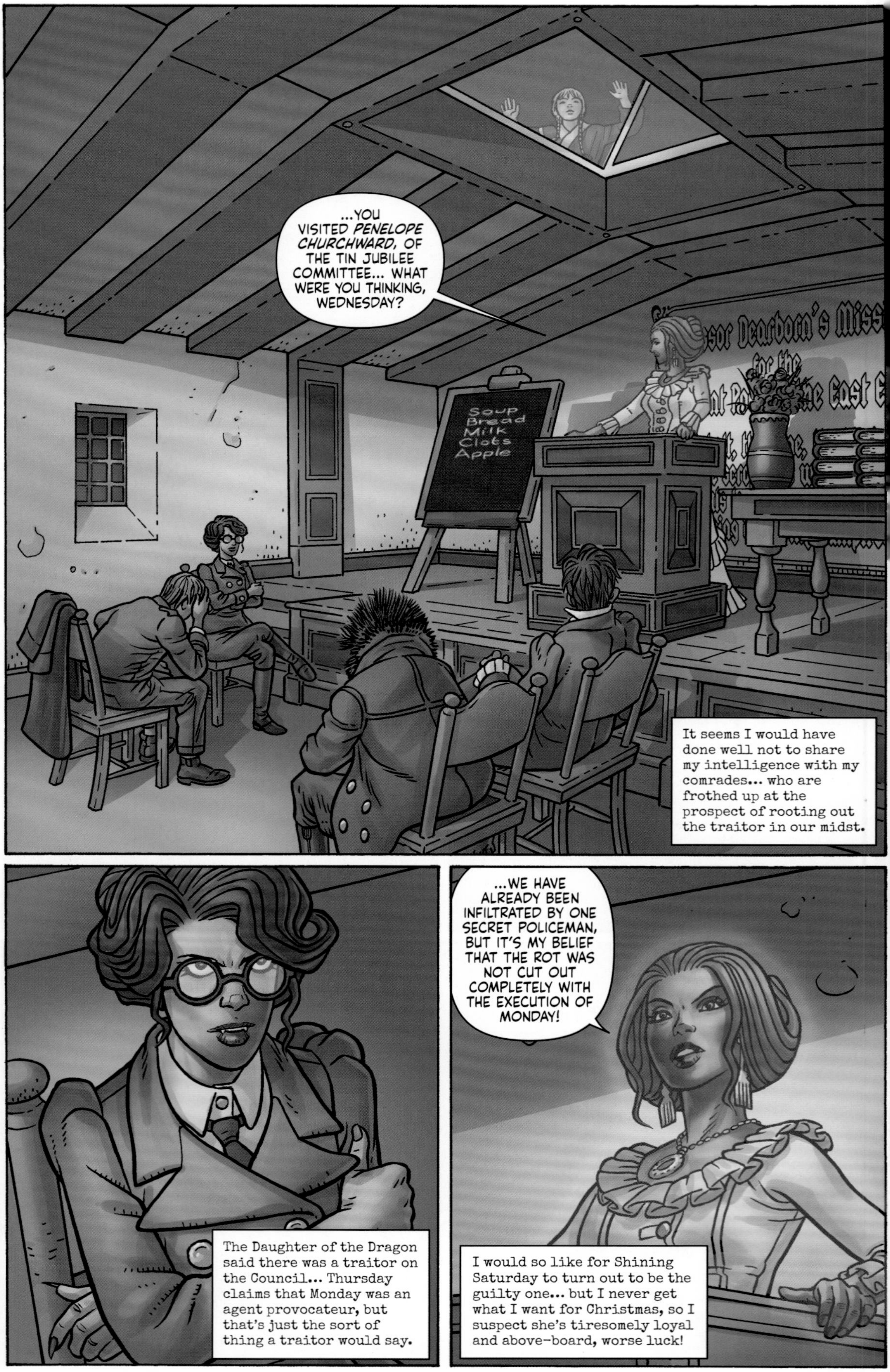
...YOU VISITED PENELOPE CHURCHWARD, OF THE TIN JUBILEE COMMITTEE... WHAT WERE YOU THINKING, WEDNESDAY?
Soup
Bread
Milk
Clots
Apple
It seems I would have done well not to share my intelligence with my comrades... who are frothed up at the prospect of rooting out the traitor in our midst.
The Daughter of the Dragon said there was a traitor on the Council... Thursday claims that Monday was an agent provocateur, but that's just the sort of thing a traitor would say.
...WE HAVE ALREADY BEEN INFILTRATED BY ONE SECRET POLICEMAN, BUT IT'S MY BELIEF THAT THE ROT WAS NOT CUT OUT COMPLETELY WITH THE EXECUTION OF MONDAY!
I would so like for Shining Saturday to turn out to be the guilty one... but I never get what I want for Christmas, so I suspect she's tiresomely loyal and above-board, worse luck!

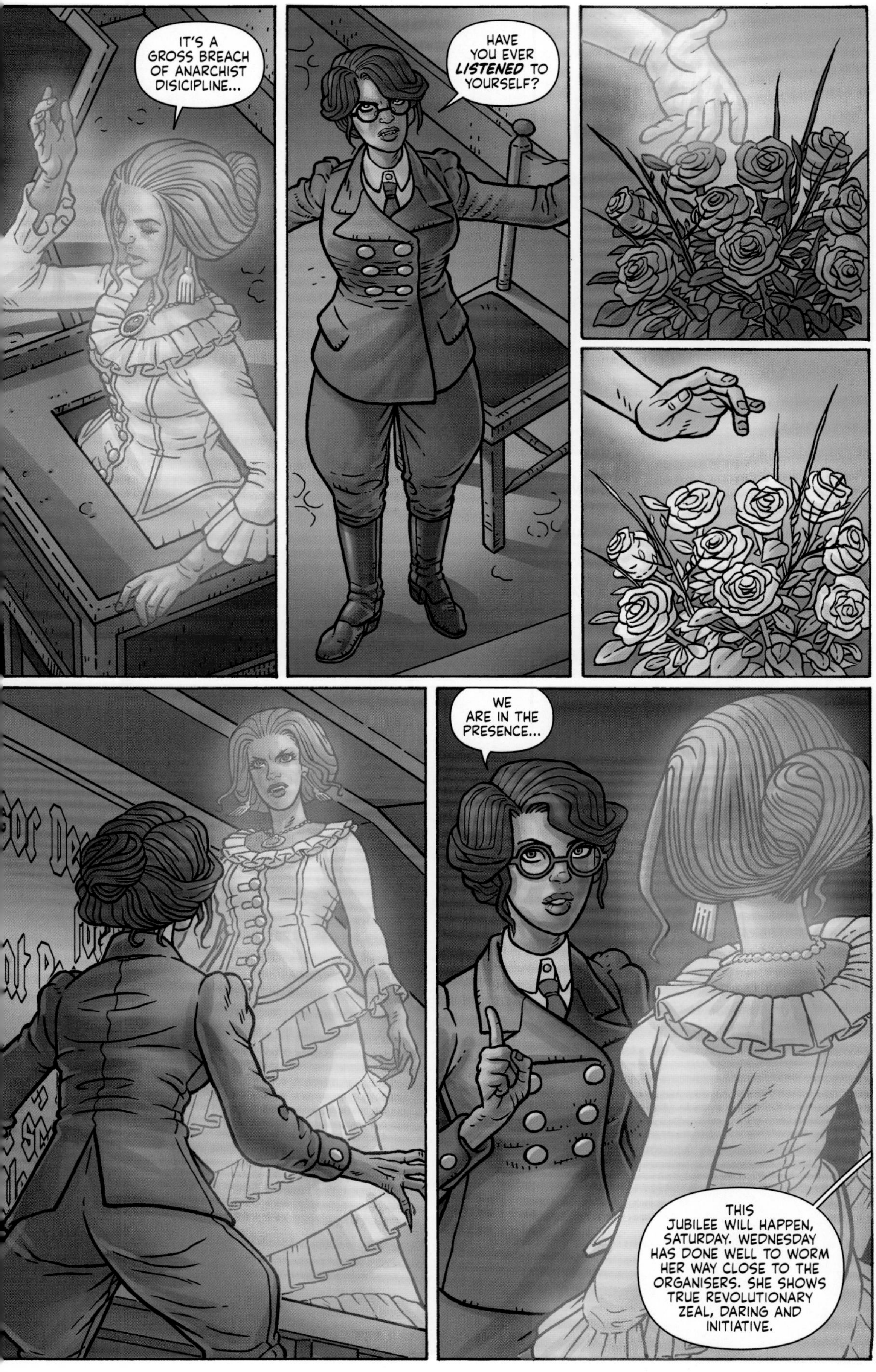
IT'S A GROSS BREACH OF ANARCHIST DISICIPLINE...
HAVE YOU EVER LISTENED TO YOURSELF?
WE ARE IN THE PRESENCE...
THIS JUBILEE WILL HAPPEN, SATURDAY. WEDNESDAY HAS DONE WELL TO WORM HER WAY CLOSE TO THE ORGANISERS. SHE SHOWS TRUE REVOLUTIONARY ZEAL, DARING AND INITIATIVE.

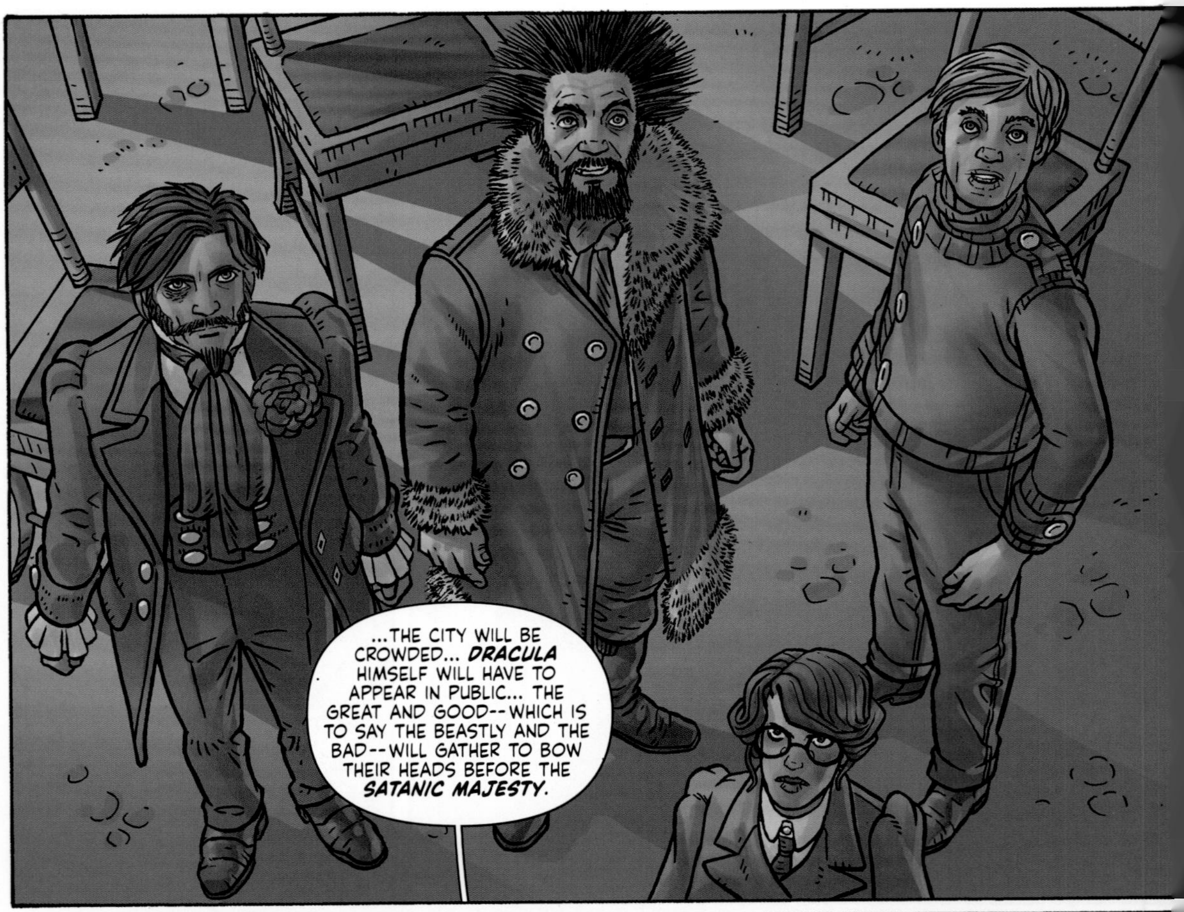
...THE CITY WILL BE CROWDED... DRACULA HIMSELF WILL HAVE TO APPEAR IN PUBLIC... THE GREAT AND GOOD--WHICH IS TO SAY THE BEASTLY AND THE BAD--WILL GATHER TO BOW THEIR HEADS BEFORE THE SATANIC MAJESTY.

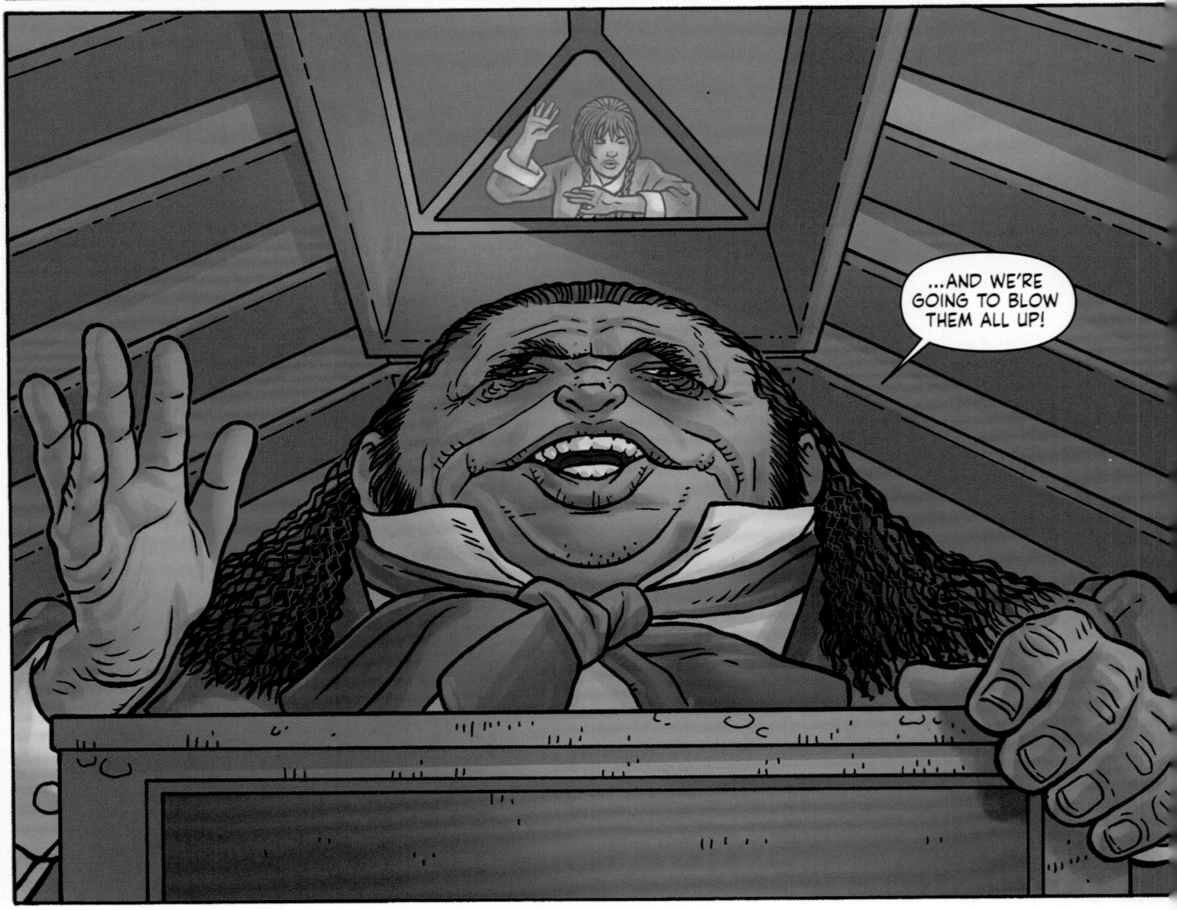
...AND WE'RE GOING TO BLOW THEM ALL UP!

CHAPTER FOUR

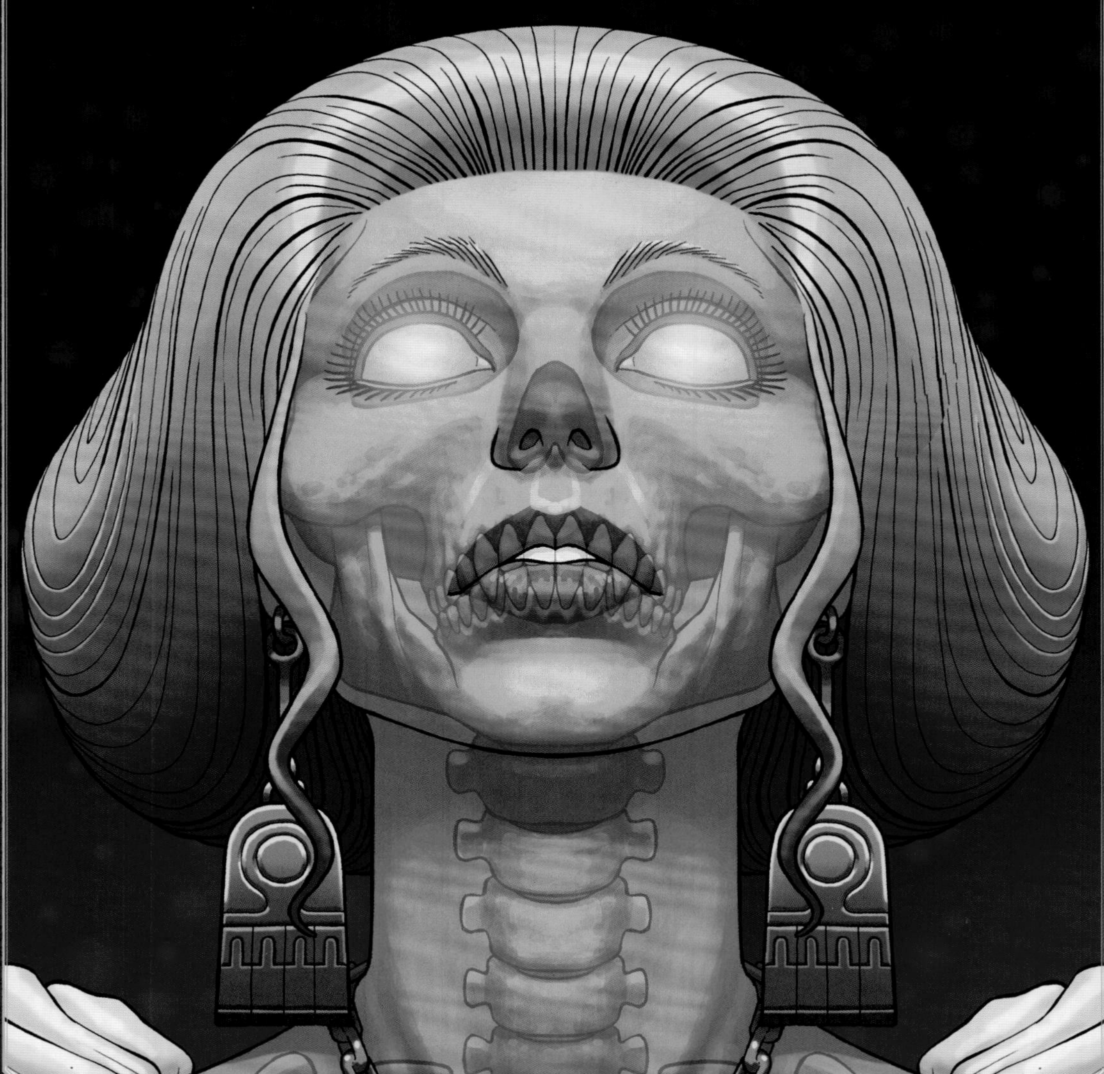

Illustration by Paul McCaffrey

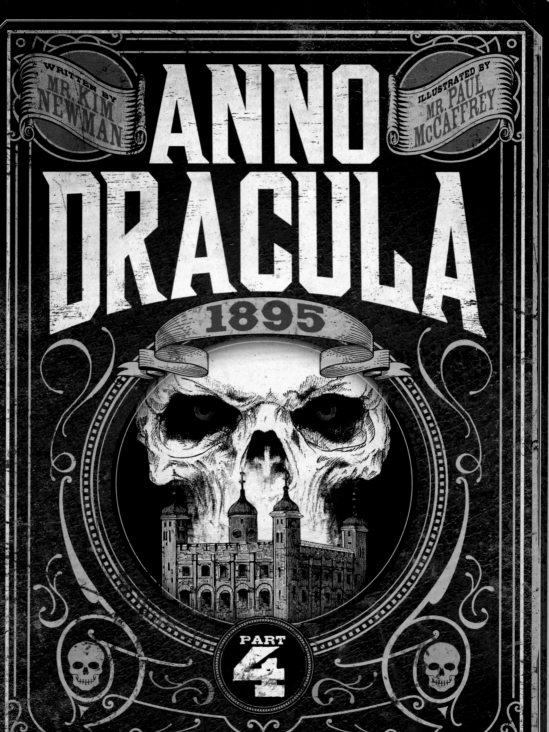

WRITTEN BY
MR. KIM
NEWMAN

ILLUSTRATED BY
MR. PAUL
McCAFFREY

ANNO DRACULA

1895

PART
4

SEVEN DAYS IN MAYHEM

Illustration by Martin Stiff

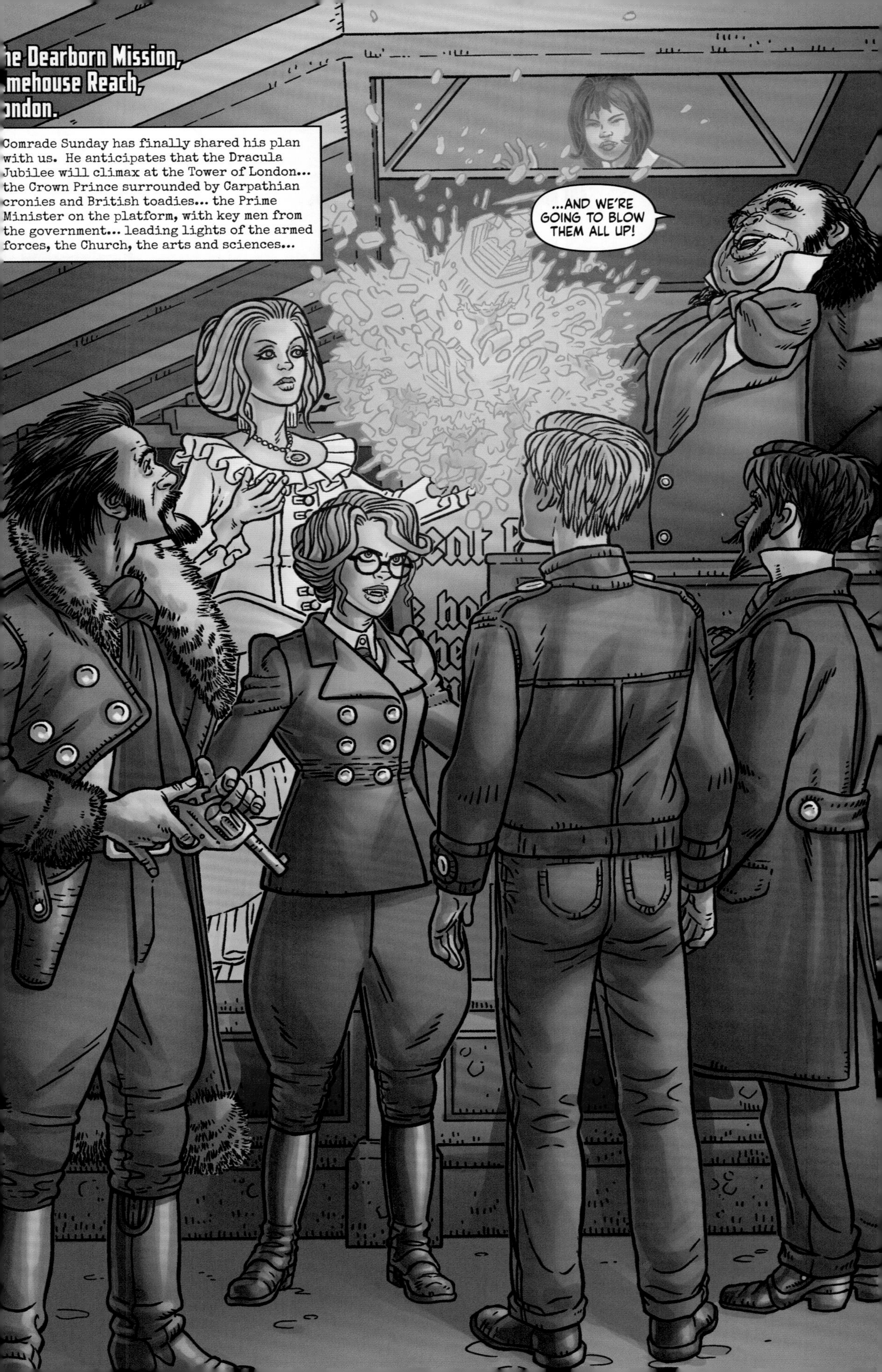
he Dearborn Mission,
mehouse Reach,
ondon.
Comrade Sunday has finally shared his plan with us. He anticipates that the Dracula Jubilee will climax at the Tower of London... the Crown Prince surrounded by Carpathian cronies and British toadies... the Prime Minister on the platform, with key men from the government... leading lights of the armed forces, the Church, the arts and sciences...
...AND WE'RE GOING TO BLOW THEM ALL UP!

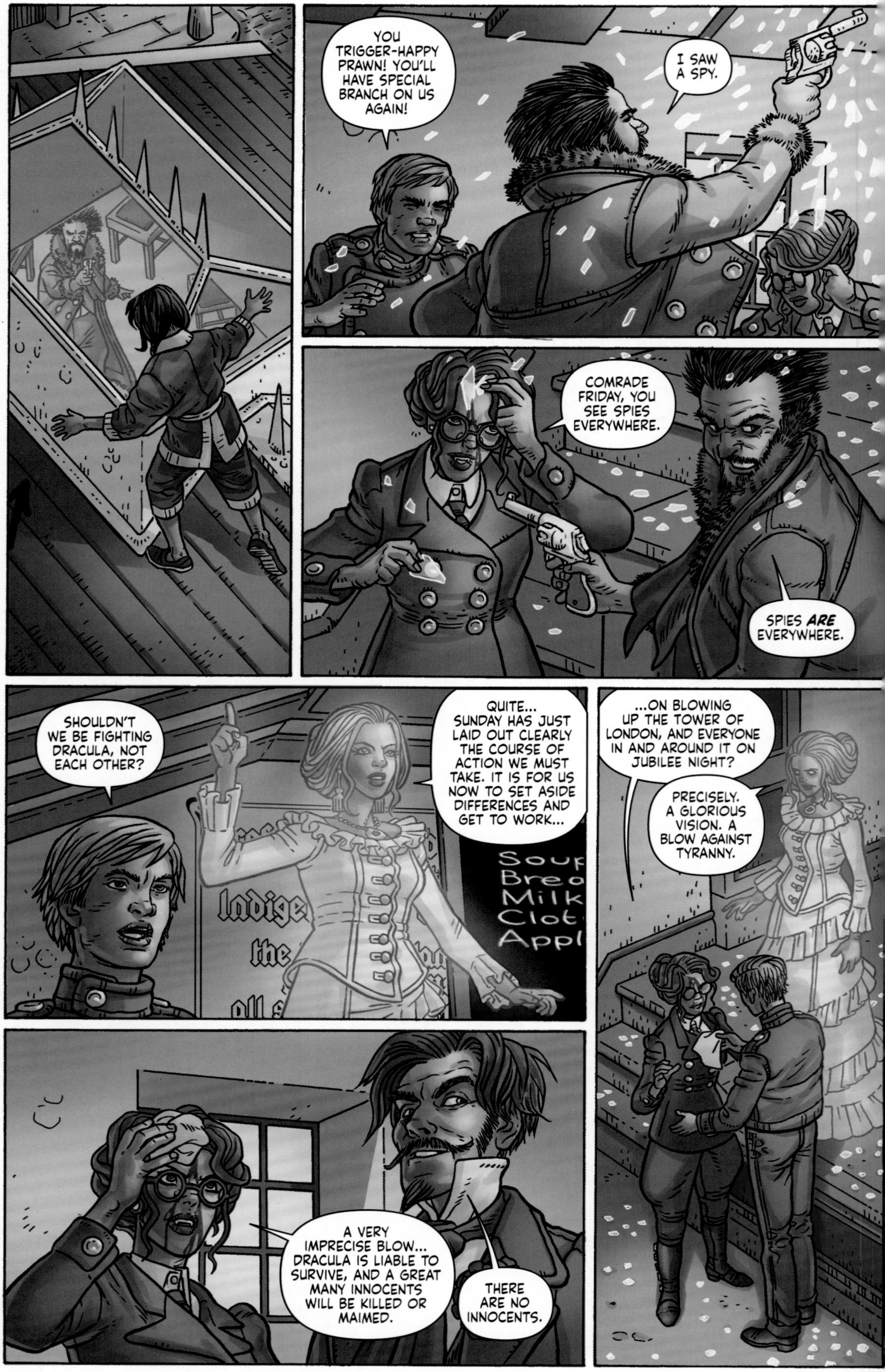

YOU TRIGGER-HAPPY PRAWN! YOU'LL HAVE SPECIAL BRANCH ON US AGAIN!
I SAW A SPY.
COMRADE FRIDAY, YOU SEE SPIES EVERYWHERE.
SPIES **ARE** EVERYWHERE.
SHOULDN'T WE BE FIGHTING DRACULA, NOT EACH OTHER?
QUITE... SUNDAY HAS JUST LAID OUT CLEARLY THE COURSE OF ACTION WE MUST TAKE. IT IS FOR US NOW TO SET ASIDE DIFFERENCES AND GET TO WORK...
...ON BLOWING UP THE TOWER OF LONDON, AND EVERYONE IN AND AROUND IT ON JUBILEE NIGHT?
PRECISELY. A GLORIOUS VISION. A BLOW AGAINST TYRANNY.
A VERY IMPRECISE BLOW... DRACULA IS LIABLE TO SURVIVE, AND A GREAT MANY INNOCENTS WILL BE KILLED OR MAIMED.
THERE ARE NO INNOCENTS.

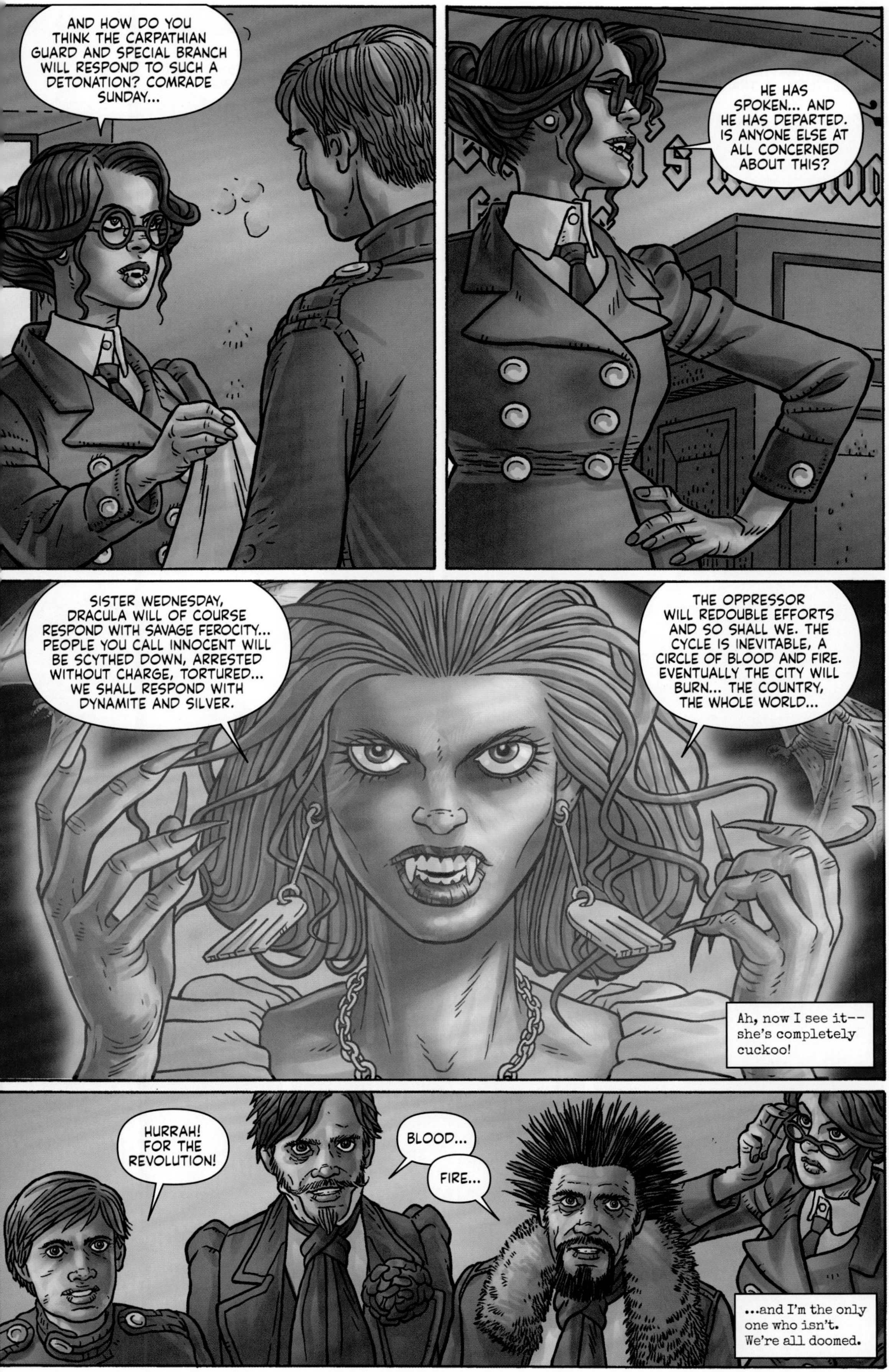
AND HOW DO YOU THINK THE CARPATHIAN GUARD AND SPECIAL BRANCH WILL RESPOND TO SUCH A DETONATION? COMRADE SUNDAY...
HE HAS SPOKEN... AND HE HAS DEPARTED. IS ANYONE ELSE AT ALL CONCERNED ABOUT THIS?
SISTER WEDNESDAY, DRACULA WILL OF COURSE RESPOND WITH SAVAGE FEROCITY... PEOPLE YOU CALL INNOCENT WILL BE SCYTHED DOWN, ARRESTED WITHOUT CHARGE, TORTURED... WE SHALL RESPOND WITH DYNAMITE AND SILVER.
THE OPPRESSOR WILL REDOUBLE EFFORTS AND SO SHALL WE. THE CYCLE IS INEVITABLE, A CIRCLE OF BLOOD AND FIRE. EVENTUALLY THE CITY WILL BURN... THE COUNTRY, THE WHOLE WORLD...
Ah, now I see it--she's completely cuckoo!
HURRAH! FOR THE REVOLUTION!
BLOOD...
FIRE...
...and I'm the only one who isn't. We're all doomed.

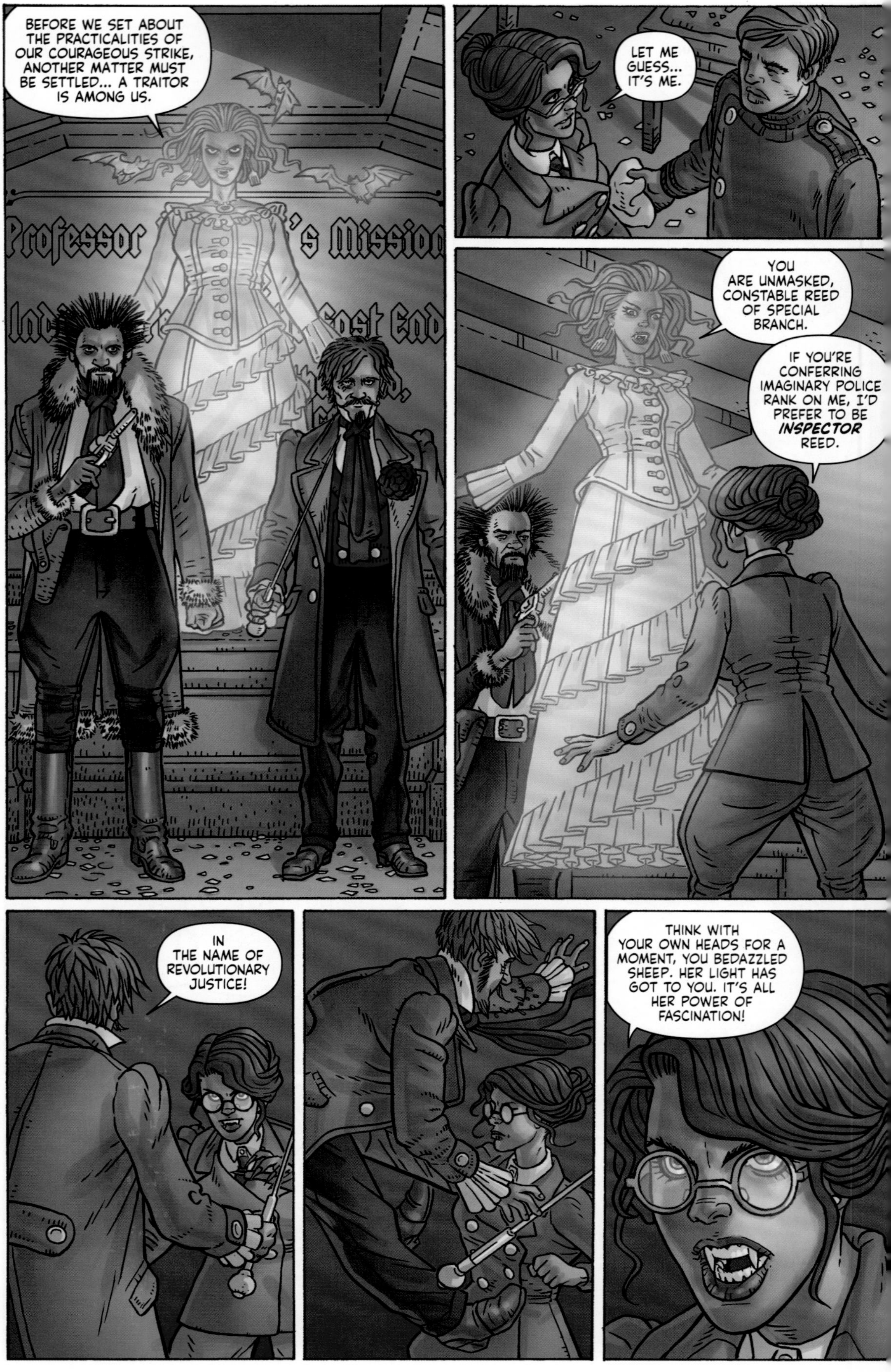
BEFORE WE SET ABOUT THE PRACTICALITIES OF OUR COURAGEOUS STRIKE, ANOTHER MATTER MUST BE SETTLED... A TRAITOR IS AMONG US.
Professor
's Mission
LET ME GUESS... IT'S ME.
YOU ARE UNMASKED, CONSTABLE REED OF SPECIAL BRANCH.
IF YOU'RE CONFERRING IMAGINARY POLICE RANK ON ME, I'D PREFER TO BE ***INSPECTOR*** REED.
IN THE NAME OF REVOLUTIONARY JUSTICE!
THINK WITH YOUR OWN HEADS FOR A MOMENT, YOU BEDAZZLED SHEEP. HER LIGHT HAS GOT TO YOU. IT'S ALL HER POWER OF FASCINATION!

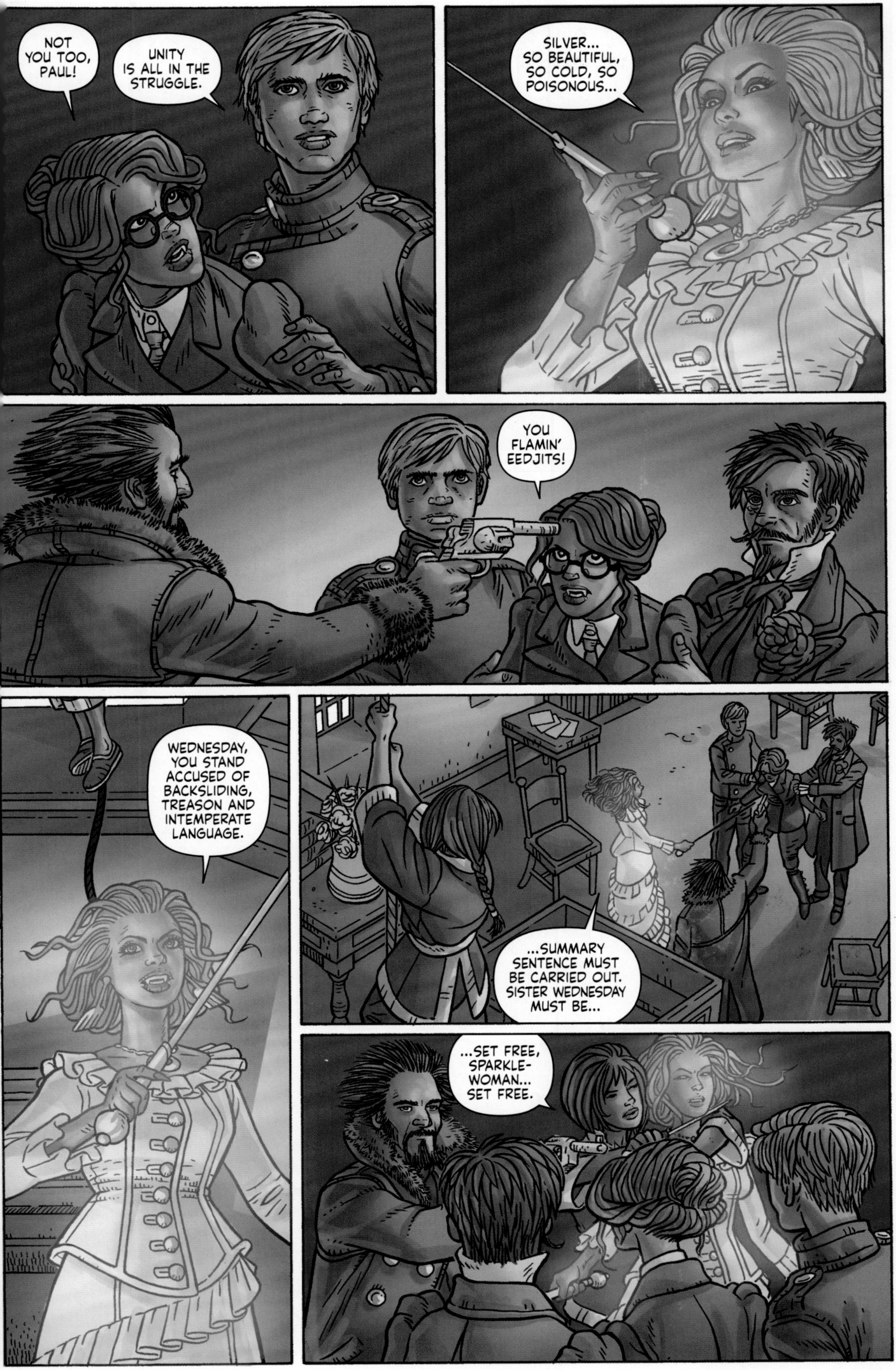
NOT YOU TOO, PAUL!
UNITY IS ALL IN THE STRUGGLE.
SILVER... SO BEAUTIFUL, SO COLD, SO POISONOUS...
YOU FLAMIN' EEDJITS!
WEDNESDAY, YOU STAND ACCUSED OF BACKSLIDING, TREASON AND INTEMPERATE LANGUAGE.
...SUMMARY SENTENCE MUST BE CARRIED OUT. SISTER WEDNESDAY MUST BE...
...SET FREE, SPARKLE-WOMAN... SET FREE.

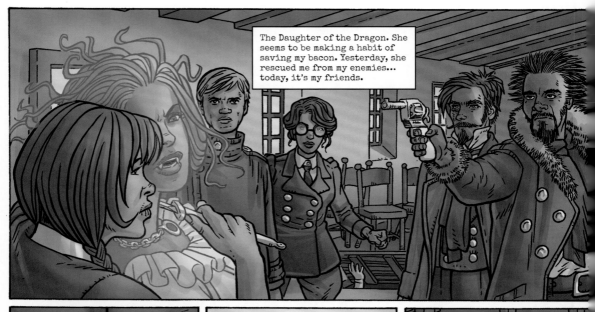

The Daughter of the Dragon. She seems to be making a habit of saving my bacon. Yesterday, she rescued me from my enemies... today, it's my friends.

What now...

JANEY MACK!

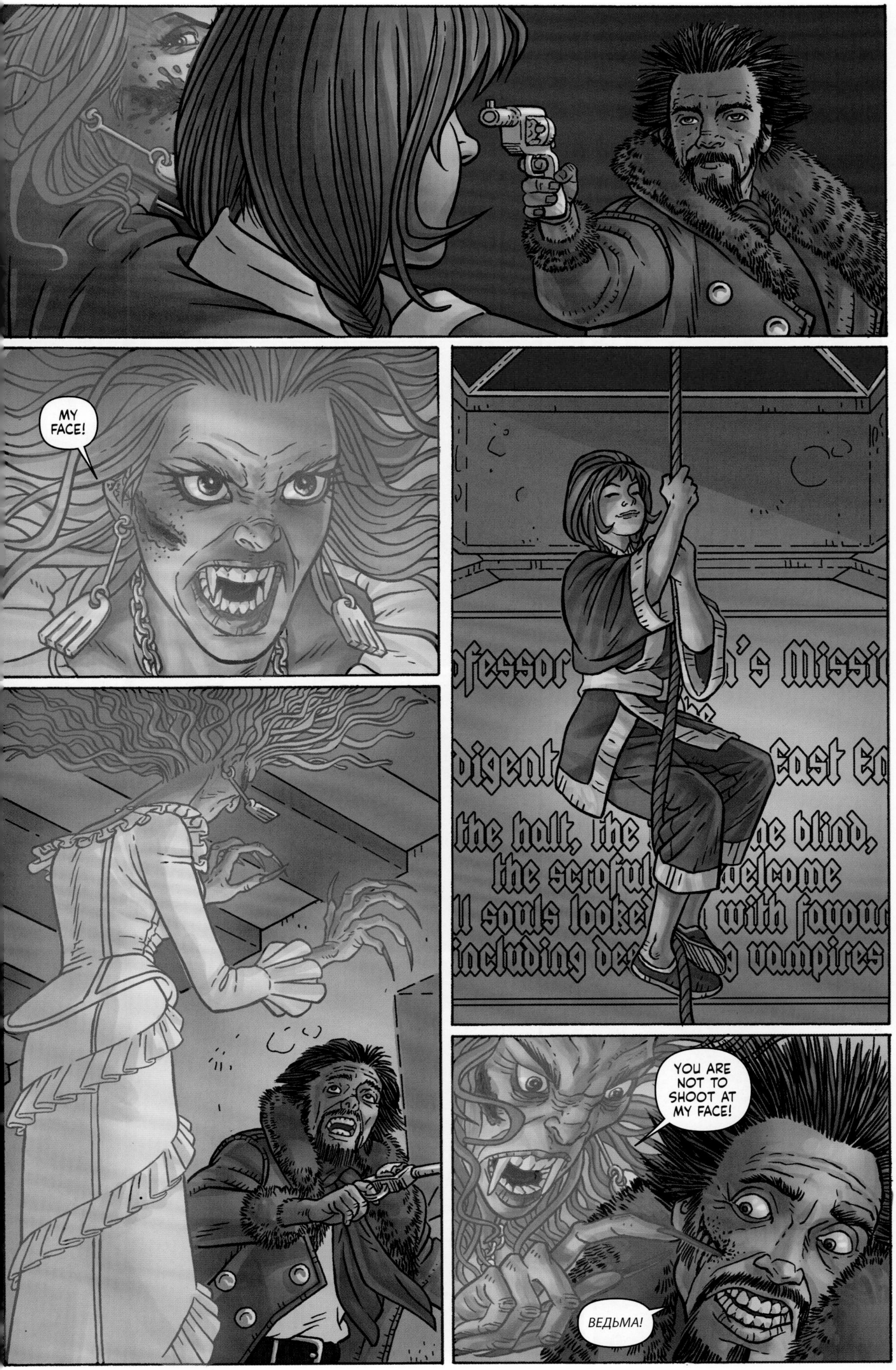
MY FACE!
ofessor h's Missi
digent East En
the halt, the e blind,
the scrofu welcome
ll souls looke with favou
including de g vampires
YOU ARE NOT TO SHOOT AT MY FACE!
ВЕДЬМА!

The River Thames,
Limehouse Reach.

MADEMOISELLE
VEP, N'EST-CE PAS?

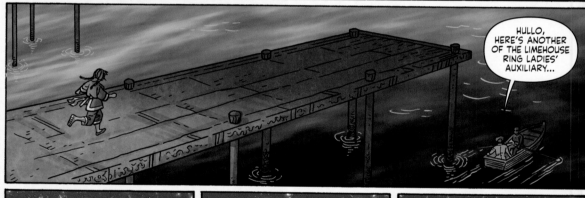

HULLO,
HERE'S ANOTHER
OF THE LIMEHOUSE
RING LADIES'
AUXILIARY...

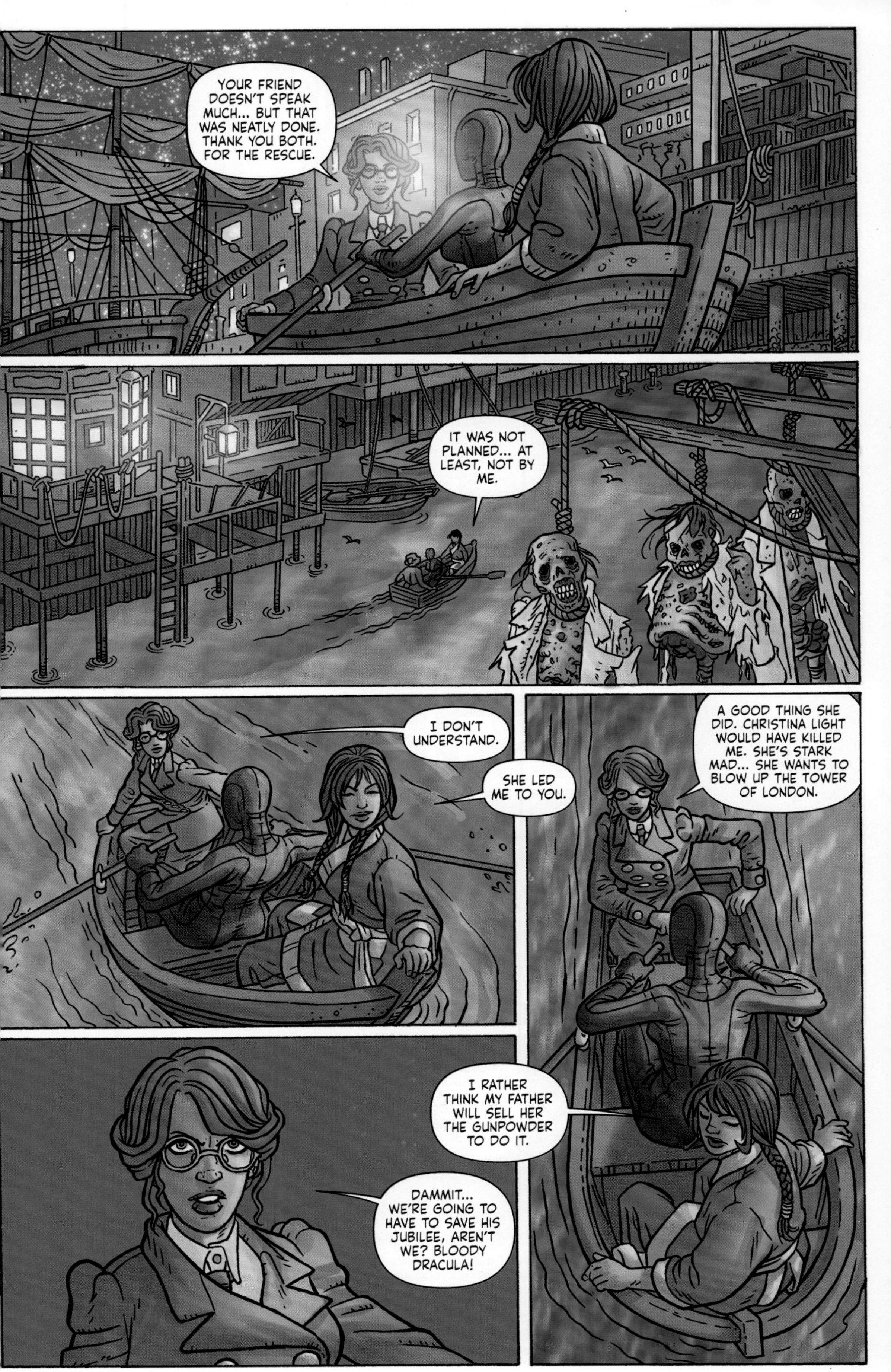
YOUR FRIEND DOESN'T SPEAK MUCH... BUT THAT WAS NEATLY DONE. THANK YOU BOTH. FOR THE RESCUE.
IT WAS NOT PLANNED... AT LEAST, NOT BY ME.
I DON'T UNDERSTAND.
SHE LED ME TO YOU.
A GOOD THING SHE DID. CHRISTINA LIGHT WOULD HAVE KILLED ME. SHE'S STARK MAD... SHE WANTS TO BLOW UP THE TOWER OF LONDON.
I RATHER THINK MY FATHER WILL SELL HER THE GUNPOWDER TO DO IT.
DAMMIT... WE'RE GOING TO HAVE TO SAVE HIS JUBILEE, AREN'T WE? BLOODY DRACULA!

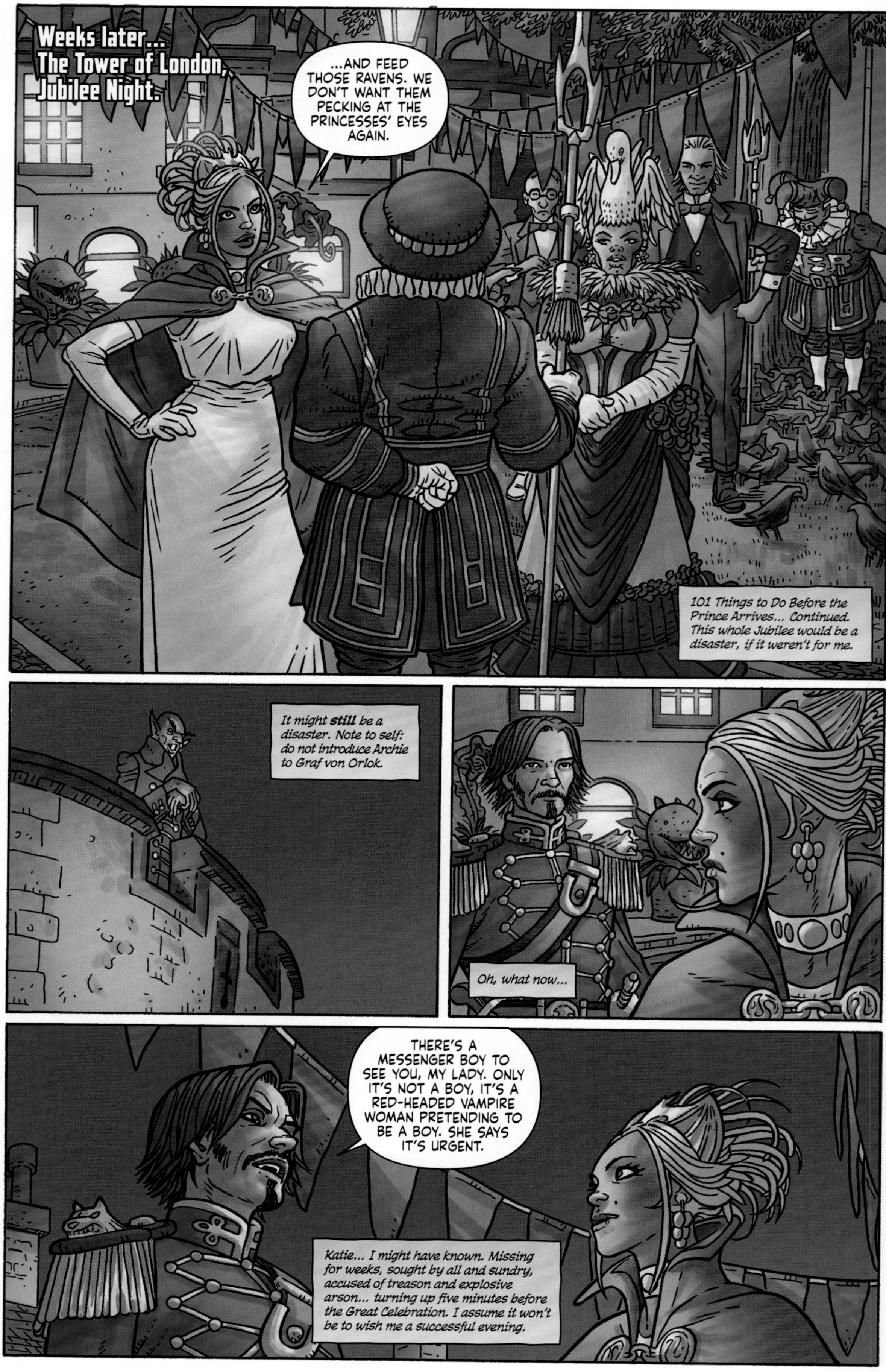
Weeks later... The Tower of London, Jubilee Night.
...AND FEED THOSE RAVENS. WE DON'T WANT THEM PECKING AT THE PRINCESSES' EYES AGAIN.
101 Things to Do Before the Prince Arrives... Continued. This whole Jubilee would be a disaster, if it weren't for me.
It might still be a disaster. Note to self: do not introduce Archie to Graf von Orlok.
Oh, what now...
THERE'S A MESSENGER BOY TO SEE YOU, MY LADY. ONLY IT'S NOT A BOY, IT'S A RED-HEADED VAMPIRE WOMAN PRETENDING TO BE A BOY. SHE SAYS IT'S URGENT.
Katie... I might have known. Missing for weeks, sought by all and sundry, accused of treason and explosive arson... turning up five minutes before the Great Celebration. I assume it won't be to wish me a successful evening.

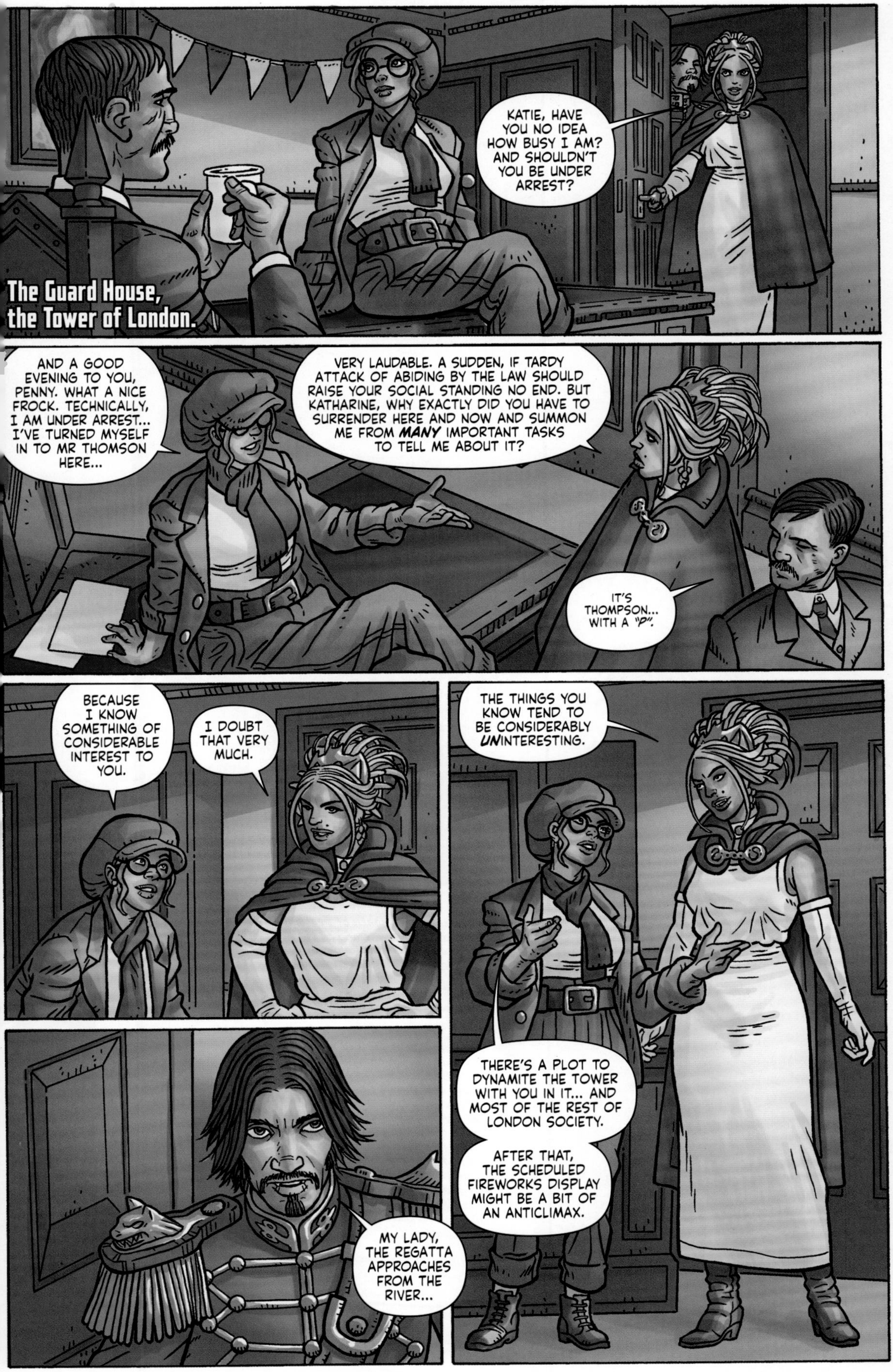
The Guard House, the Tower of London.
KATIE, HAVE YOU NO IDEA HOW BUSY I AM? AND SHOULDN'T YOU BE UNDER ARREST?
AND A GOOD EVENING TO YOU, PENNY. WHAT A NICE FROCK. TECHNICALLY, I AM UNDER ARREST... I'VE TURNED MYSELF IN TO MR THOMSON HERE...
VERY LAUDABLE. A SUDDEN, IF TARDY ATTACK OF ABIDING BY THE LAW SHOULD RAISE YOUR SOCIAL STANDING NO END. BUT KATHARINE, WHY EXACTLY DID YOU HAVE TO SURRENDER HERE AND NOW AND SUMMON ME FROM MANY IMPORTANT TASKS TO TELL ME ABOUT IT?
IT'S THOMPSON... WITH A "P".
BECAUSE I KNOW SOMETHING OF CONSIDERABLE INTEREST TO YOU.
I DOUBT THAT VERY MUCH.
THE THINGS YOU KNOW TEND TO BE CONSIDERABLY UNINTERESTING.
THERE'S A PLOT TO DYNAMITE THE TOWER WITH YOU IN IT... AND MOST OF THE REST OF LONDON SOCIETY.
AFTER THAT, THE SCHEDULED FIREWORKS DISPLAY MIGHT BE A BIT OF AN ANTICLIMAX.
MY LADY, THE REGATTA APPROACHES FROM THE RIVER...

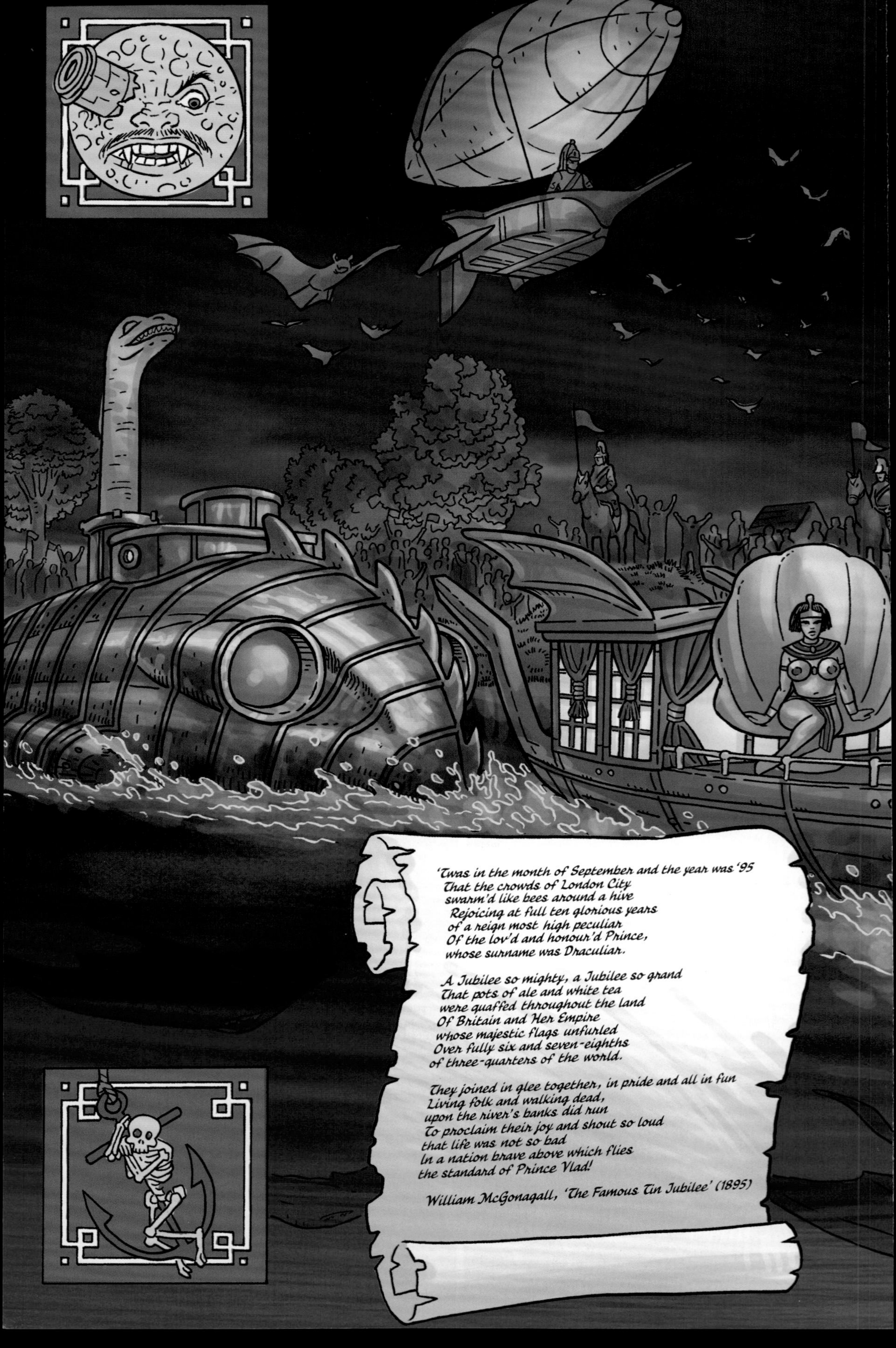
'Twas in the month of September and the year was '95
That the crowds of London City
swarm'd like bees around a hive
Rejoicing at full ten glorious years
of a reign most high peculiar
Of the lov'd and honour'd Prince,
whose surname was Draculiar.

A Jubilee so mighty, a Jubilee so grand
That pots of ale and white tea
were quaffed throughout the land
Of Britain and Her Empire
whose majestic flags unfurled
Over fully six and seven-eighths
of three-quarters of the world.

They joined in glee together, in pride and all in fun
Living folk and walking dead,
upon the river's banks did run
To proclaim their joy and shout so loud
that life was not so bad
In a nation brave above which flies
the standard of Prince Vlad!

William McGonagall, 'The Famous Tin Jubilee' (1895)

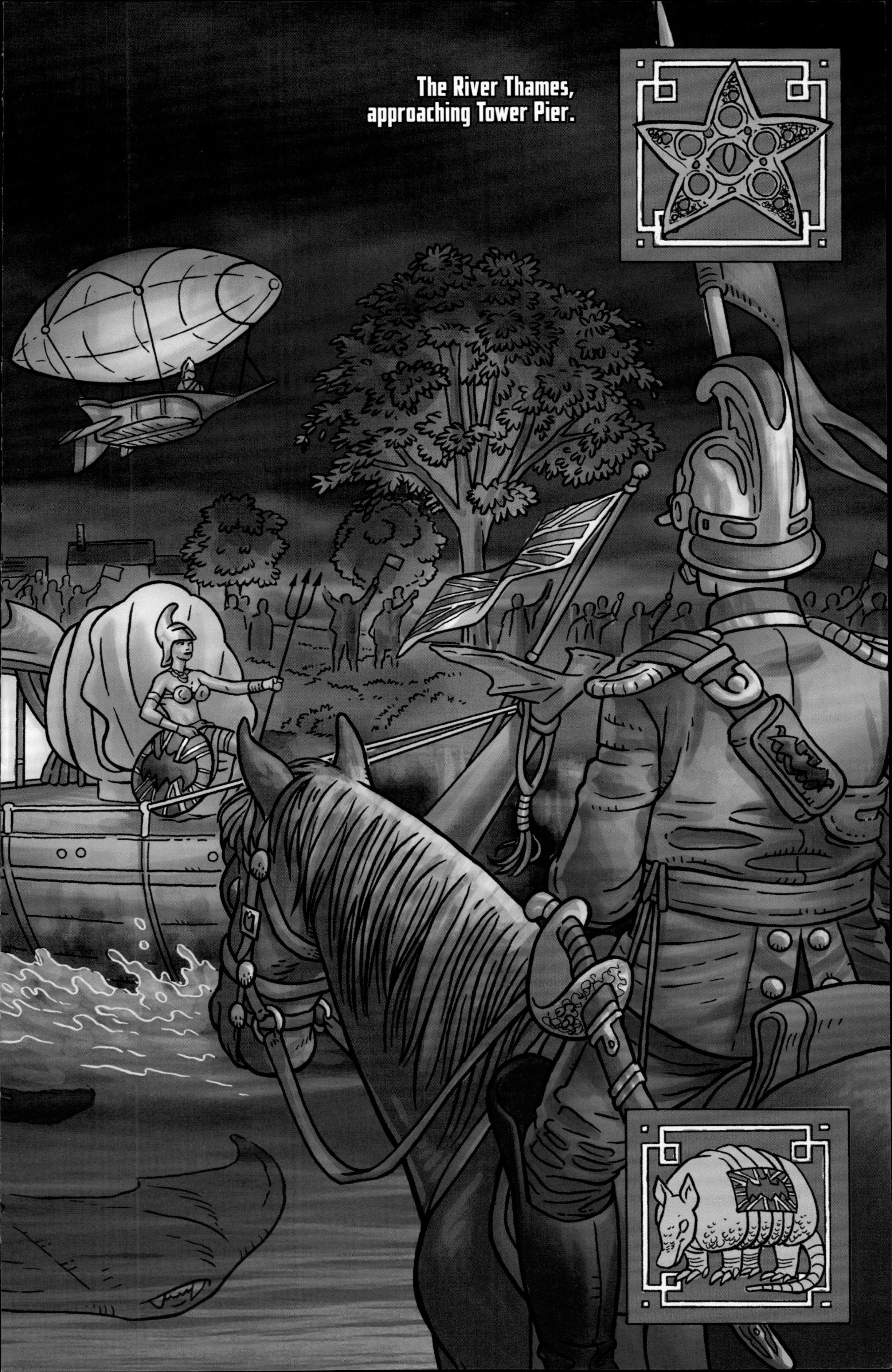
The River Thames,
approaching Tower Pier.

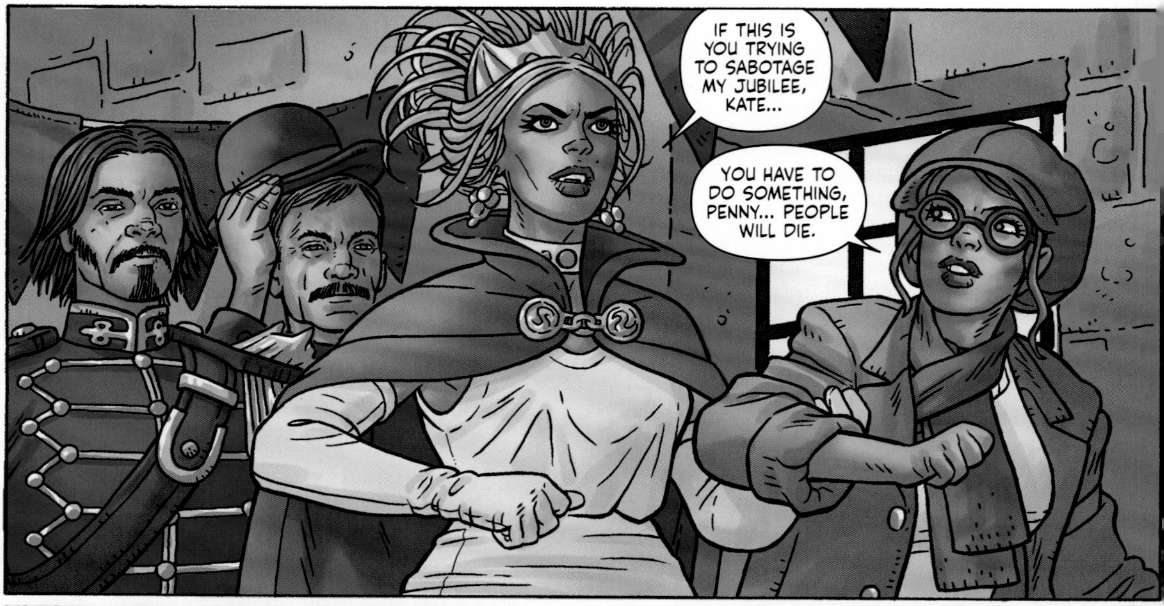
IF THIS IS YOU TRYING TO SABOTAGE MY JUBILEE, KATE...
YOU HAVE TO DO SOMETHING, PENNY... PEOPLE WILL DIE.

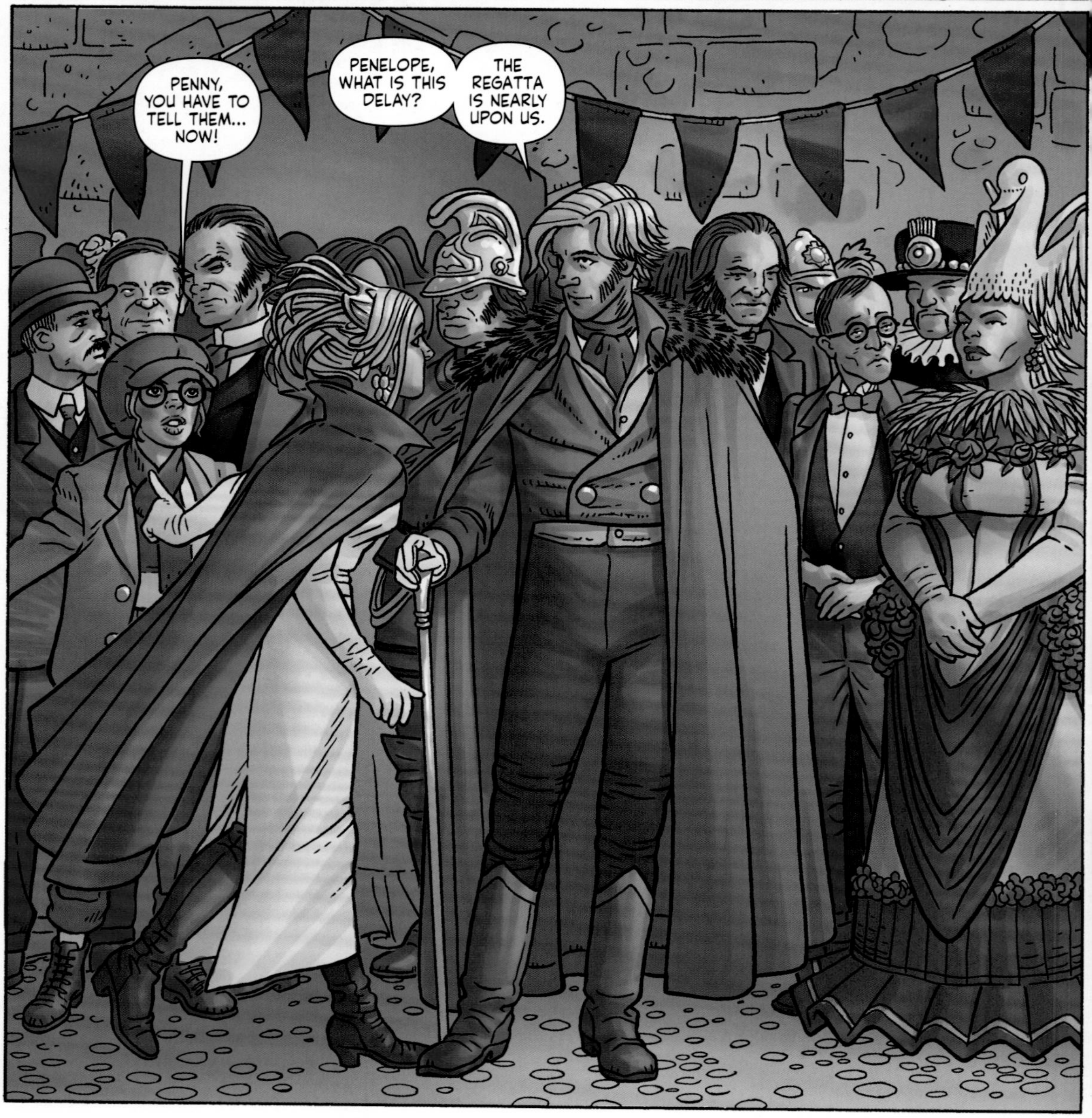
PENNY, YOU HAVE TO TELL THEM... NOW!
PENELOPE, WHAT IS THIS DELAY?
THE REGATTA IS NEARLY UPON US.

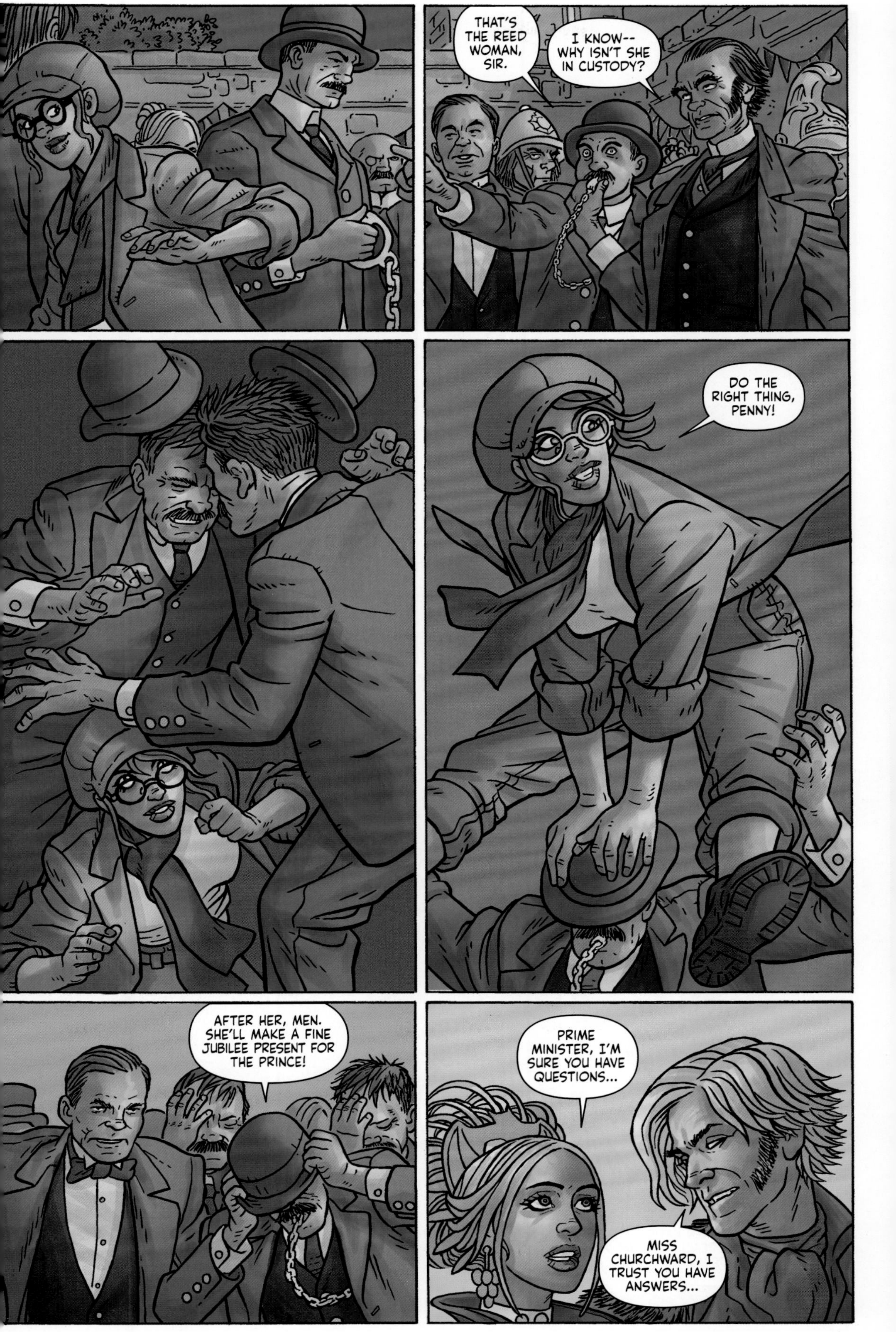
THAT'S THE REED WOMAN, SIR.
I KNOW-- WHY ISN'T SHE IN CUSTODY?
DO THE RIGHT THING, PENNY!
AFTER HER, MEN. SHE'LL MAKE A FINE JUBILEE PRESENT FOR THE PRINCE!
PRIME MINISTER, I'M SURE YOU HAVE QUESTIONS...
MISS CHURCHWARD, I TRUST YOU HAVE ANSWERS...

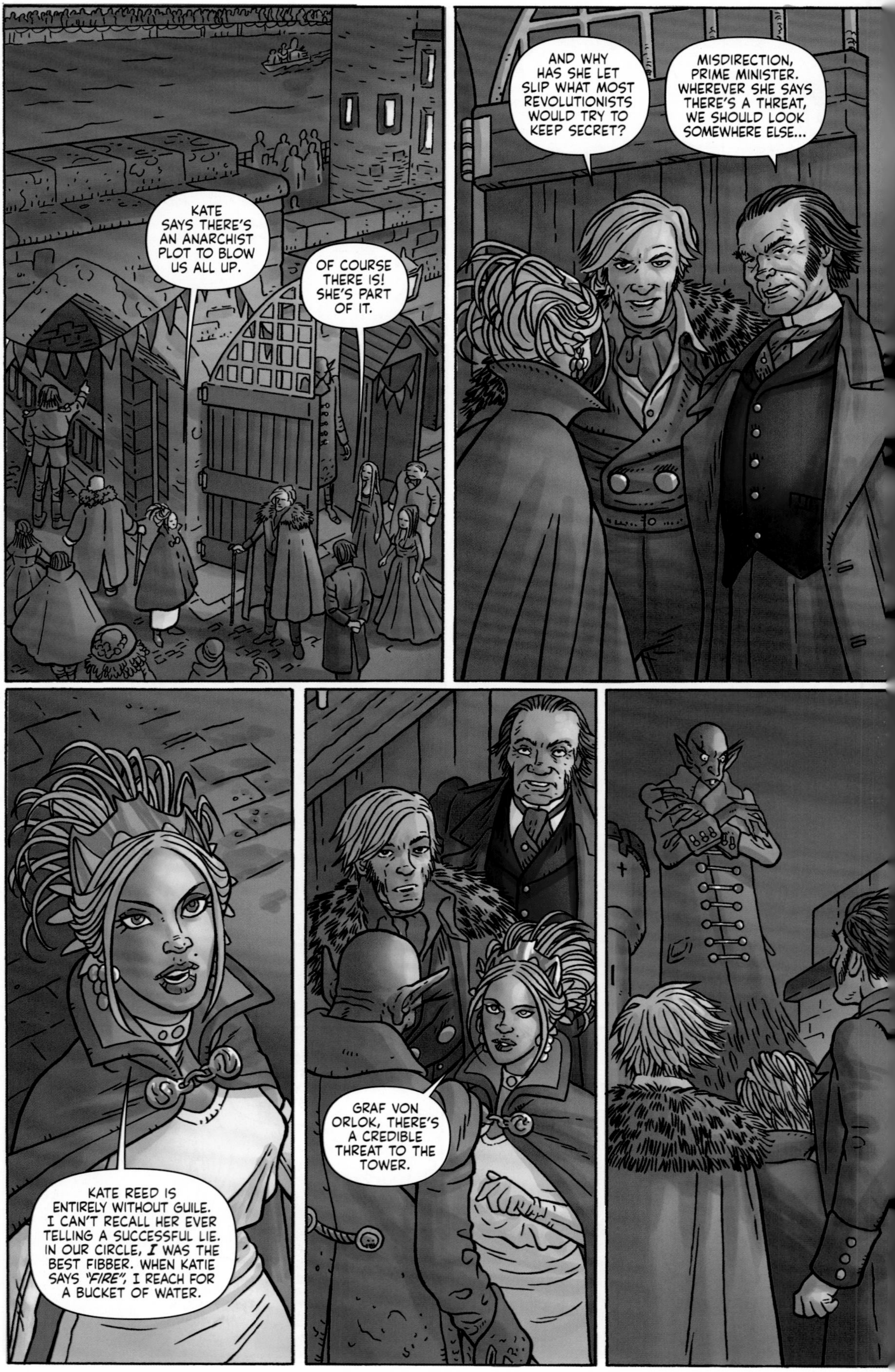
KATE SAYS THERE'S AN ANARCHIST PLOT TO BLOW US ALL UP.
OF COURSE THERE IS! SHE'S PART OF IT.
AND WHY HAS SHE LET SLIP WHAT MOST REVOLUTIONISTS WOULD TRY TO KEEP SECRET?
MISDIRECTION, PRIME MINISTER. WHEREVER SHE SAYS THERE'S A THREAT, WE SHOULD LOOK SOMEWHERE ELSE...
KATE REED IS ENTIRELY WITHOUT GUILE. I CAN'T RECALL HER EVER TELLING A SUCCESSFUL LIE. IN OUR CIRCLE, *I* WAS THE BEST FIBBER. WHEN KATIE SAYS *"FIRE"*, I REACH FOR A BUCKET OF WATER.
GRAF VON ORLOK, THERE'S A CREDIBLE THREAT TO THE TOWER.

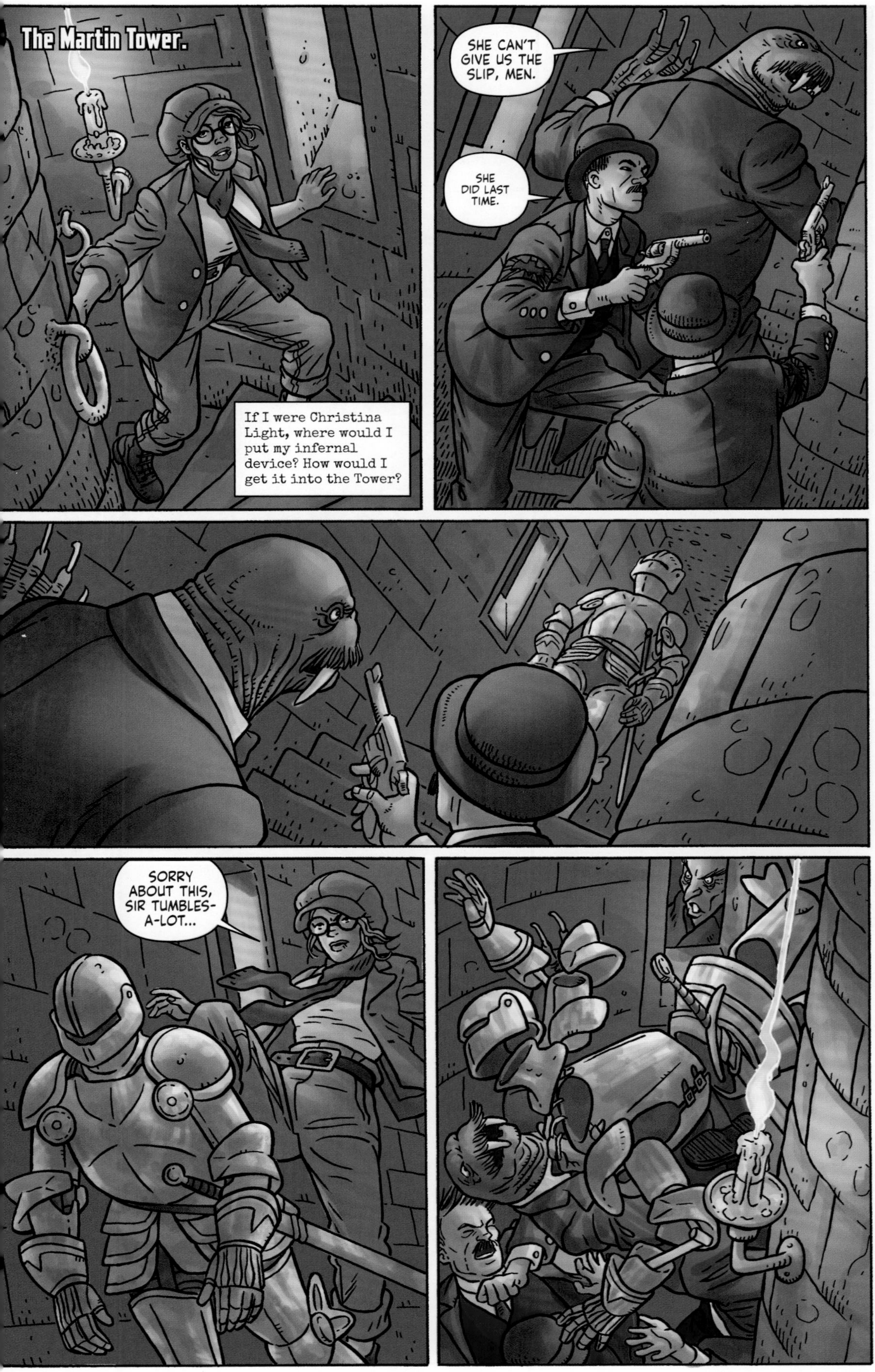

The Martin Tower.
If I were Christina Light, where would I put my infernal device? How would I get it into the Tower?
SHE CAN'T GIVE US THE SLIP, MEN.
SHE DID LAST TIME.
SORRY ABOUT THIS, SIR TUMBLES-A-LOT...

The Jewel Room.

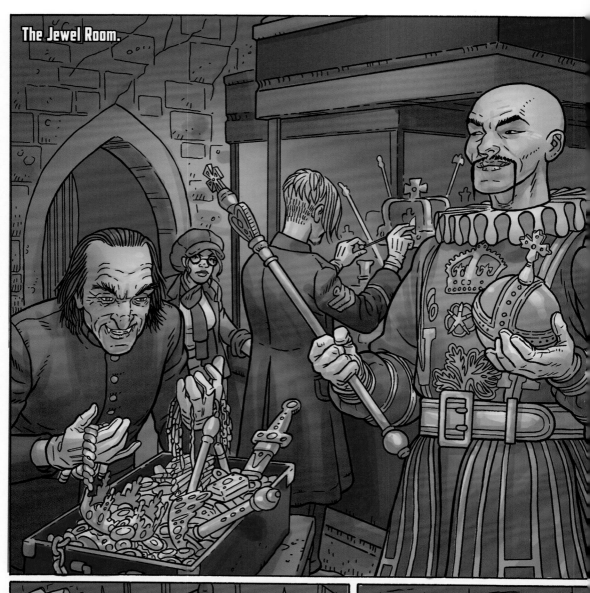

DON'T MIND ME, GENTLEMEN... SO FAR AS I'M CONCERNED, MOST OF THOSE BAUBLES ARE ALREADY STOLEN PROPERTY.

Good thing vampires can see in the dark...

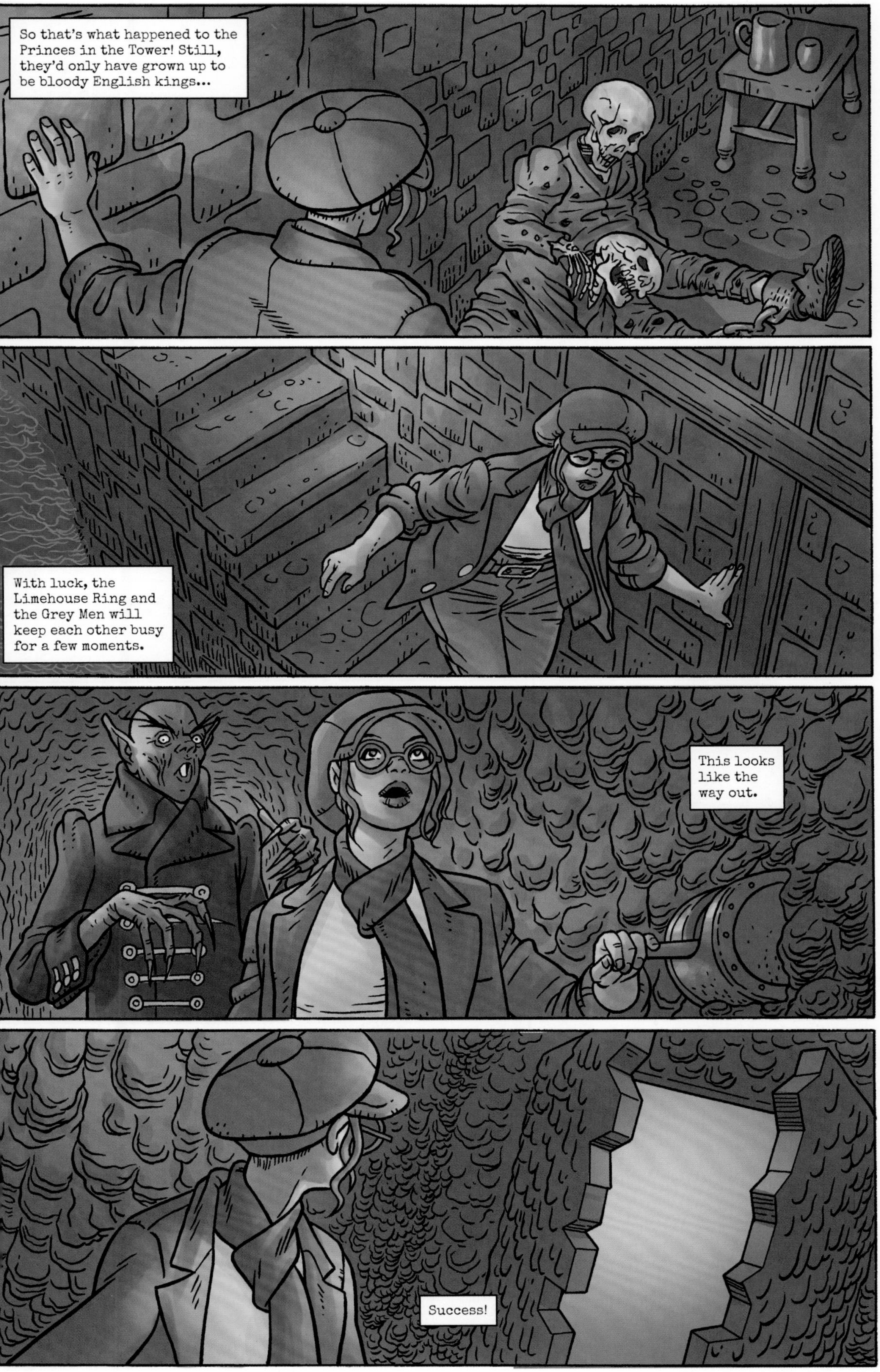
So that's what happened to the Princes in the Tower! Still, they'd only have grown up to be bloody English kings...
With luck, the Limehouse Ring and the Grey Men will keep each other busy for a few moments.
This looks like the way out.
Success!

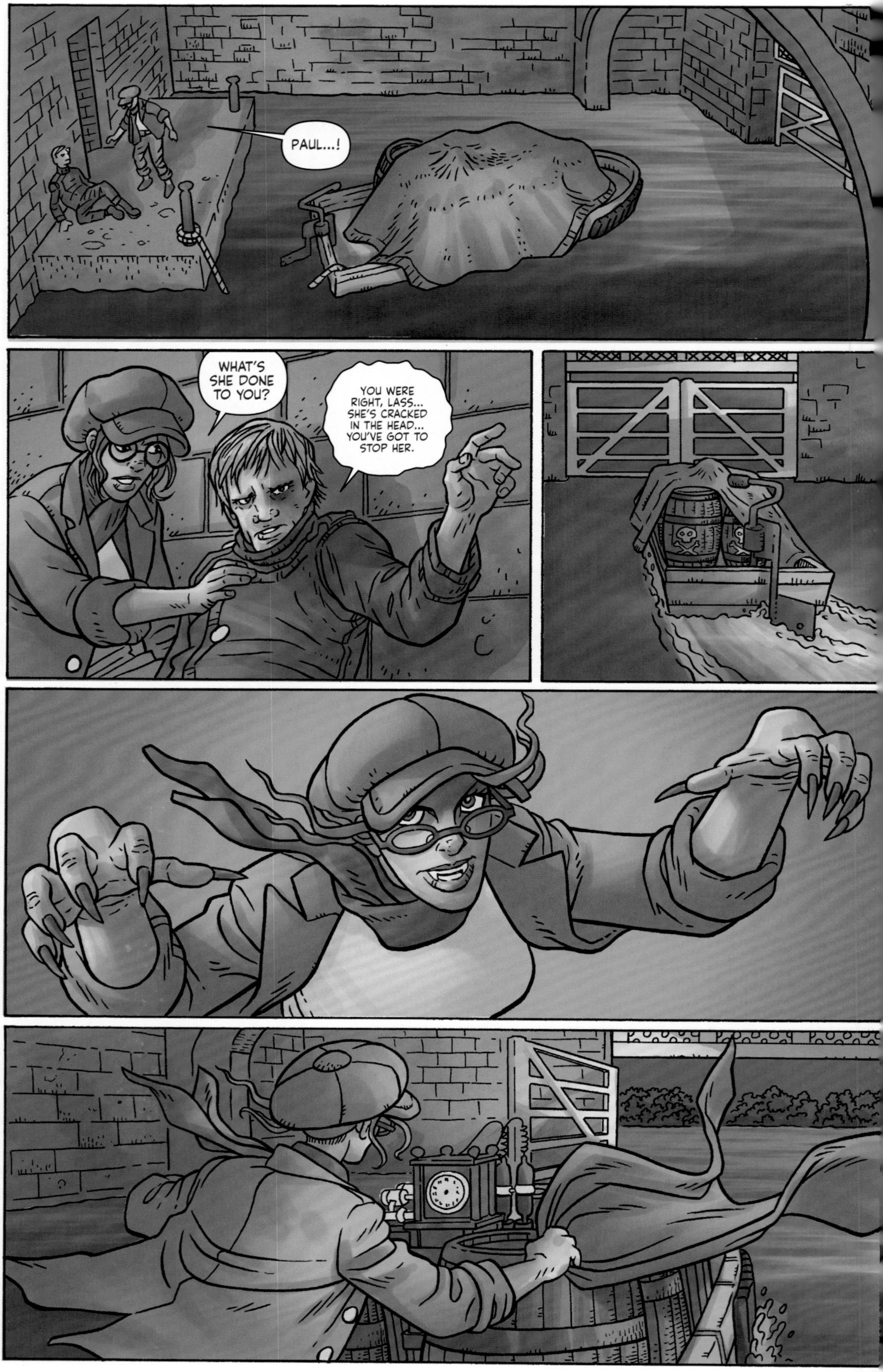
PAUL...!
WHAT'S SHE DONE TO YOU?
YOU WERE RIGHT, LASS... SHE'S CRACKED IN THE HEAD... YOU'VE GOT TO STOP HER.

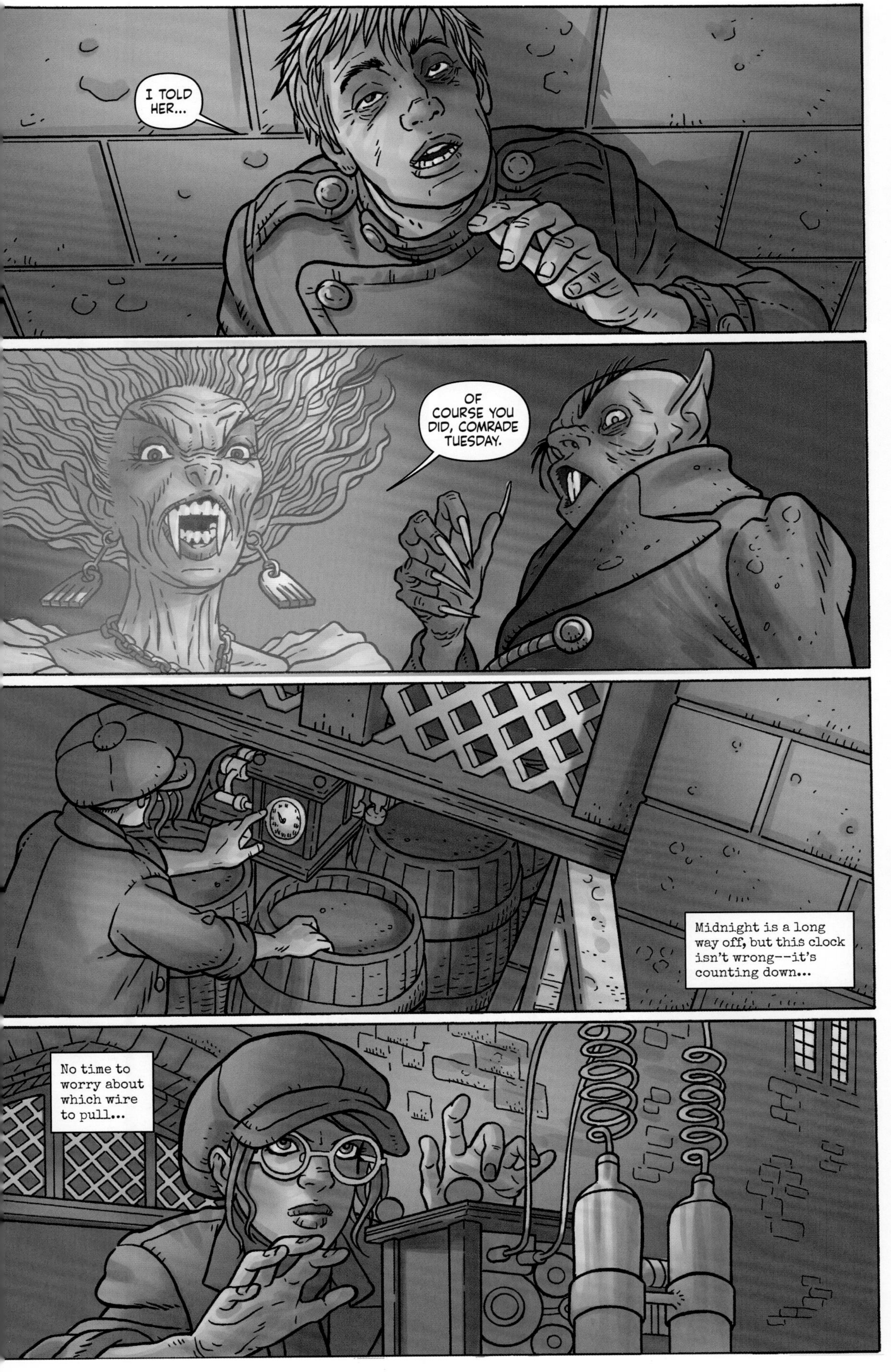

I TOLD HER...
OF COURSE YOU DID, COMRADE TUESDAY.
Midnight is a long way off, but this clock isn't wrong--it's counting down...
No time to worry about which wire to pull...

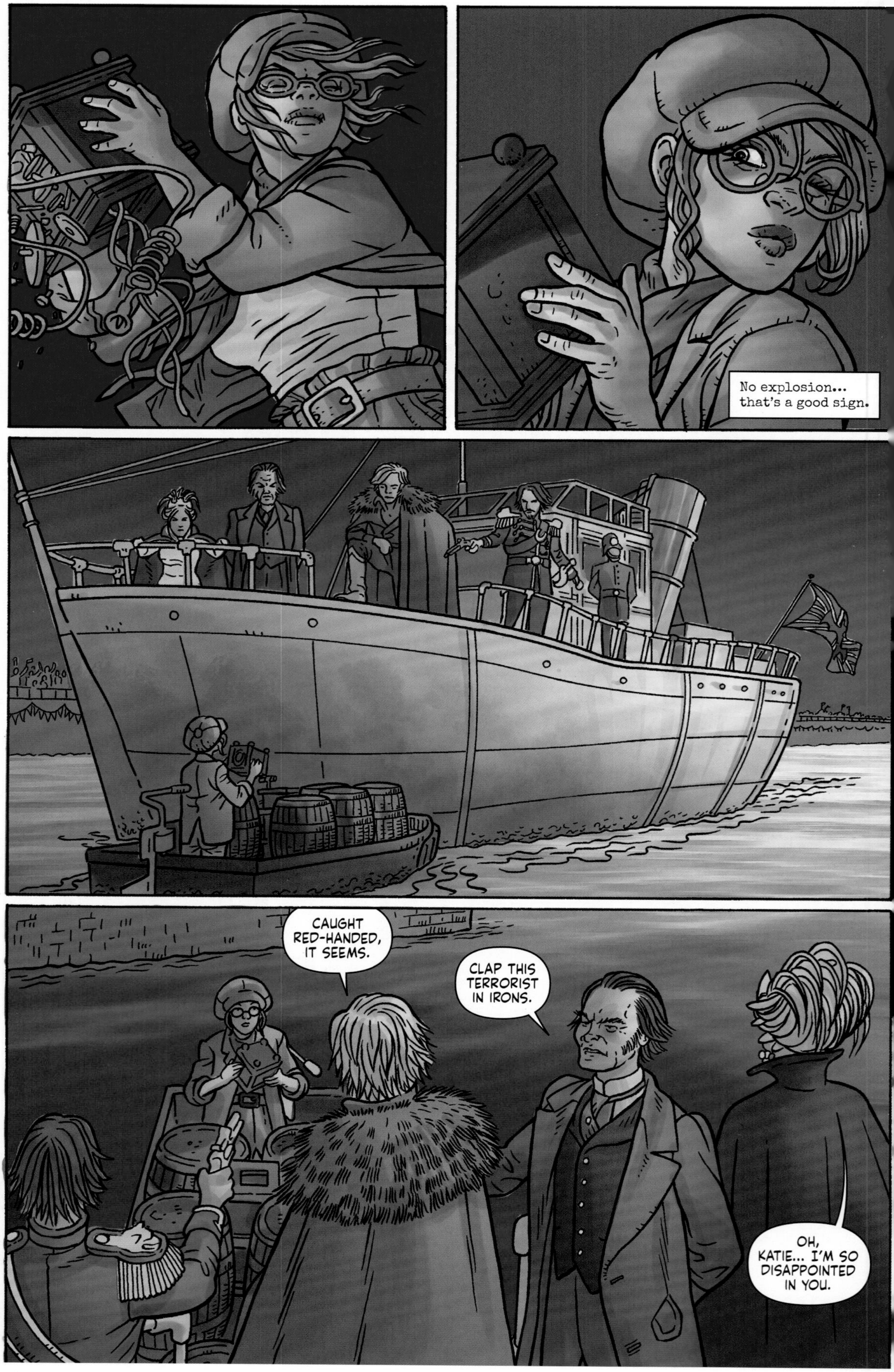
No explosion...
that's a good sign.
CAUGHT RED-HANDED, IT SEEMS.
CLAP THIS TERRORIST IN IRONS.
OH, KATIE... I'M SO DISAPPOINTED IN YOU.

CHAPTER FIVE

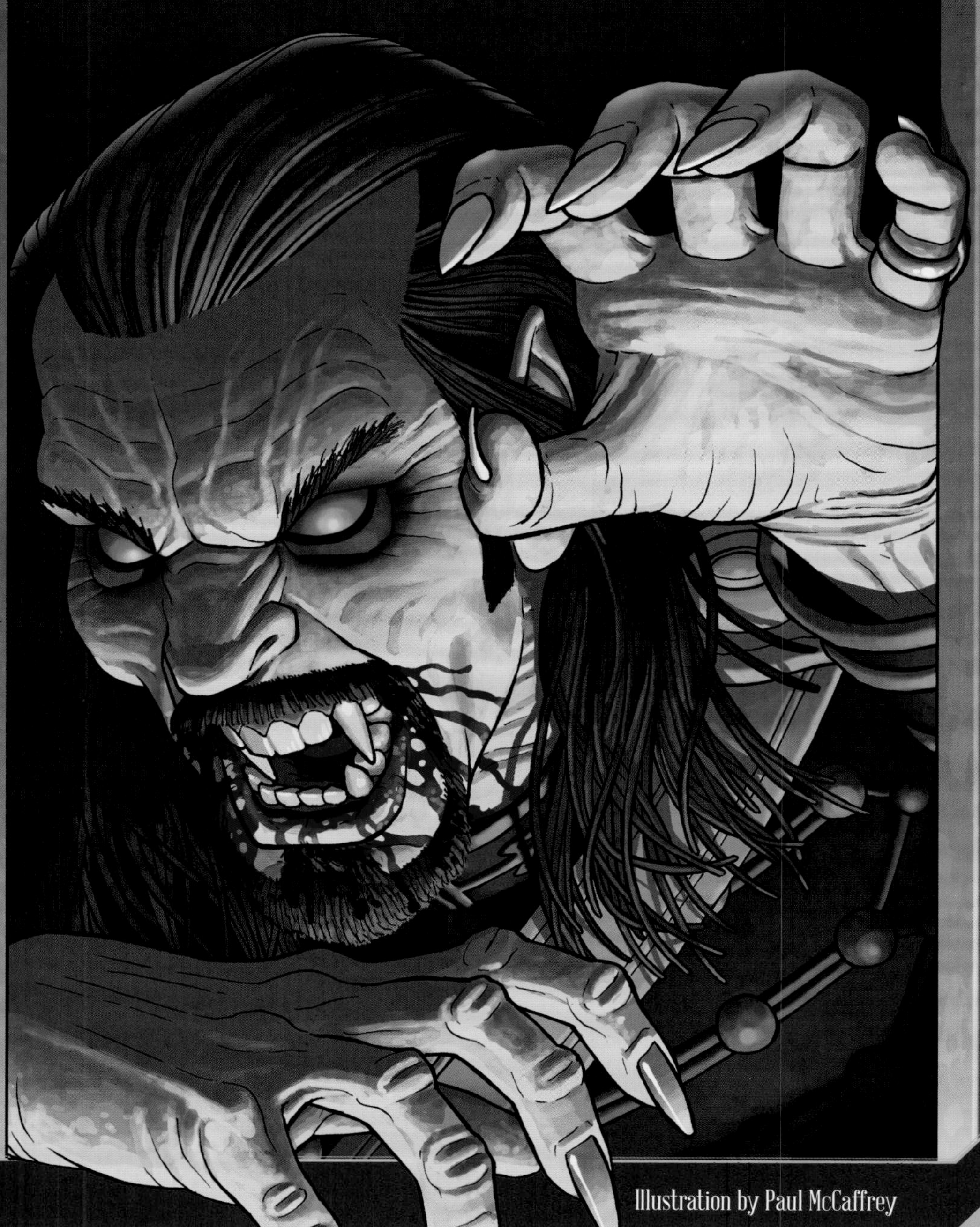

Illustration by Paul McCaffrey

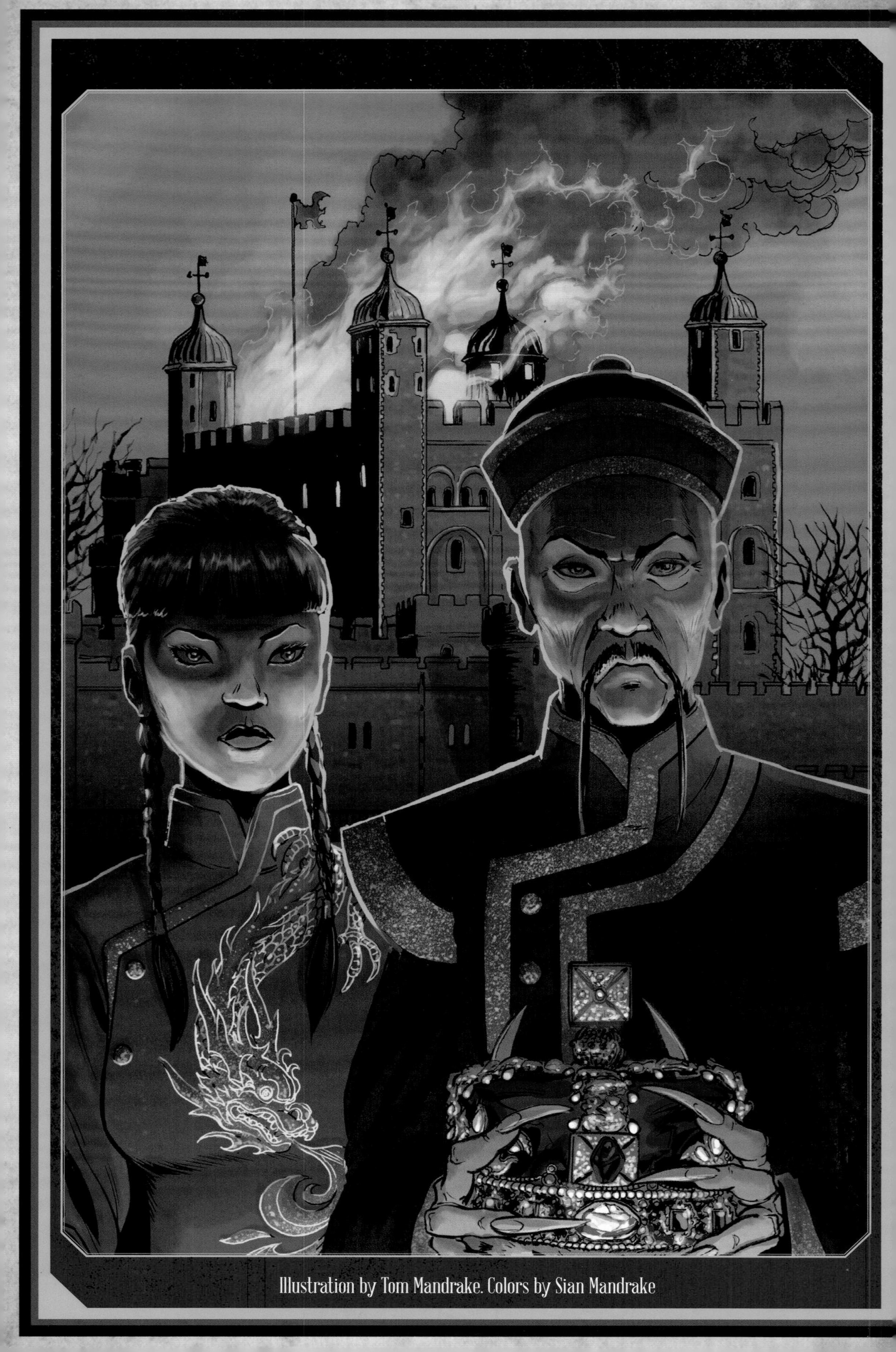

Illustration by Tom Mandrake. Colors by Sian Mandrake

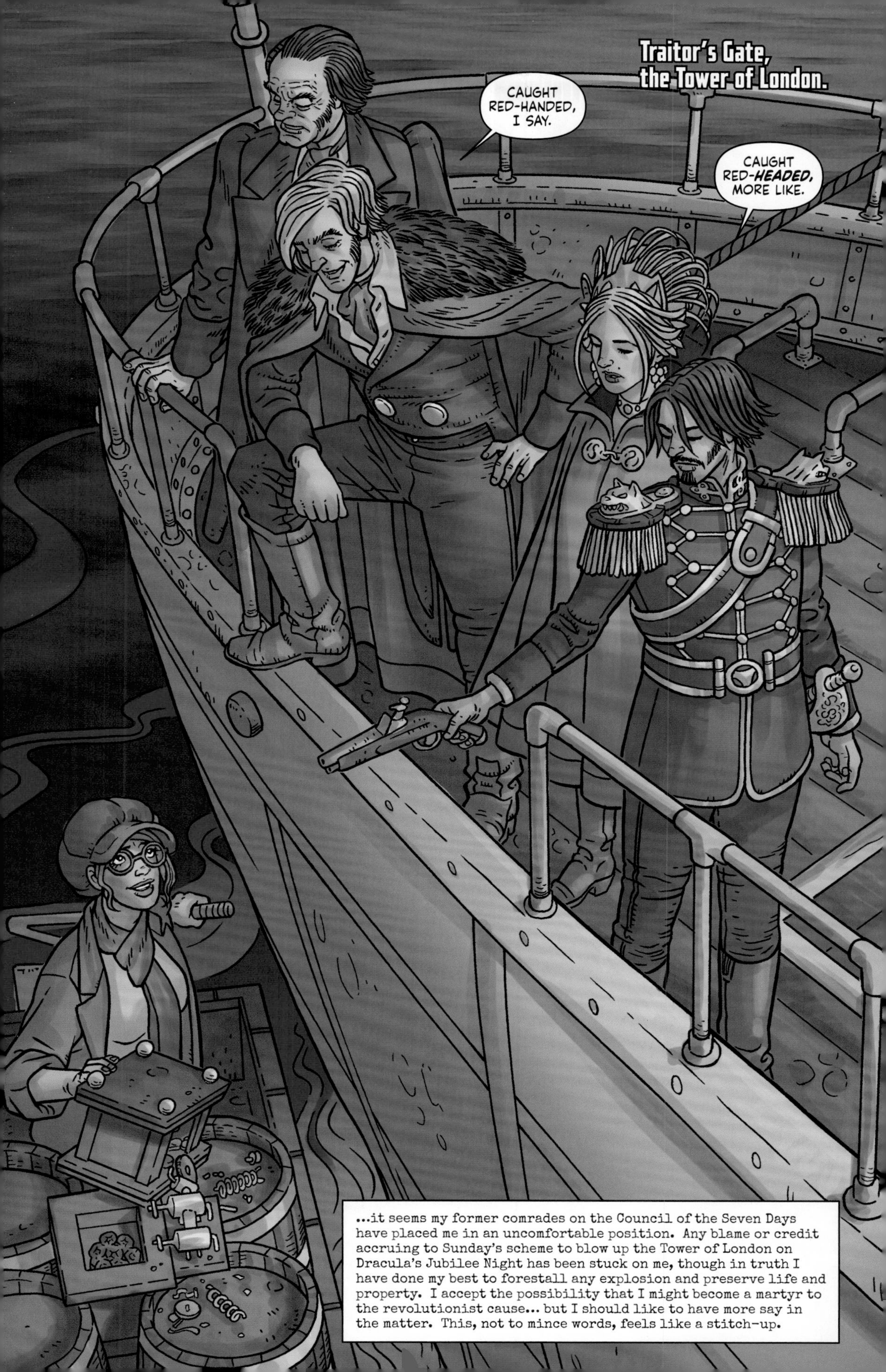
Traitor's Gate, the Tower of London.
CAUGHT RED-HANDED, I SAY.
CAUGHT RED-HEADED, MORE LIKE.
...it seems my former comrades on the Council of the Seven Days have placed me in an uncomfortable position. Any blame or credit accruing to Sunday's scheme to blow up the Tower of London on Dracula's Jubilee Night has been stuck on me, though in truth I have done my best to forestall any explosion and preserve life and property. I accept the possibility that I might become a martyr to the revolutionist cause... but I should like to have more say in the matter. This, not to mince words, feels like a stitch-up.

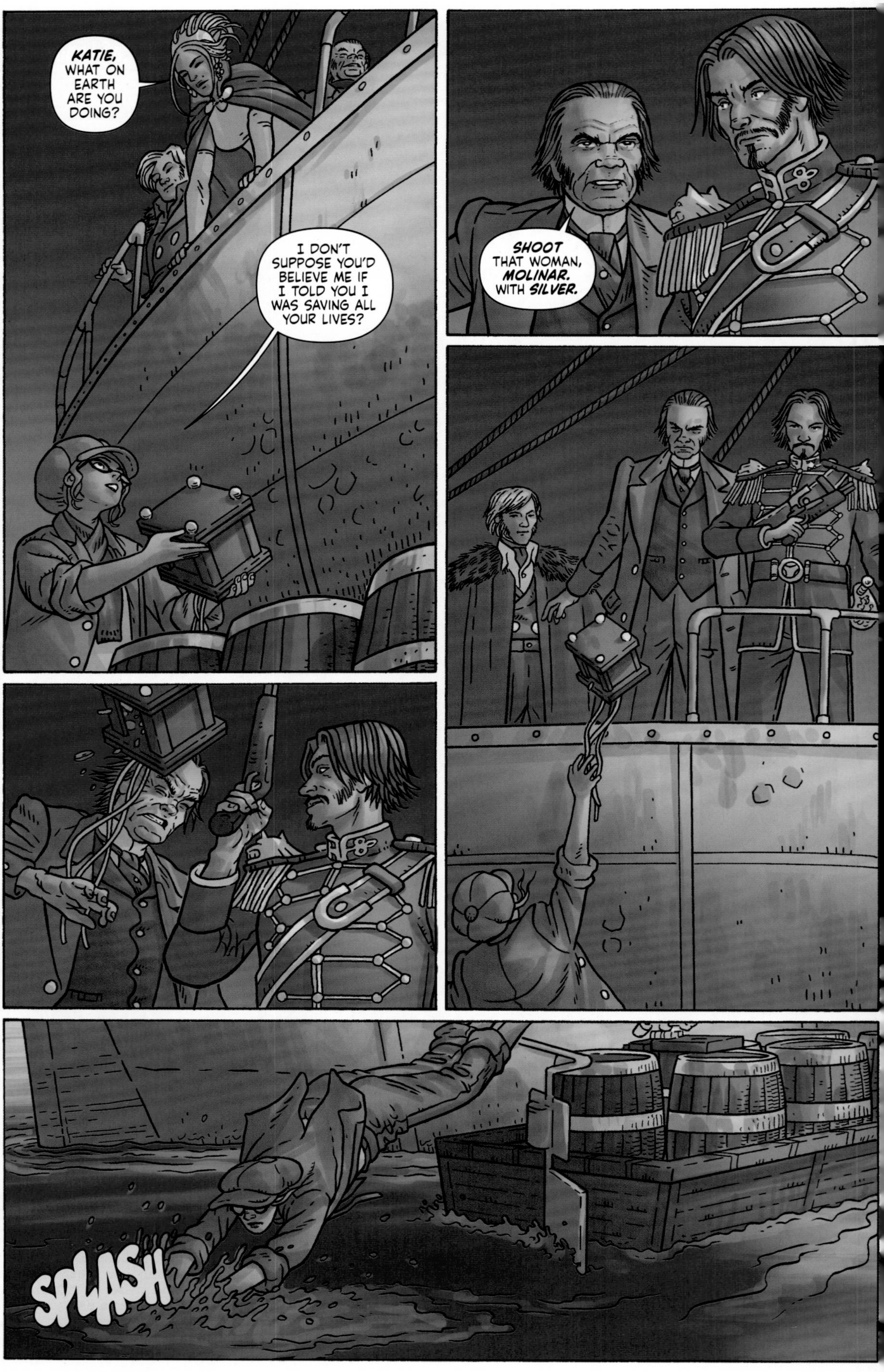
KATIE, WHAT ON EARTH ARE YOU DOING?
I DON'T SUPPOSE YOU'D BELIEVE ME IF I TOLD YOU I WAS SAVING ALL YOUR LIVES?
SHOOT THAT WOMAN, MOLINAR. WITH SILVER.
SPLASH

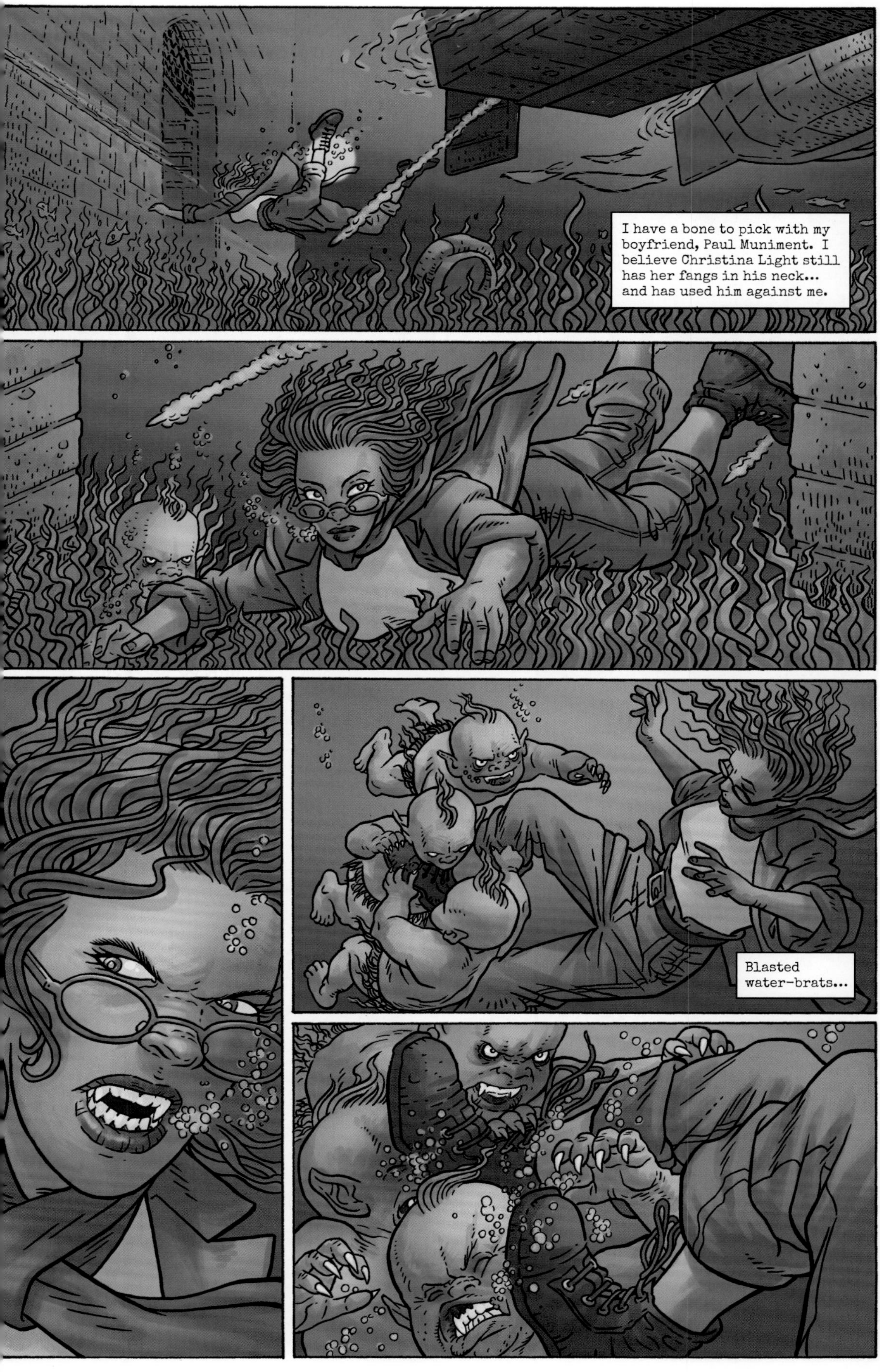
I have a bone to pick with my boyfriend, Paul Muniment. I believe Christina Light still has her fangs in his neck... and has used him against me.
Blasted water-brats...

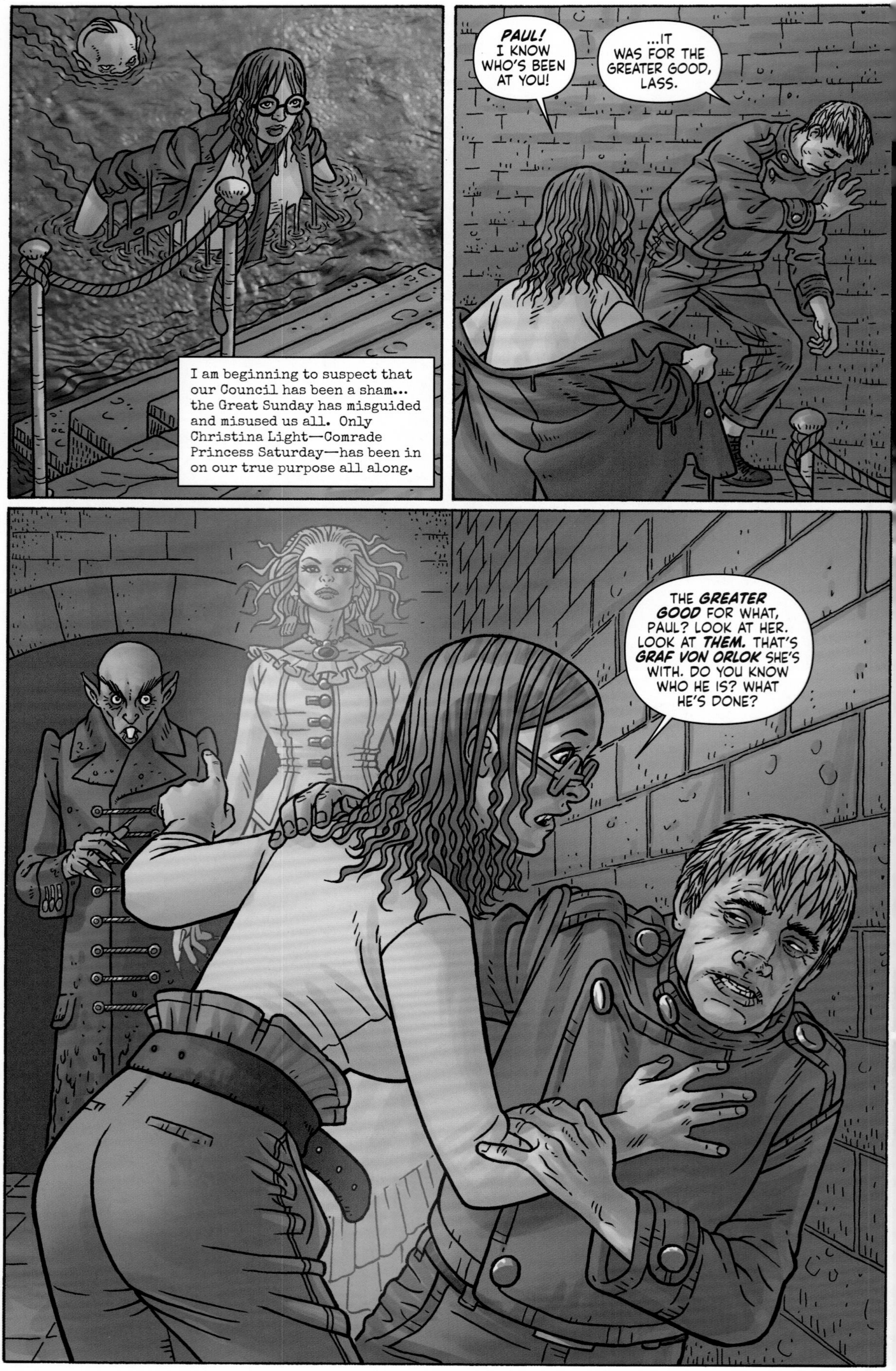
I am beginning to suspect that our Council has been a sham... the Great Sunday has misguided and misused us all. Only Christina Light—Comrade Princess Saturday—has been in on our true purpose all along.
PAUL! I KNOW WHO'S BEEN AT YOU!
...IT WAS FOR THE GREATER GOOD, LASS.
THE GREATER GOOD FOR WHAT, PAUL? LOOK AT HER. LOOK AT THEM. THAT'S GRAF VON ORLOK SHE'S WITH. DO YOU KNOW WHO HE IS? WHAT HE'S DONE?

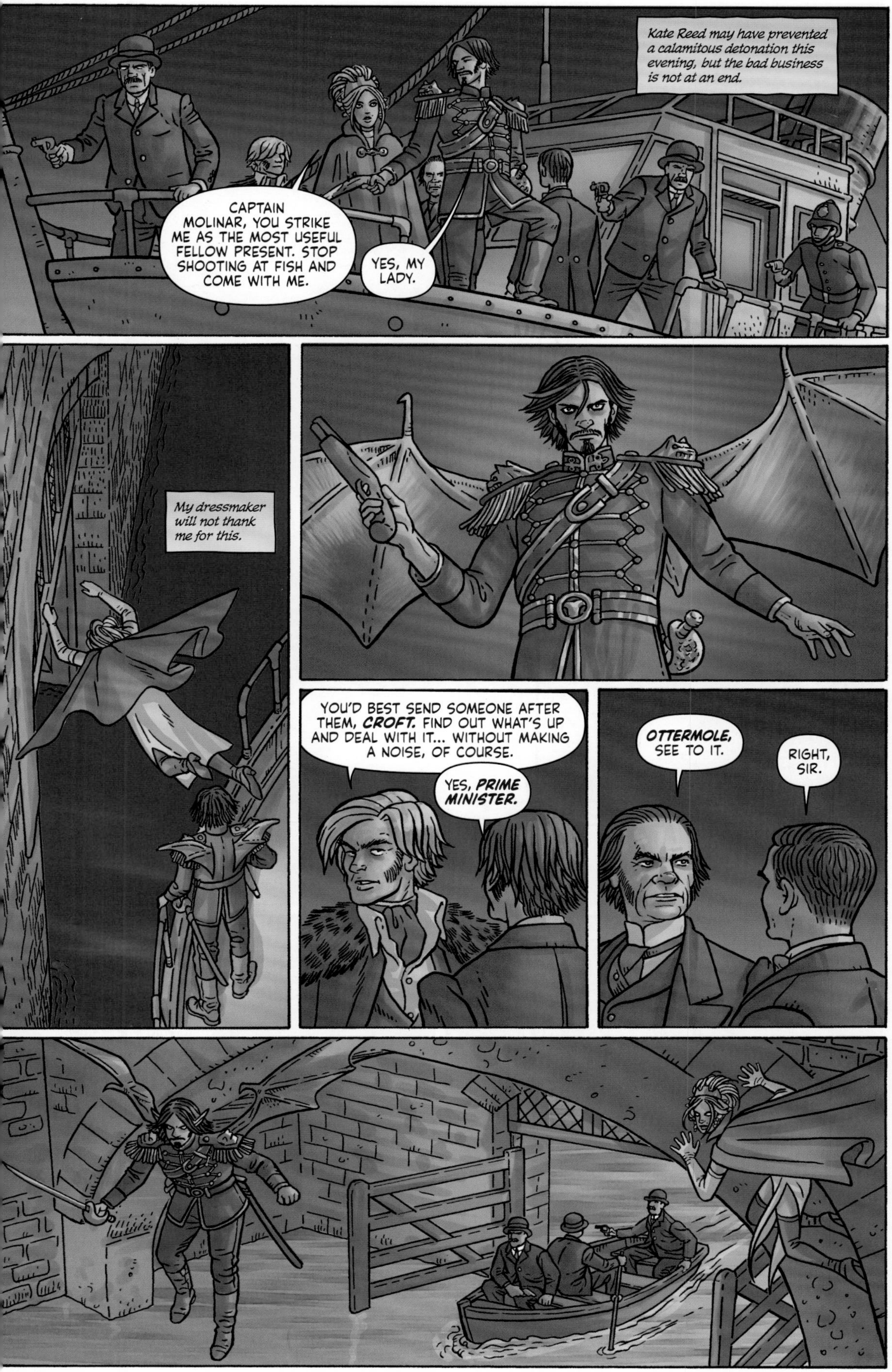

Kate Reed may have prevented a calamitous detonation this evening, but the bad business is not at an end.
CAPTAIN MOLINAR, YOU STRIKE ME AS THE MOST USEFUL FELLOW PRESENT. STOP SHOOTING AT FISH AND COME WITH ME.
YES, MY LADY.
My dressmaker will not thank me for this.
YOU'D BEST SEND SOMEONE AFTER THEM, CROFT. FIND OUT WHAT'S UP AND DEAL WITH IT... WITHOUT MAKING A NOISE, OF COURSE.
YES, PRIME MINISTER.
OTTERMOLE, SEE TO IT.
RIGHT, SIR.

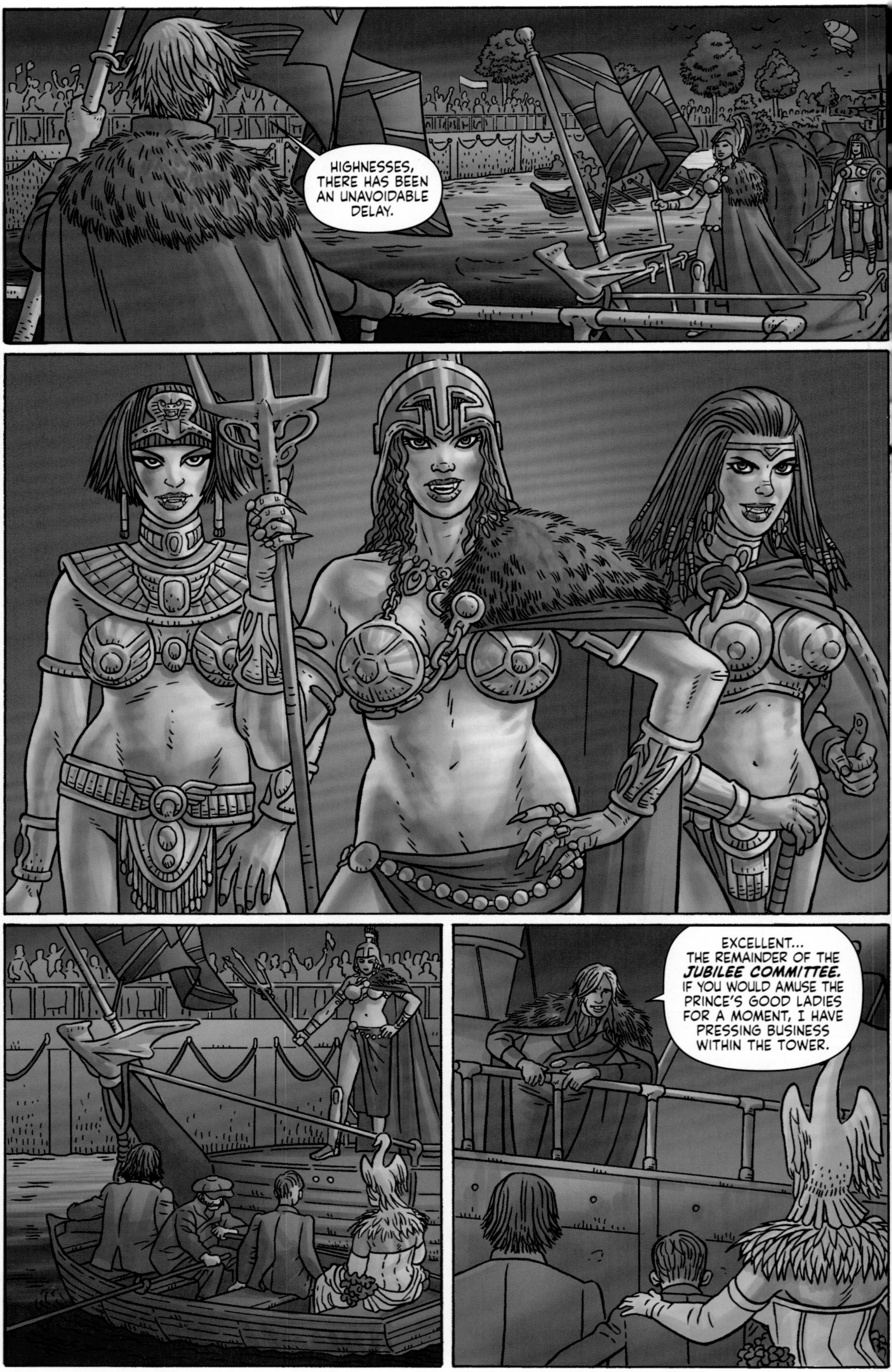
HIGHNESSES, THERE HAS BEEN AN UNAVOIDABLE DELAY.
EXCELLENT... THE REMAINDER OF THE *JUBILEE COMMITTEE.* IF YOU WOULD AMUSE THE PRINCE'S GOOD LADIES FOR A MOMENT, I HAVE PRESSING BUSINESS WITHIN THE TOWER.

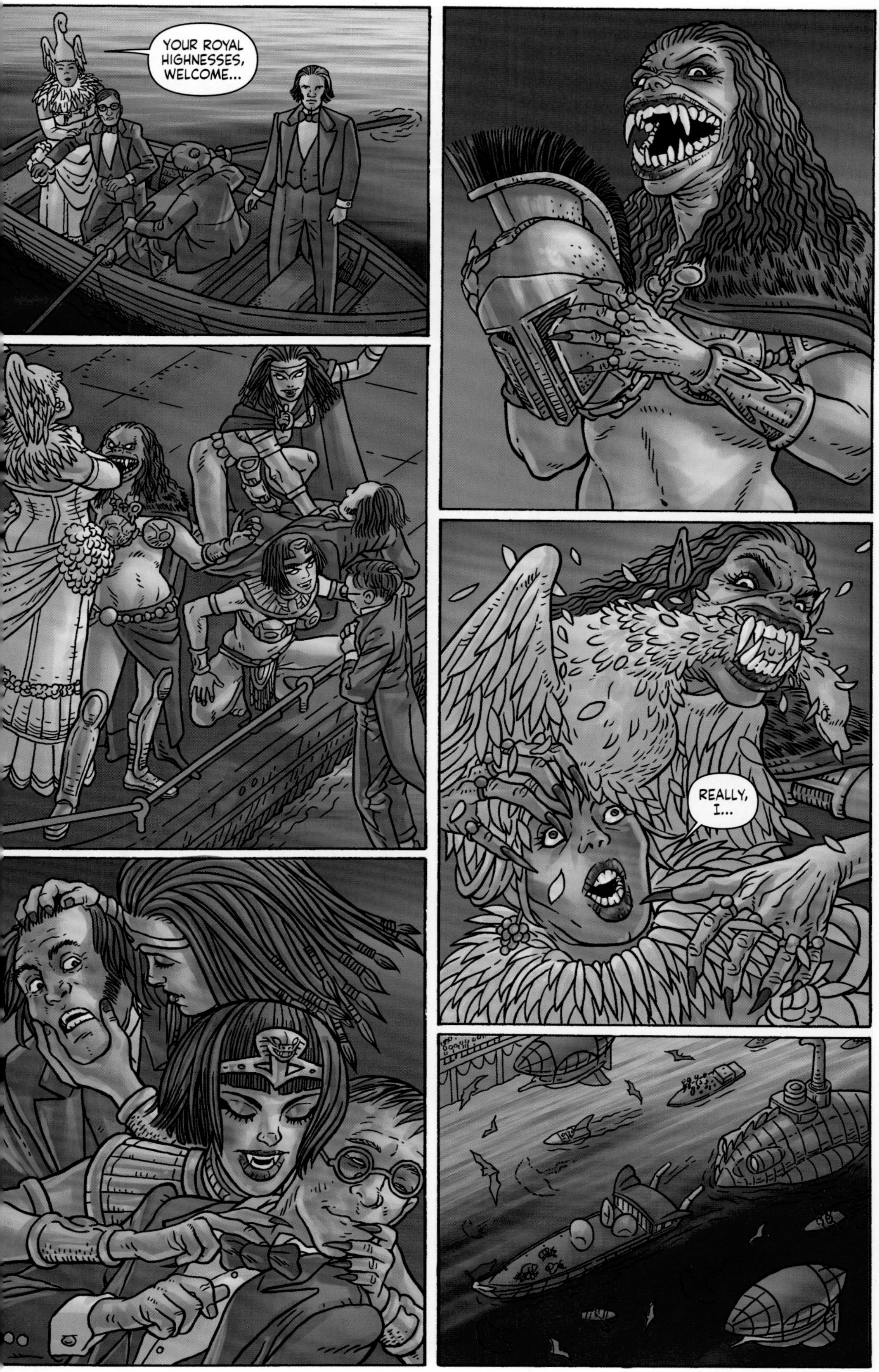
YOUR ROYAL HIGHNESSES, WELCOME...
REALLY, I...

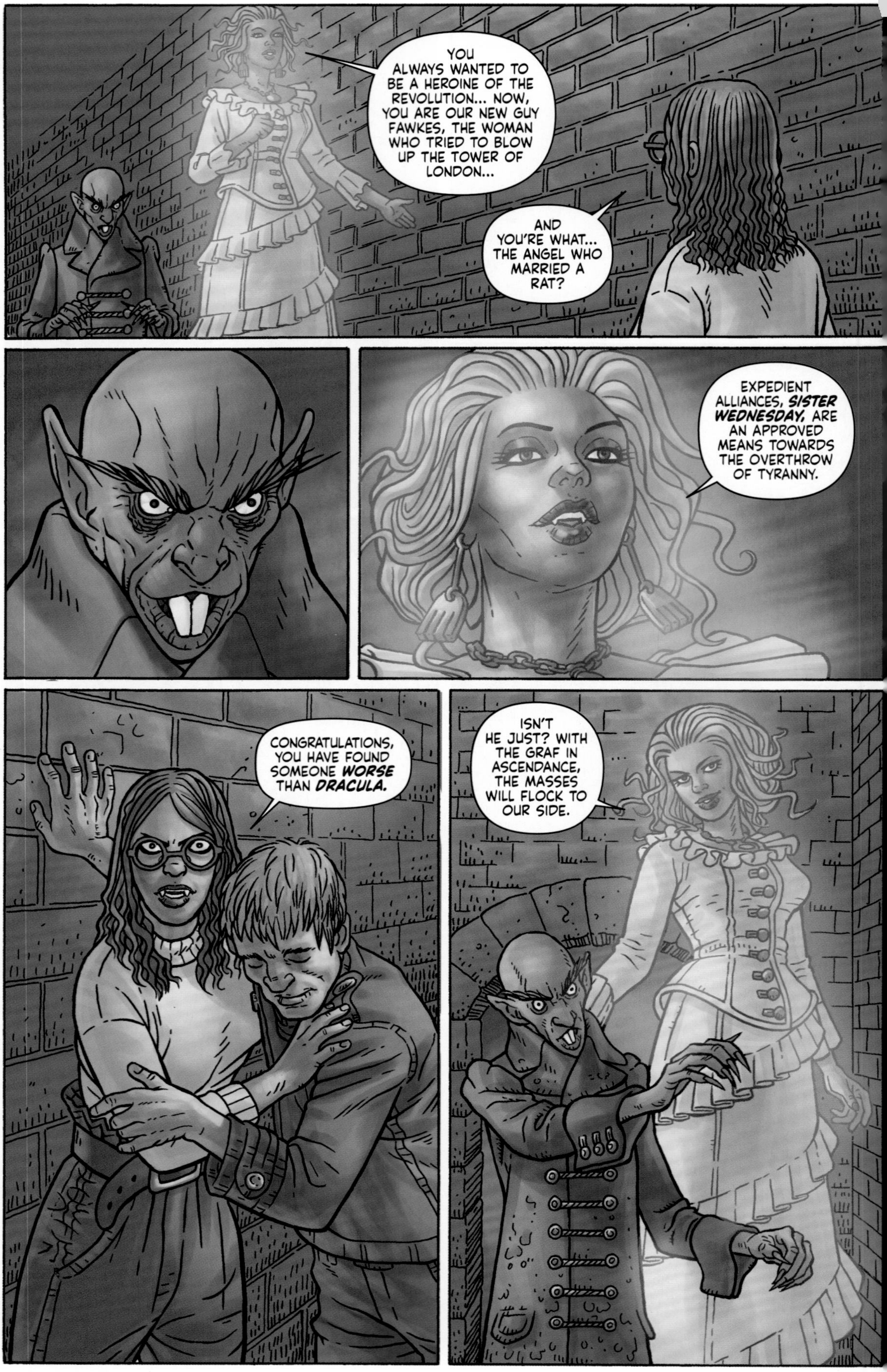
YOU ALWAYS WANTED TO BE A HEROINE OF THE REVOLUTION... NOW, YOU ARE OUR NEW GUY FAWKES, THE WOMAN WHO TRIED TO BLOW UP THE TOWER OF LONDON...
AND YOU'RE WHAT... THE ANGEL WHO MARRIED A RAT?
EXPEDIENT ALLIANCES, ***SISTER WEDNESDAY,*** ARE AN APPROVED MEANS TOWARDS THE OVERTHROW OF TYRANNY.
CONGRATULATIONS, YOU HAVE FOUND SOMEONE ***WORSE*** THAN ***DRACULA.***
ISN'T HE JUST? WITH THE GRAF IN ASCENDANCE, THE MASSES WILL FLOCK TO OUR SIDE.

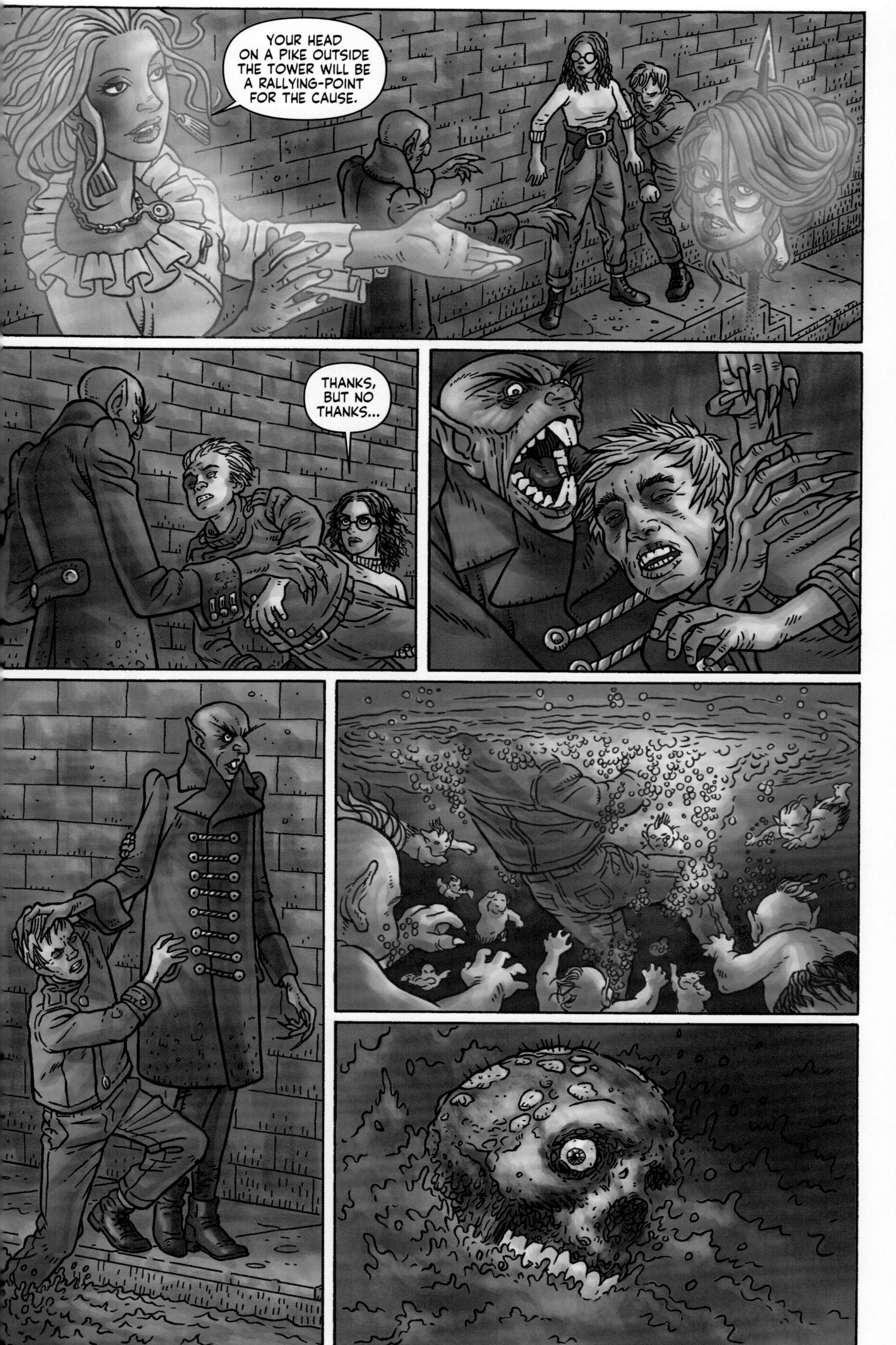
YOUR HEAD ON A PIKE OUTSIDE THE TOWER WILL BE A RALLYING-POINT FOR THE CAUSE.
THANKS, BUT NO THANKS...

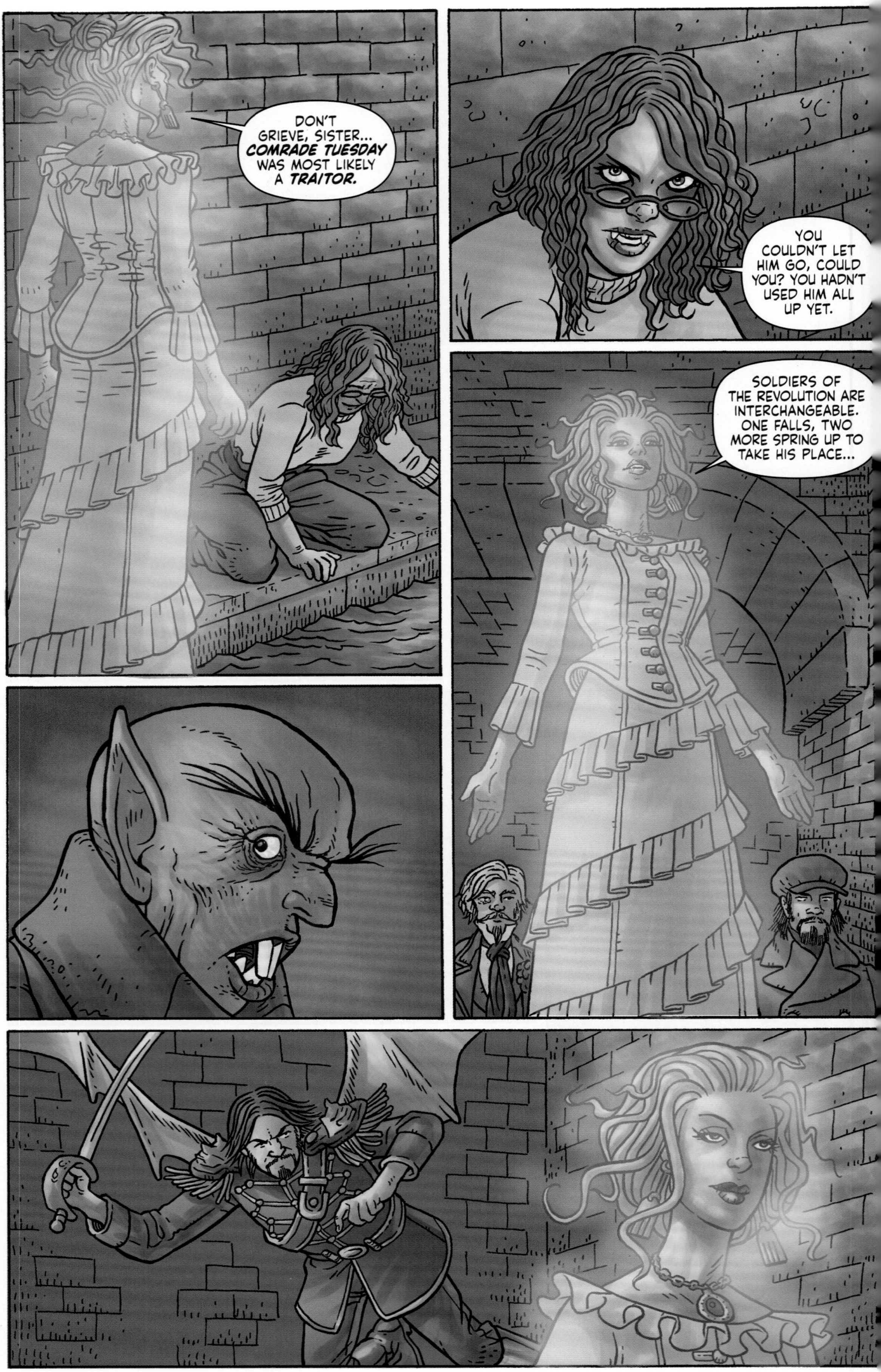
DON'T GRIEVE, SISTER... COMRADE TUESDAY WAS MOST LIKELY A TRAITOR.
YOU COULDN'T LET HIM GO, COULD YOU? YOU HADN'T USED HIM ALL UP YET.
SOLDIERS OF THE REVOLUTION ARE INTERCHANGEABLE. ONE FALLS, TWO MORE SPRING UP TO TAKE HIS PLACE...

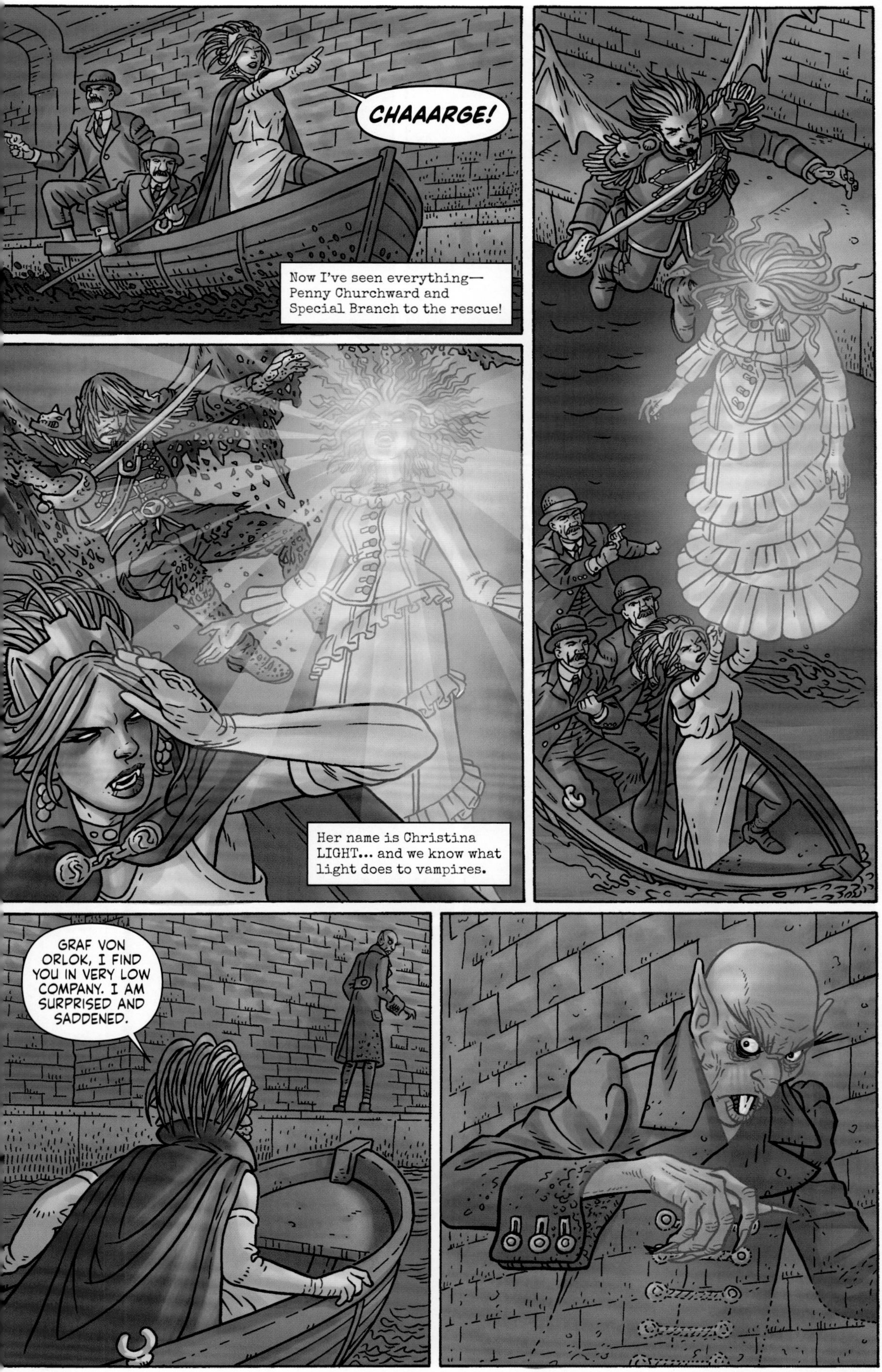

CHAAARGE!
Now I've seen everything—Penny Churchward and Special Branch to the rescue!
Her name is Christina LIGHT... and we know what light does to vampires.
GRAF VON ORLOK, I FIND YOU IN VERY LOW COMPANY. I AM SURPRISED AND SADDENED.

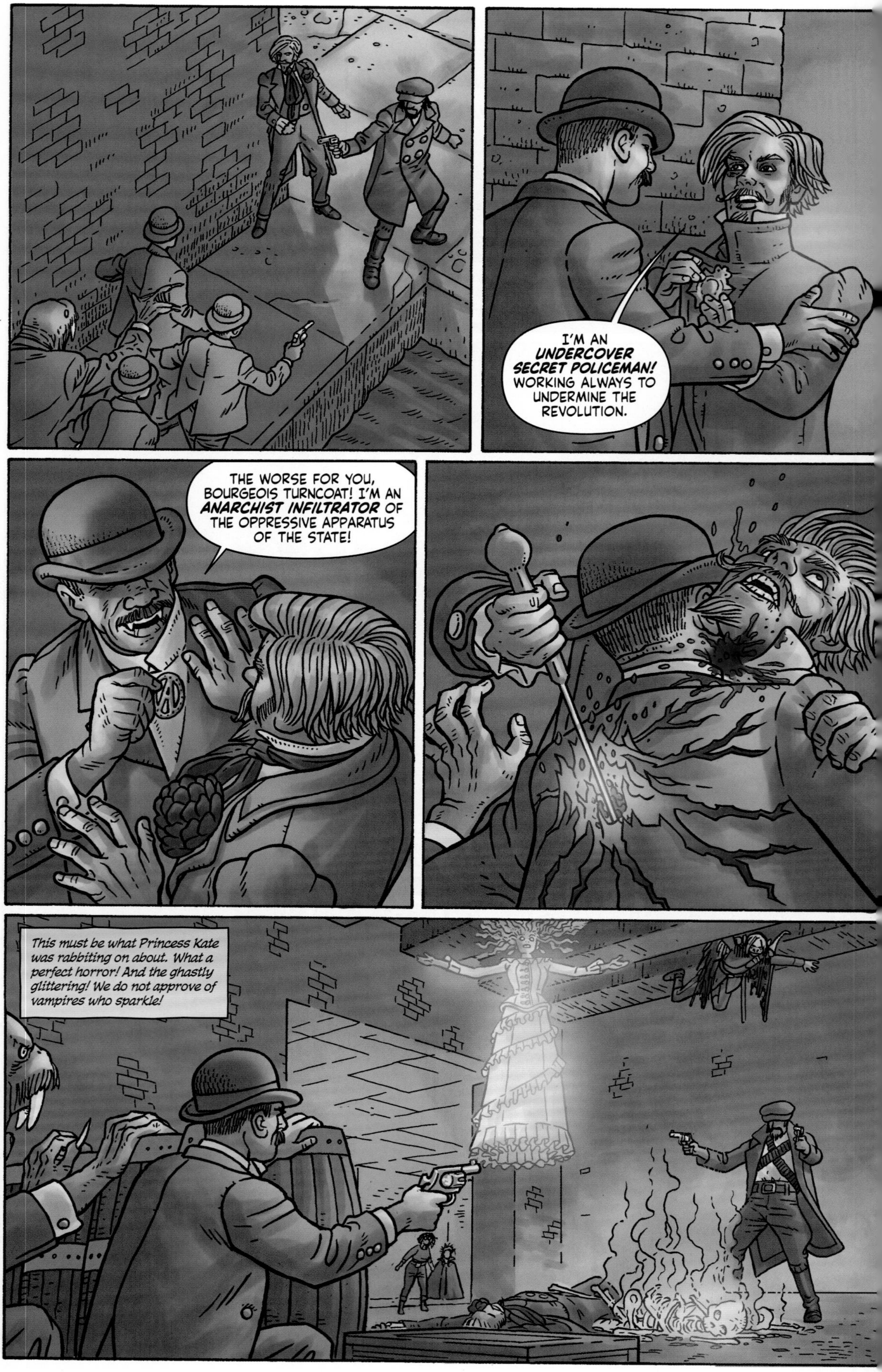

I'M AN UNDERCOVER SECRET POLICEMAN! WORKING ALWAYS TO UNDERMINE THE REVOLUTION.
THE WORSE FOR YOU, BOURGEOIS TURNCOAT! I'M AN ANARCHIST INFILTRATOR OF THE OPPRESSIVE APPARATUS OF THE STATE!
This must be what Princess Kate was rabbiting on about. What a perfect horror! And the ghastly glittering! We do not approve of vampires who sparkle!

UNWORTHY DAUGHTER, SEE WE ARE NOT FOLLOWED. DO NOT DISGRACE MY NAME BY GETTING KILLED OR ARRESTED.

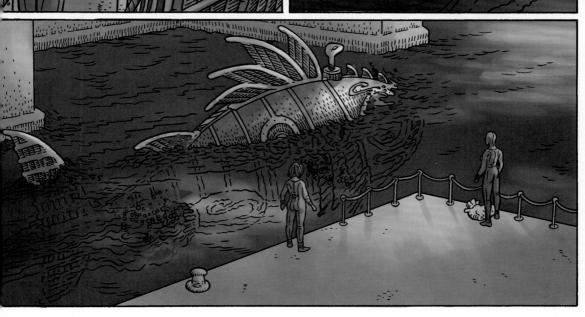

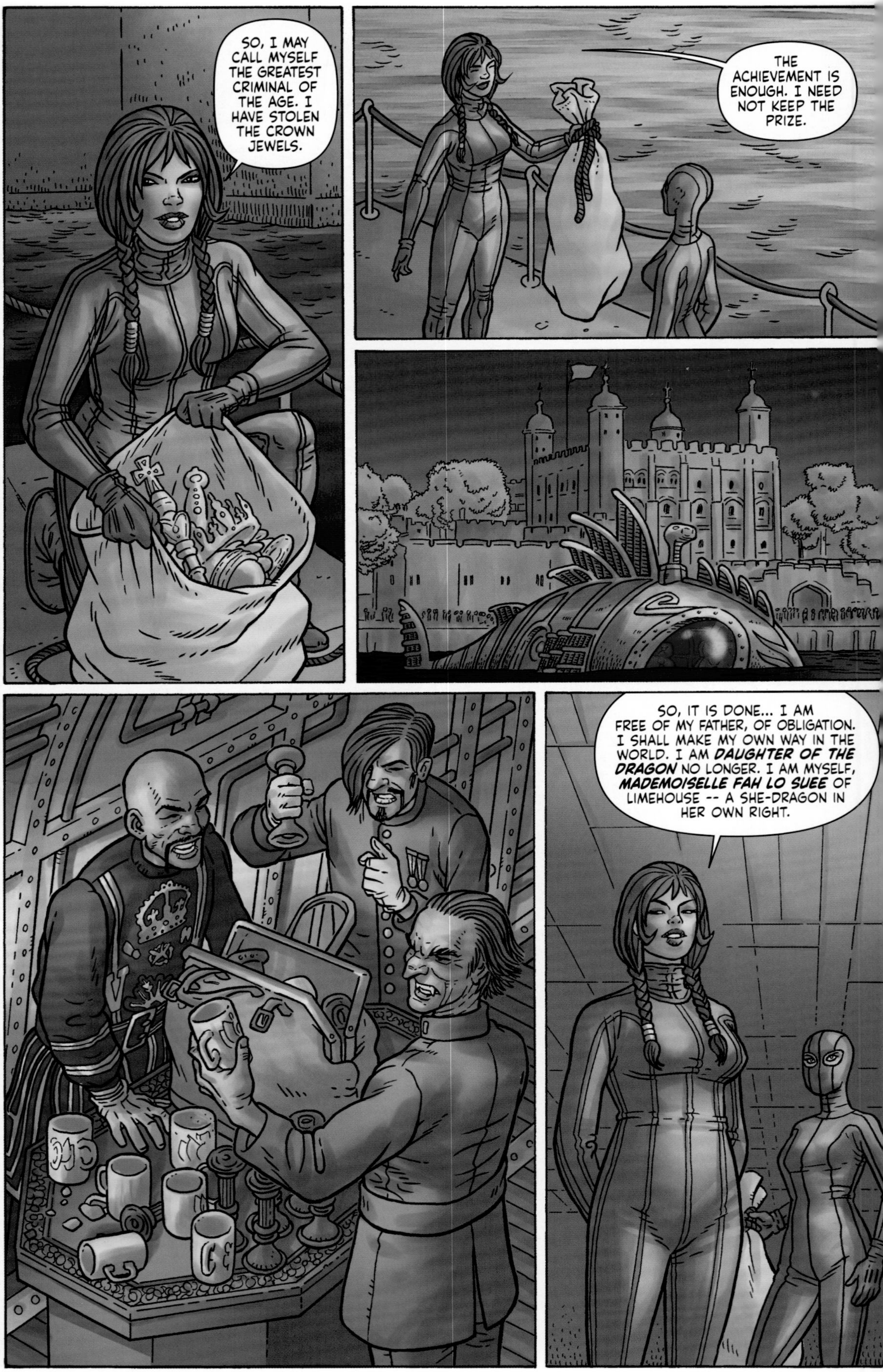
SO, I MAY CALL MYSELF THE GREATEST CRIMINAL OF THE AGE. I HAVE STOLEN THE CROWN JEWELS.
THE ACHIEVEMENT IS ENOUGH. I NEED NOT KEEP THE PRIZE.
SO, IT IS DONE... I AM FREE OF MY FATHER, OF OBLIGATION. I SHALL MAKE MY OWN WAY IN THE WORLD. I AM ***DAUGHTER OF THE DRAGON*** NO LONGER. I AM MYSELF, ***MADEMOISELLE FAH LO SUEE*** OF LIMEHOUSE -- A SHE-DRAGON IN HER OWN RIGHT.

For Mr Mycroft Holmes,
c/o The Diogenes Club, Pall Mall.

Here are some trinkets saved from
barbarians and thieves, to be held in
trust for a more worthy monarch
than the monster who presently
occupies the throne of England.

Fondest regards,

"Irma Vep"
- a name taken as a mask

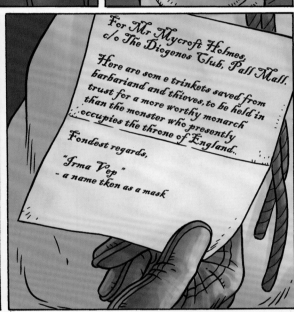

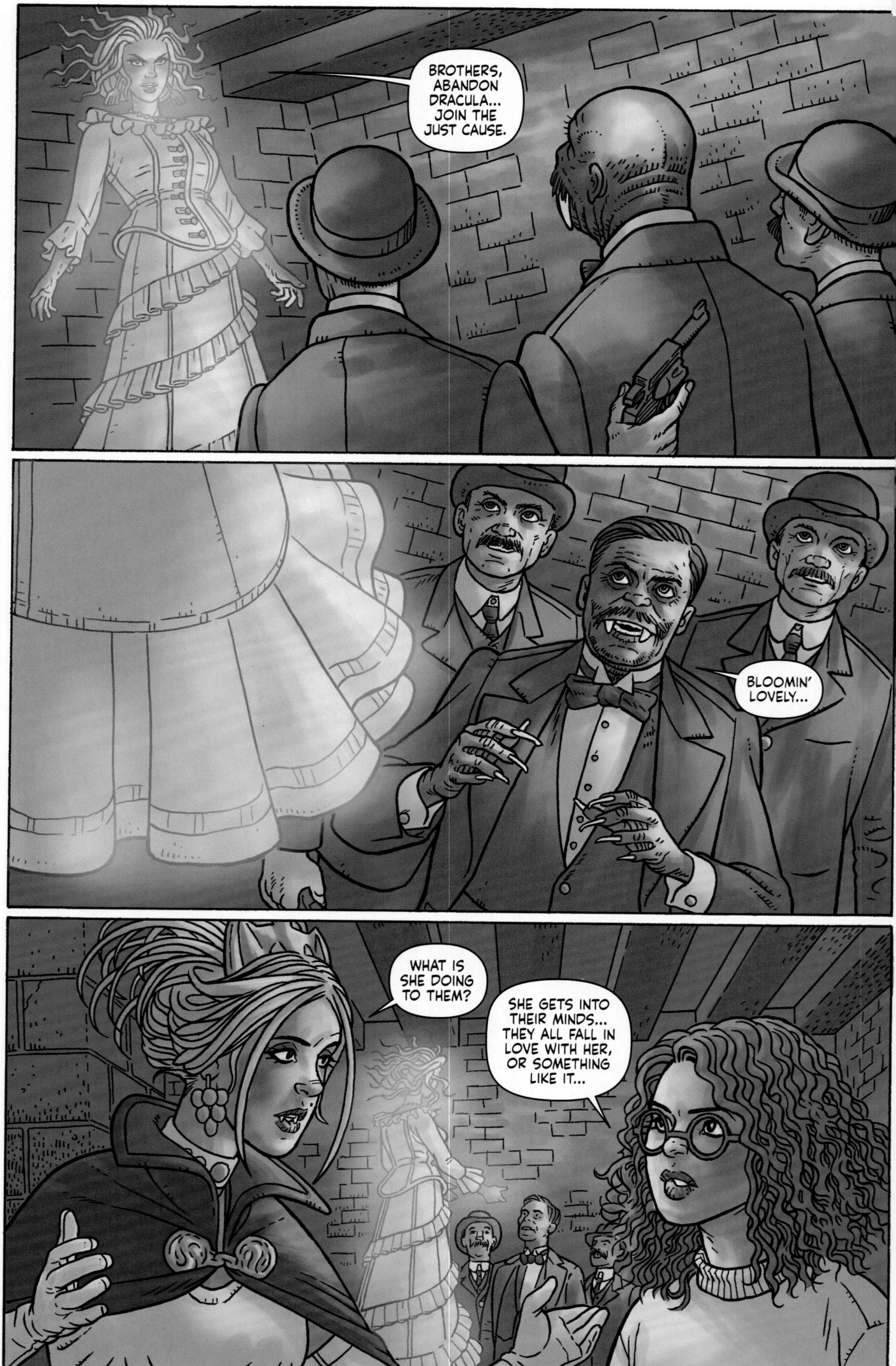
BROTHERS, ABANDON DRACULA... JOIN THE JUST CAUSE.
BLOOMIN' LOVELY...
WHAT IS SHE DOING TO THEM?
SHE GETS INTO THEIR MINDS... THEY ALL FALL IN LOVE WITH HER, OR SOMETHING LIKE IT...

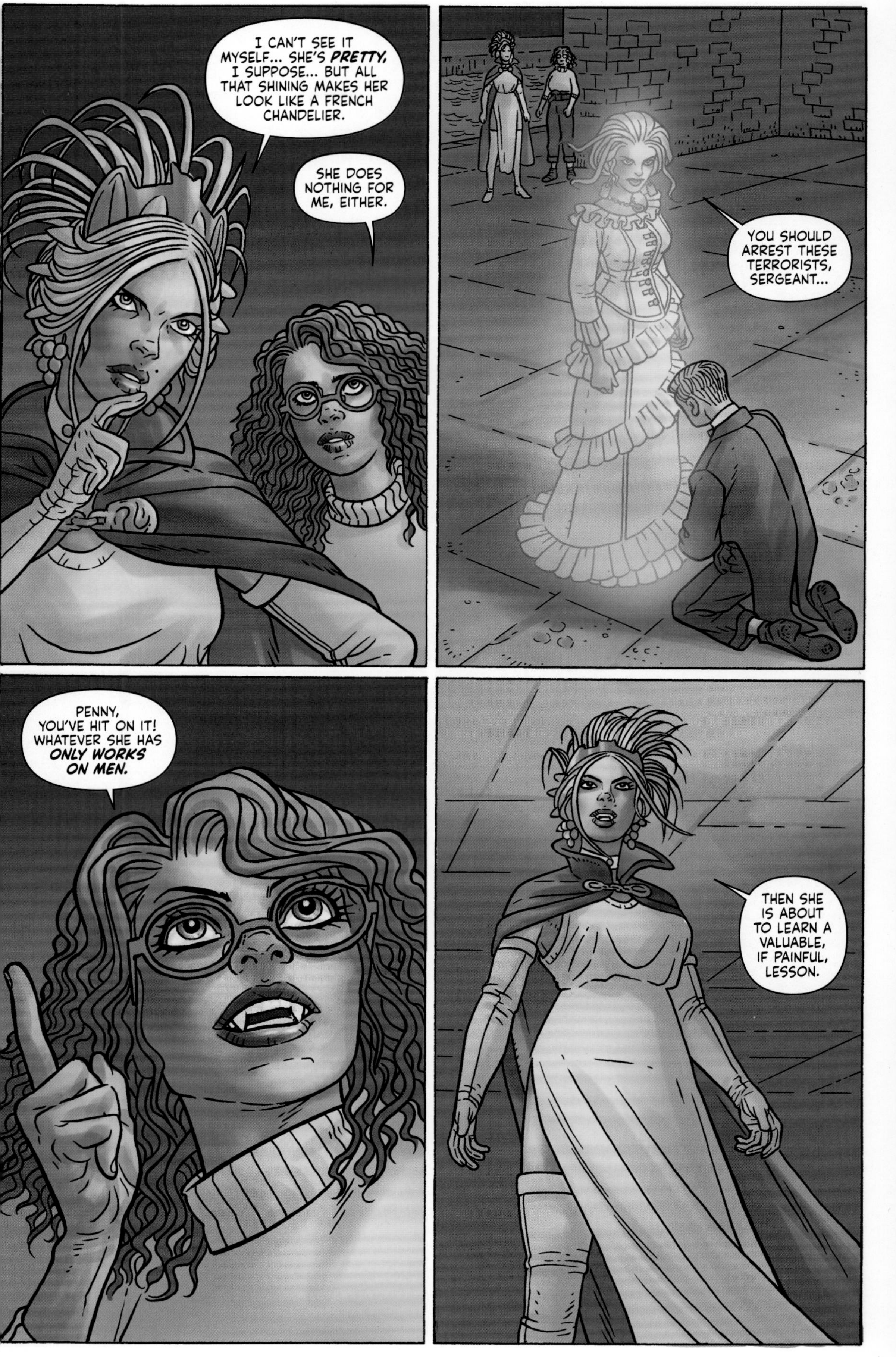
I CAN'T SEE IT MYSELF... SHE'S PRETTY, I SUPPOSE... BUT ALL THAT SHINING MAKES HER LOOK LIKE A FRENCH CHANDELIER.
SHE DOES NOTHING FOR ME, EITHER.
YOU SHOULD ARREST THESE TERRORISTS, SERGEANT...
PENNY, YOU'VE HIT ON IT! WHATEVER SHE HAS ONLY WORKS ON MEN.
THEN SHE IS ABOUT TO LEARN A VALUABLE, IF PAINFUL, LESSON.

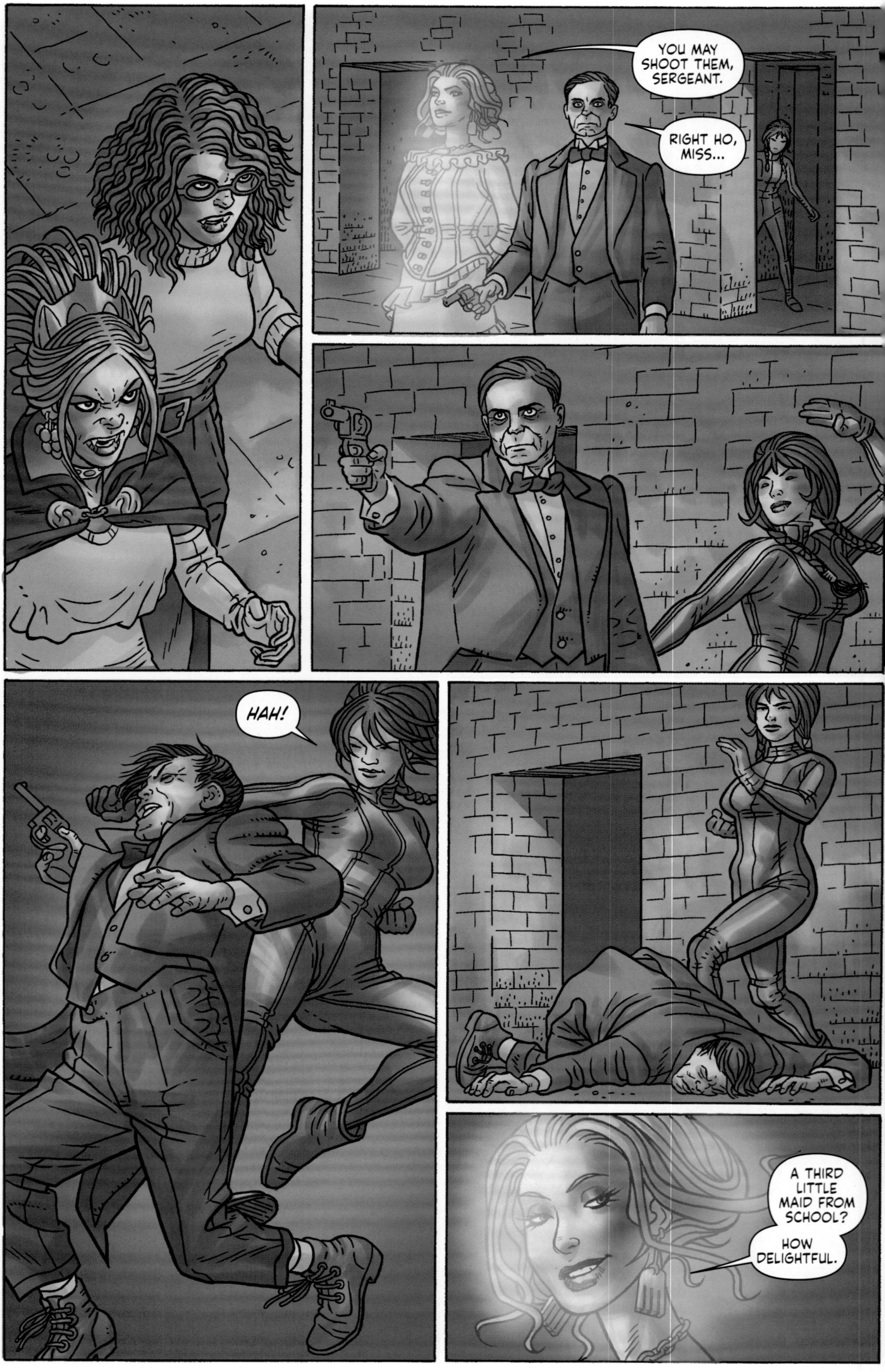
YOU MAY SHOOT THEM, SERGEANT.
RIGHT HO, MISS...
HAH!
A THIRD LITTLE MAID FROM SCHOOL?
HOW DELIGHTFUL.

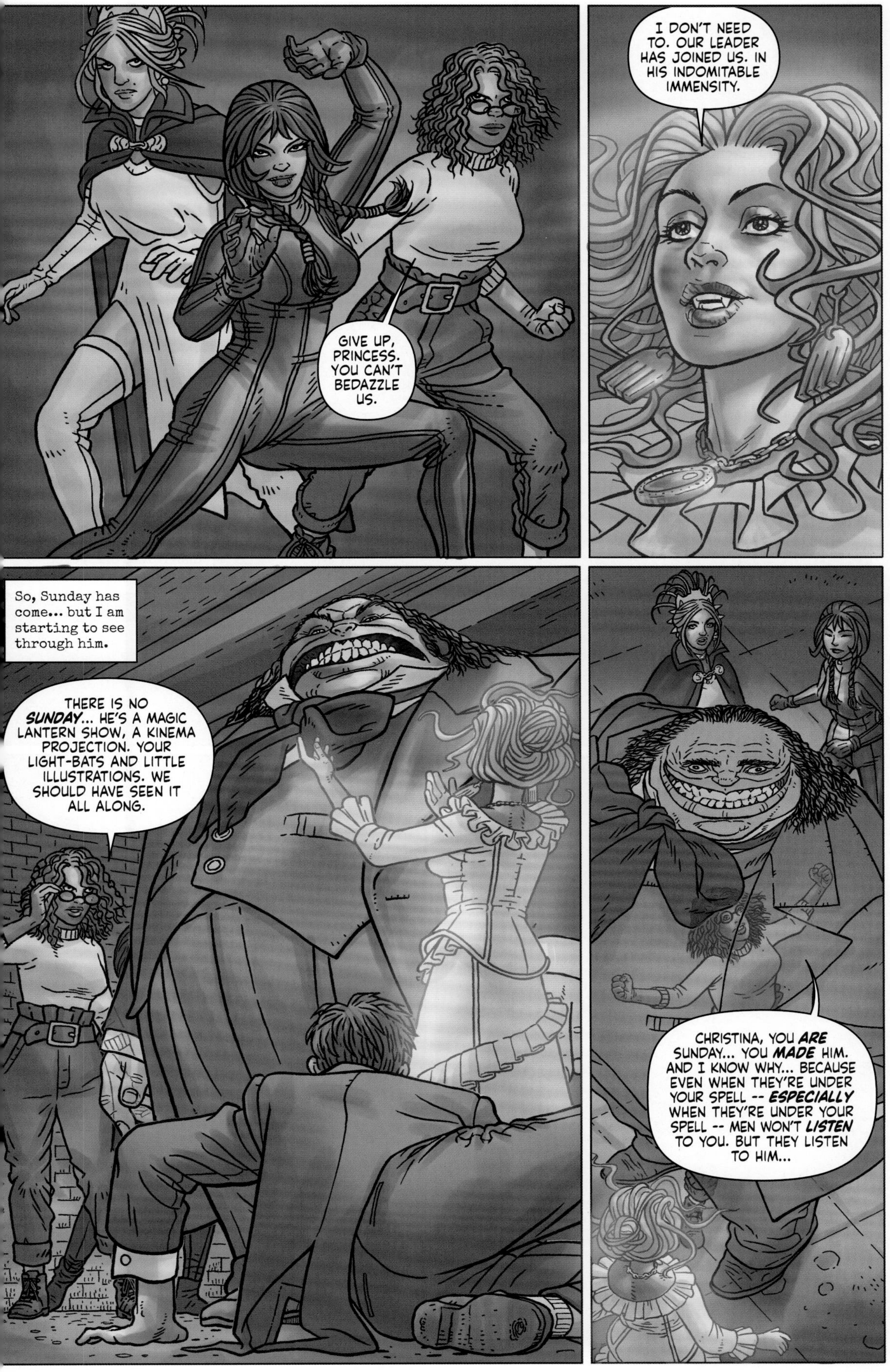
GIVE UP, PRINCESS. YOU CAN'T BEDAZZLE US.
I DON'T NEED TO. OUR LEADER HAS JOINED US. IN HIS INDOMITABLE IMMENSITY.
So, Sunday has come... but I am starting to see through him.
THERE IS NO SUNDAY... HE'S A MAGIC LANTERN SHOW, A KINEMA PROJECTION. YOUR LIGHT-BATS AND LITTLE ILLUSTRATIONS. WE SHOULD HAVE SEEN IT ALL ALONG.
CHRISTINA, YOU ARE SUNDAY... YOU MADE HIM. AND I KNOW WHY... BECAUSE EVEN WHEN THEY'RE UNDER YOUR SPELL -- ESPECIALLY WHEN THEY'RE UNDER YOUR SPELL -- MEN WON'T LISTEN TO YOU. BUT THEY LISTEN TO HIM...

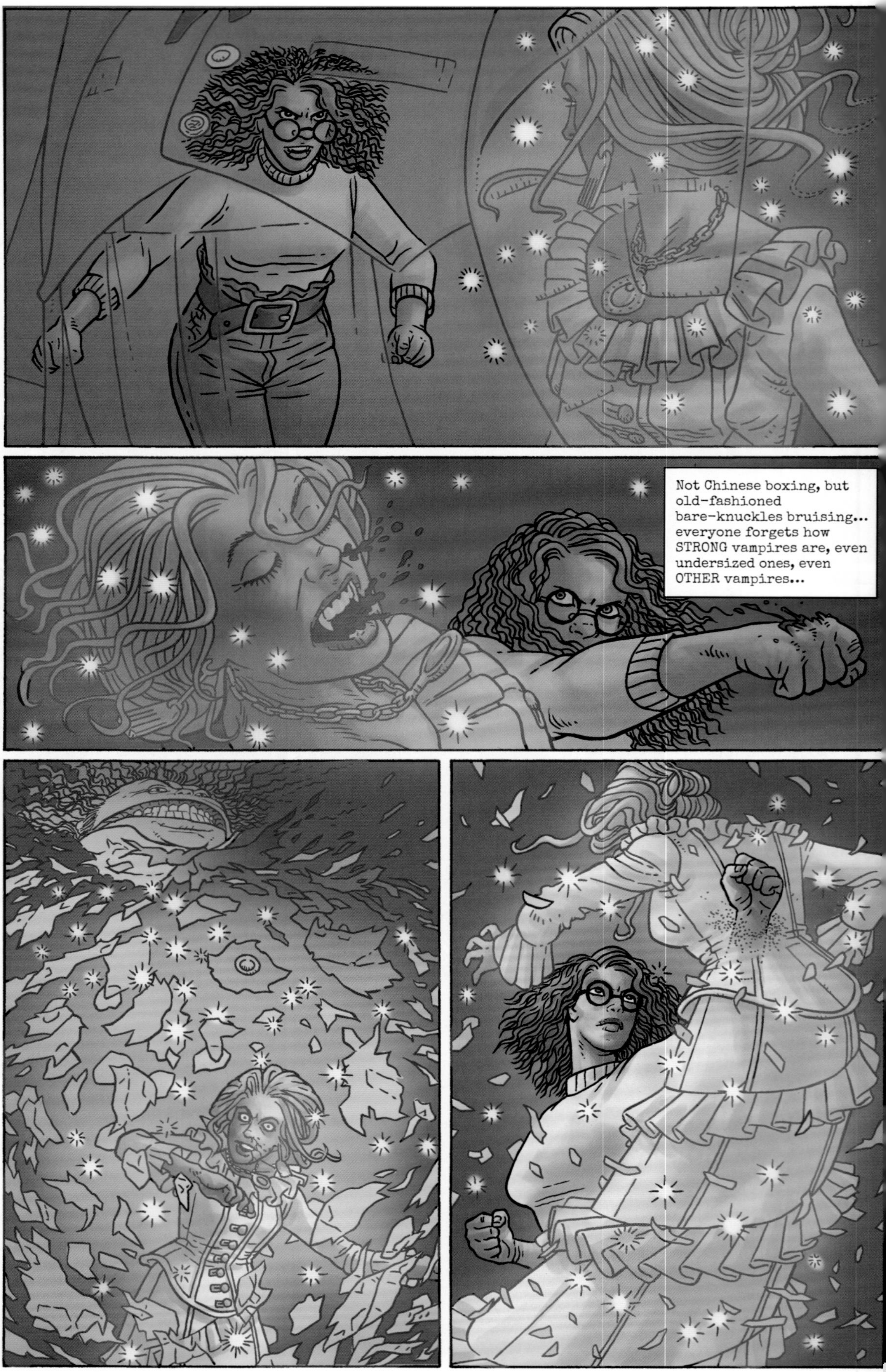
Not Chinese boxing, but old-fashioned bare-knuckles bruising... everyone forgets how STRONG vampires are, even undersized ones, even OTHER vampires...

WHAT'S WRONG WITH HER?

SHE CAN'T CHANGE BACK... SHE'S PARTLY LIGHT. LET'S HOPE SHE'S STUCK THAT WAY.

THAT'S POLICE PROPERTY, MISS.

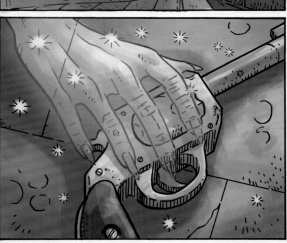

GRAF VON ORLOK... IT CAN STILL BE DONE... YOU CAN STILL RISE.

THERE'S ENOUGH DYNAMITE AND POWDER TO BRING DOWN THE TOWER AND DRACULA AND ALL THE ROT WITH IT...

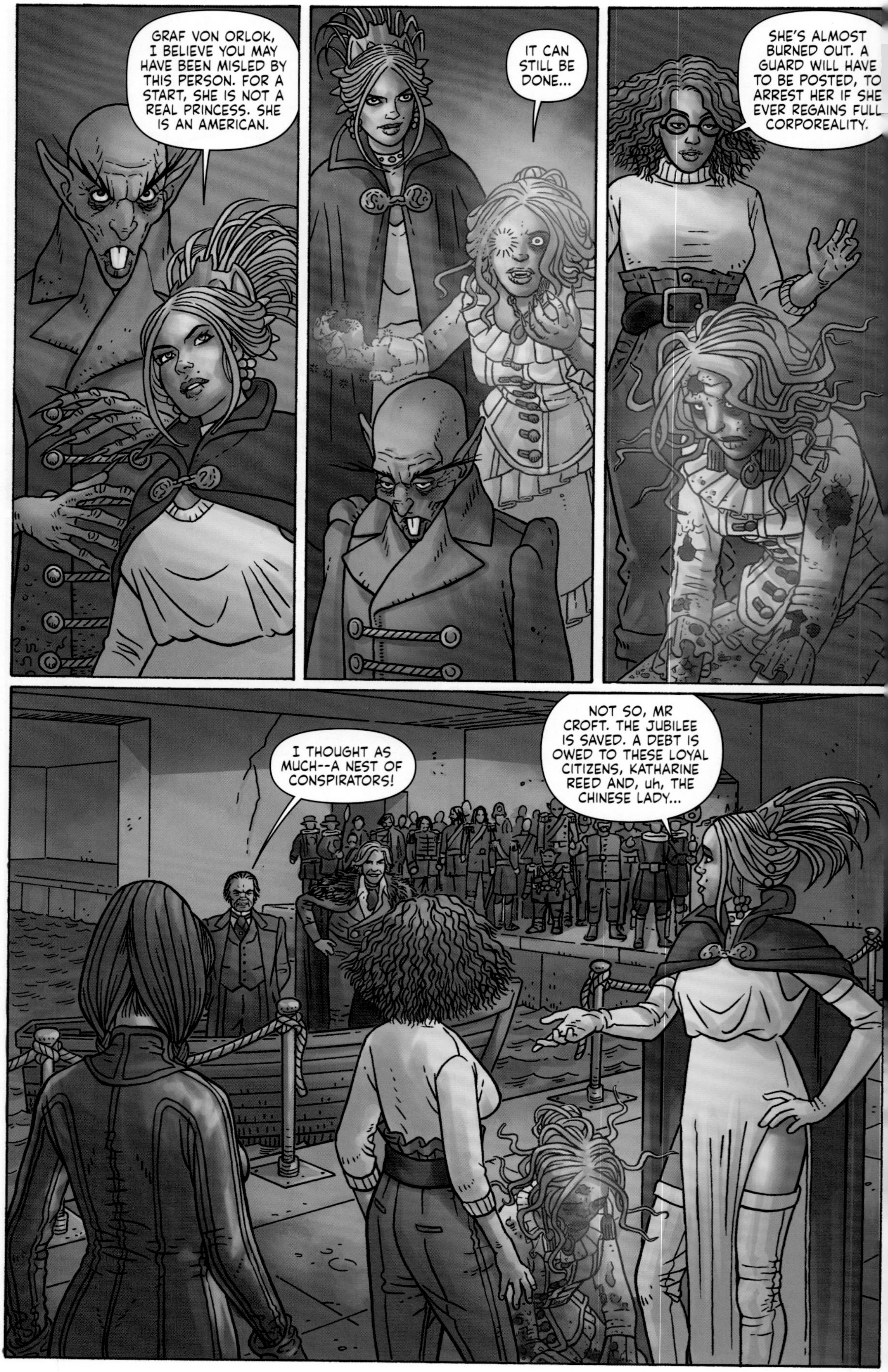
GRAF VON ORLOK, I BELIEVE YOU MAY HAVE BEEN MISLED BY THIS PERSON. FOR A START, SHE IS NOT A REAL PRINCESS. SHE IS AN AMERICAN.
IT CAN STILL BE DONE...
SHE'S ALMOST BURNED OUT. A GUARD WILL HAVE TO BE POSTED, TO ARREST HER IF SHE EVER REGAINS FULL CORPOREALITY.
I THOUGHT AS MUCH--A NEST OF CONSPIRATORS!
NOT SO, MR CROFT. THE JUBILEE IS SAVED. A DEBT IS OWED TO THESE LOYAL CITIZENS, KATHARINE REED AND, uh, THE CHINESE LADY...

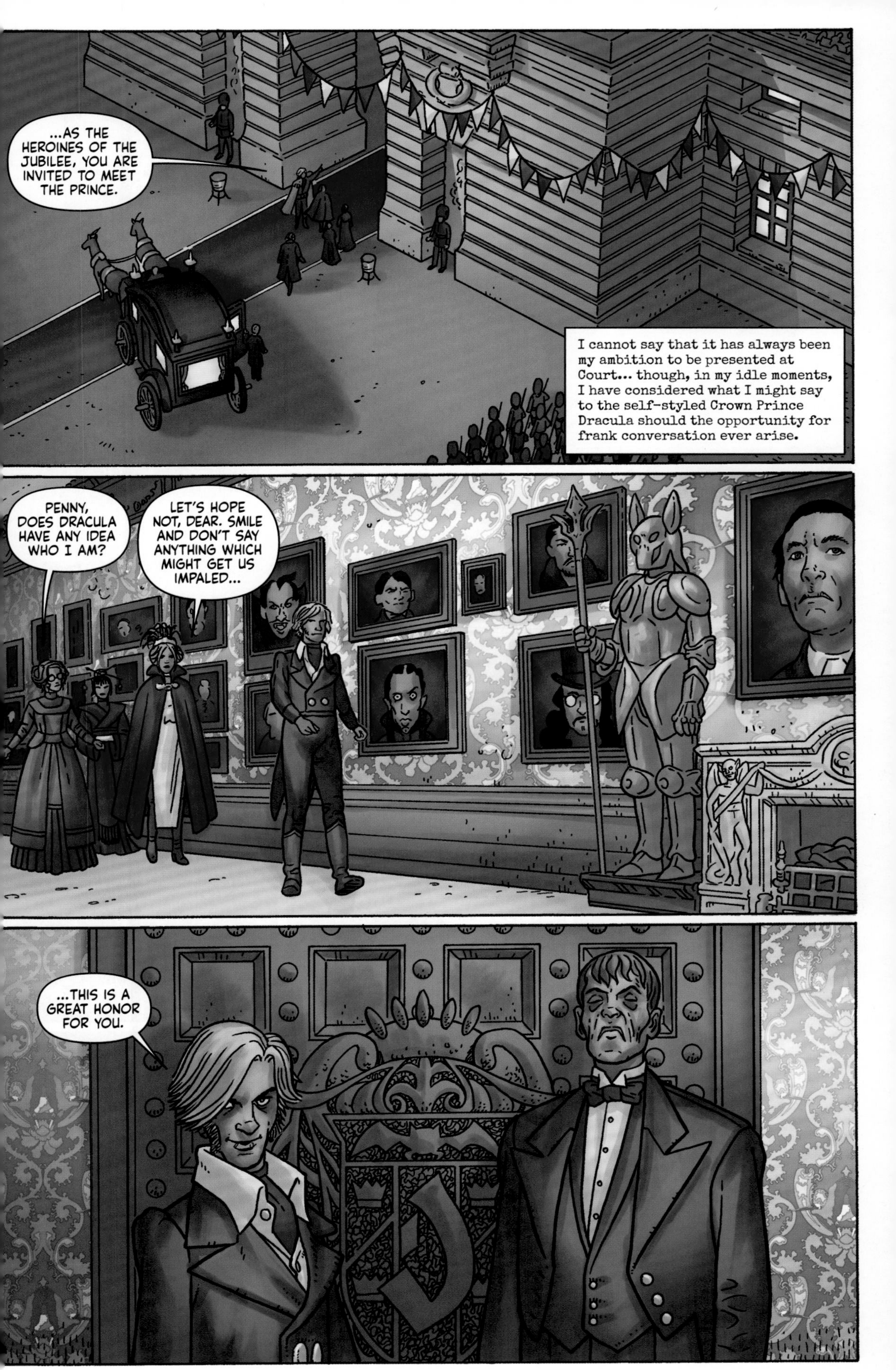
...AS THE HEROINES OF THE JUBILEE, YOU ARE INVITED TO MEET THE PRINCE.
I cannot say that it has always been my ambition to be presented at Court... though, in my idle moments, I have considered what I might say to the self-styled Crown Prince Dracula should the opportunity for frank conversation ever arise.
PENNY, DOES DRACULA HAVE ANY IDEA WHO I AM?
LET'S HOPE NOT, DEAR. SMILE AND DON'T SAY ANYTHING WHICH MIGHT GET US IMPALED...
...THIS IS A GREAT HONOR FOR YOU.

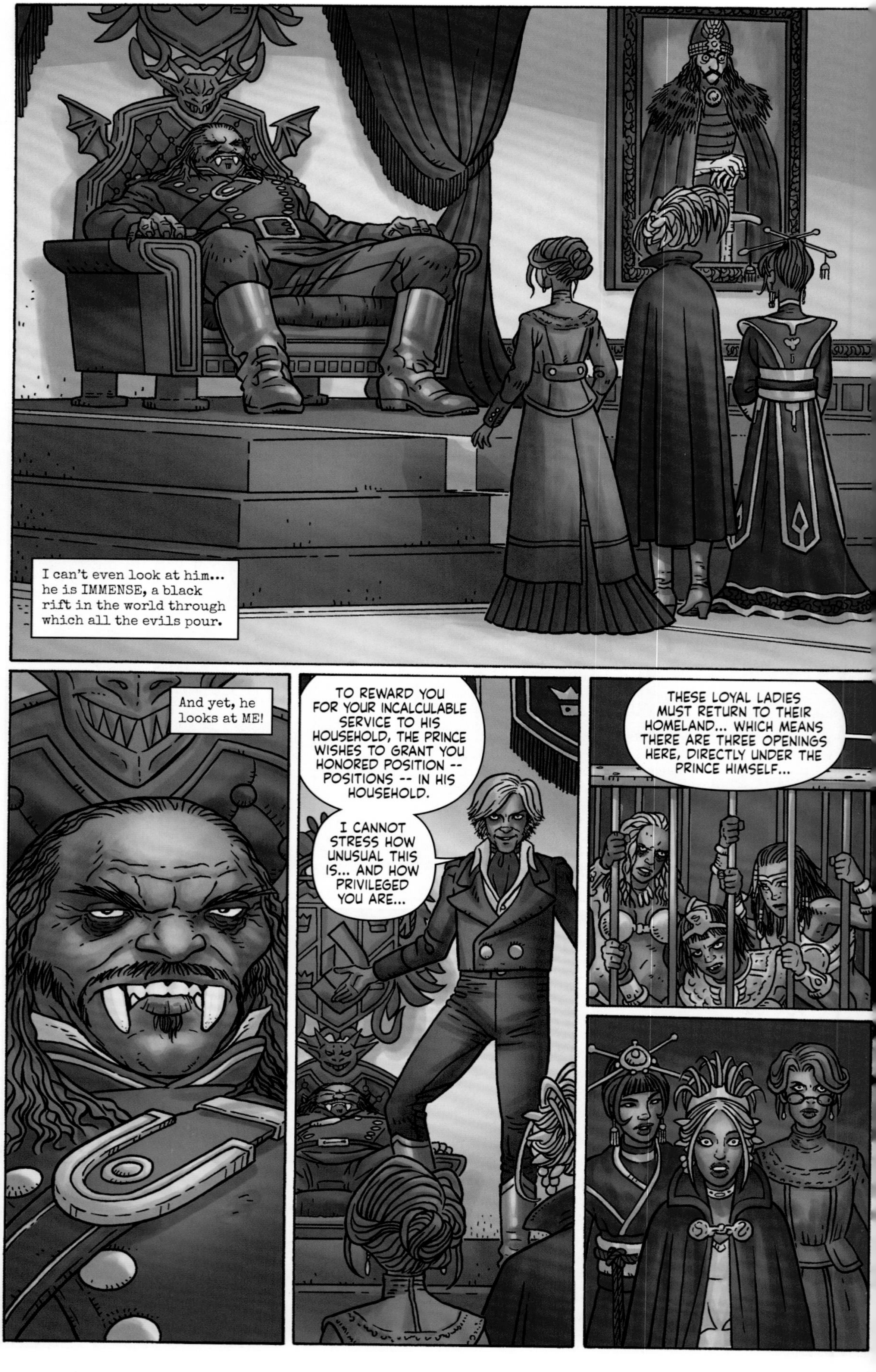
I can't even look at him... he is IMMENSE, a black rift in the world through which all the evils pour.
And yet, he looks at ME!
TO REWARD YOU FOR YOUR INCALCULABLE SERVICE TO HIS HOUSEHOLD, THE PRINCE WISHES TO GRANT YOU HONORED POSITION -- POSITIONS -- IN HIS HOUSEHOLD.
I CANNOT STRESS HOW UNUSUAL THIS IS... AND HOW PRIVILEGED YOU ARE...
THESE LOYAL LADIES MUST RETURN TO THEIR HOMELAND... WHICH MEANS THERE ARE THREE OPENINGS HERE, DIRECTLY UNDER THE PRINCE HIMSELF...

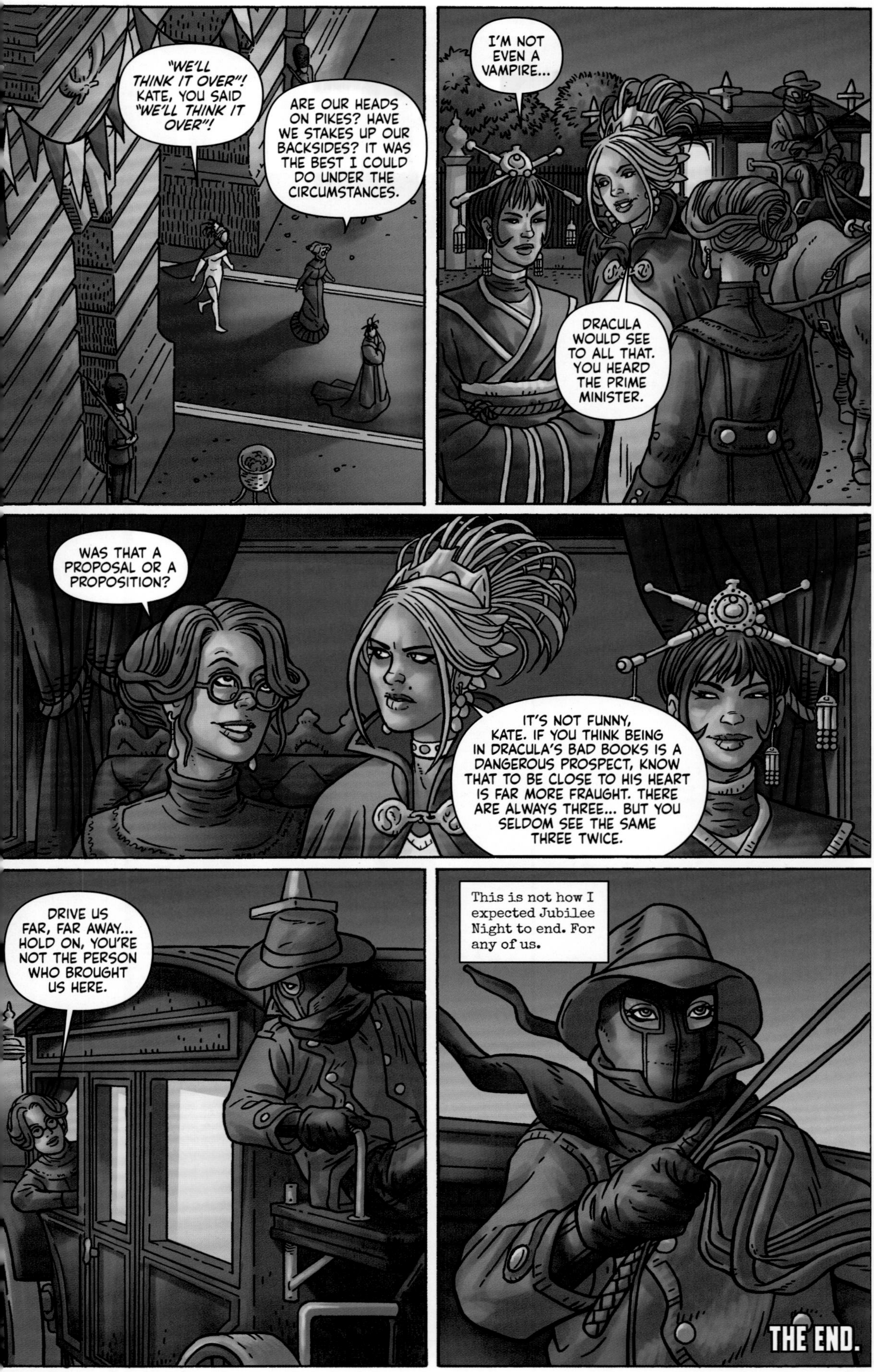
"WE'LL THINK IT OVER"! KATE, YOU SAID "WE'LL THINK IT OVER"!
ARE OUR HEADS ON PIKES? HAVE WE STAKES UP OUR BACKSIDES? IT WAS THE BEST I COULD DO UNDER THE CIRCUMSTANCES.
I'M NOT EVEN A VAMPIRE...
DRACULA WOULD SEE TO ALL THAT. YOU HEARD THE PRIME MINISTER.
WAS THAT A PROPOSAL OR A PROPOSITION?
IT'S NOT FUNNY, KATE. IF YOU THINK BEING IN DRACULA'S BAD BOOKS IS A DANGEROUS PROSPECT, KNOW THAT TO BE CLOSE TO HIS HEART IS FAR MORE FRAUGHT. THERE ARE ALWAYS THREE... BUT YOU SELDOM SEE THE SAME THREE TWICE.
DRIVE US FAR, FAR AWAY... HOLD ON, YOU'RE NOT THE PERSON WHO BROUGHT US HERE.
This is not how I expected Jubilee Night to end. For any of us.
THE END.

COVER GALLERY

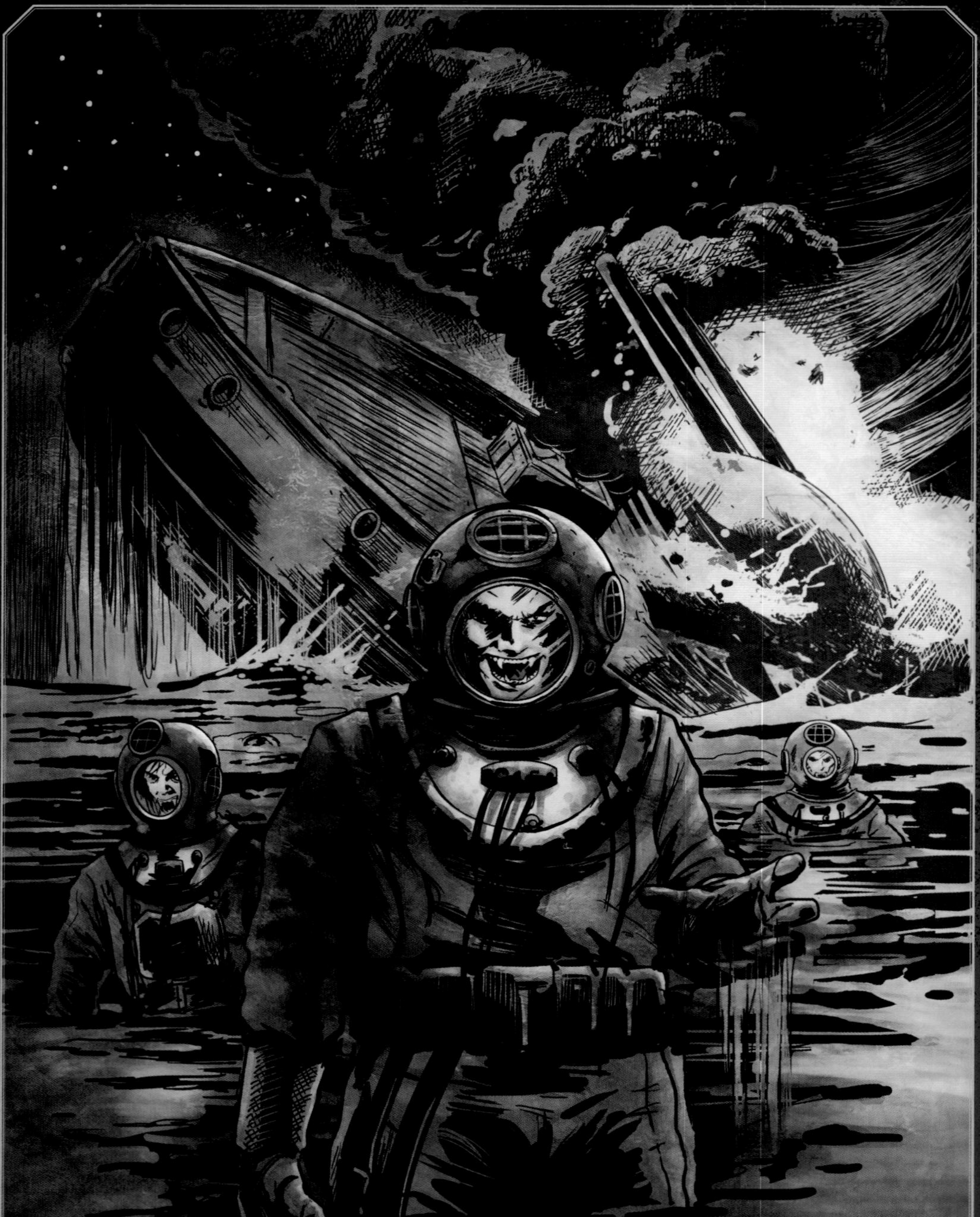

Issue #1. Variant cover C by Brian Williamson

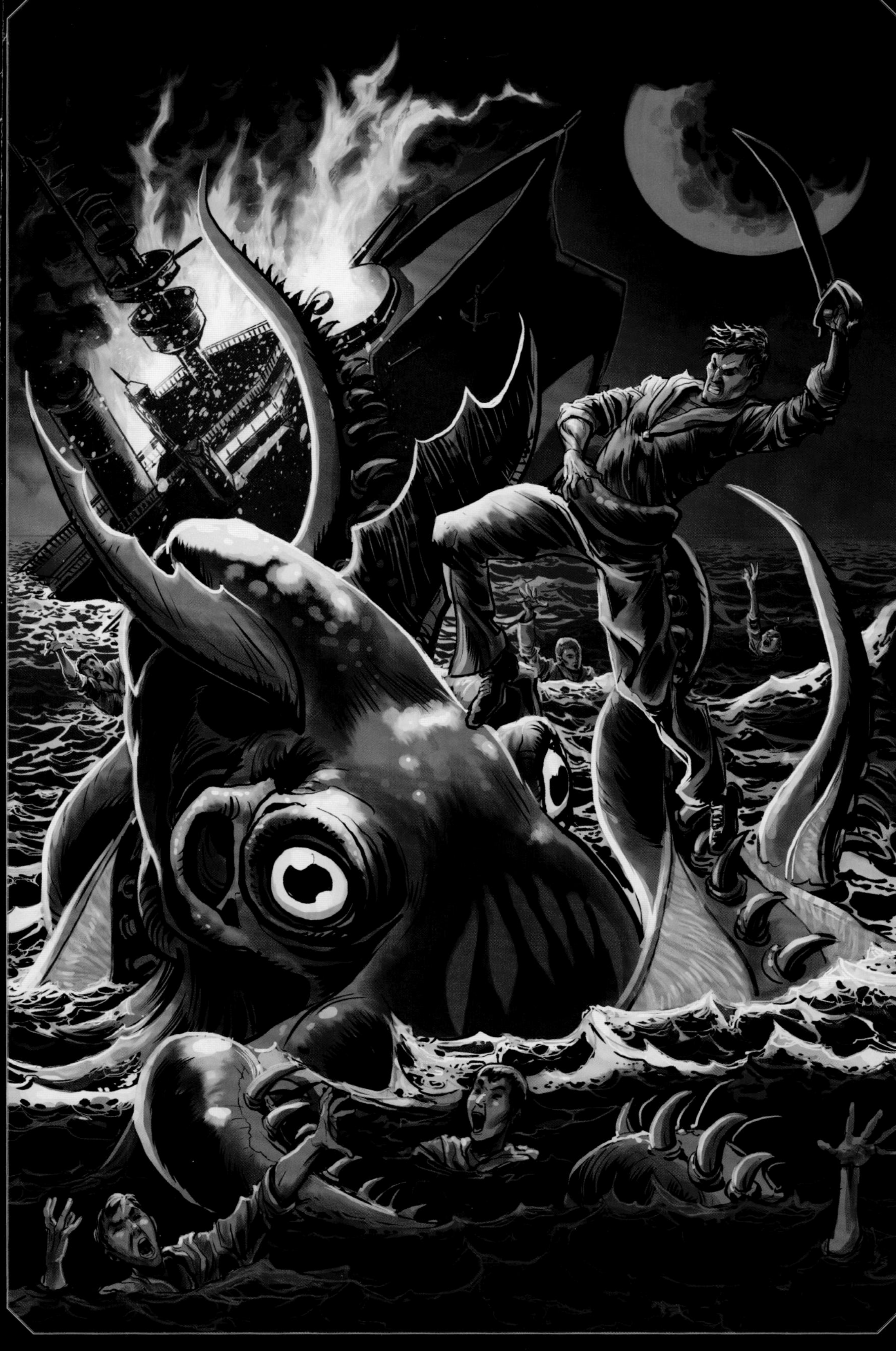

Issue #1. Variant cover D by Jeff Zornow

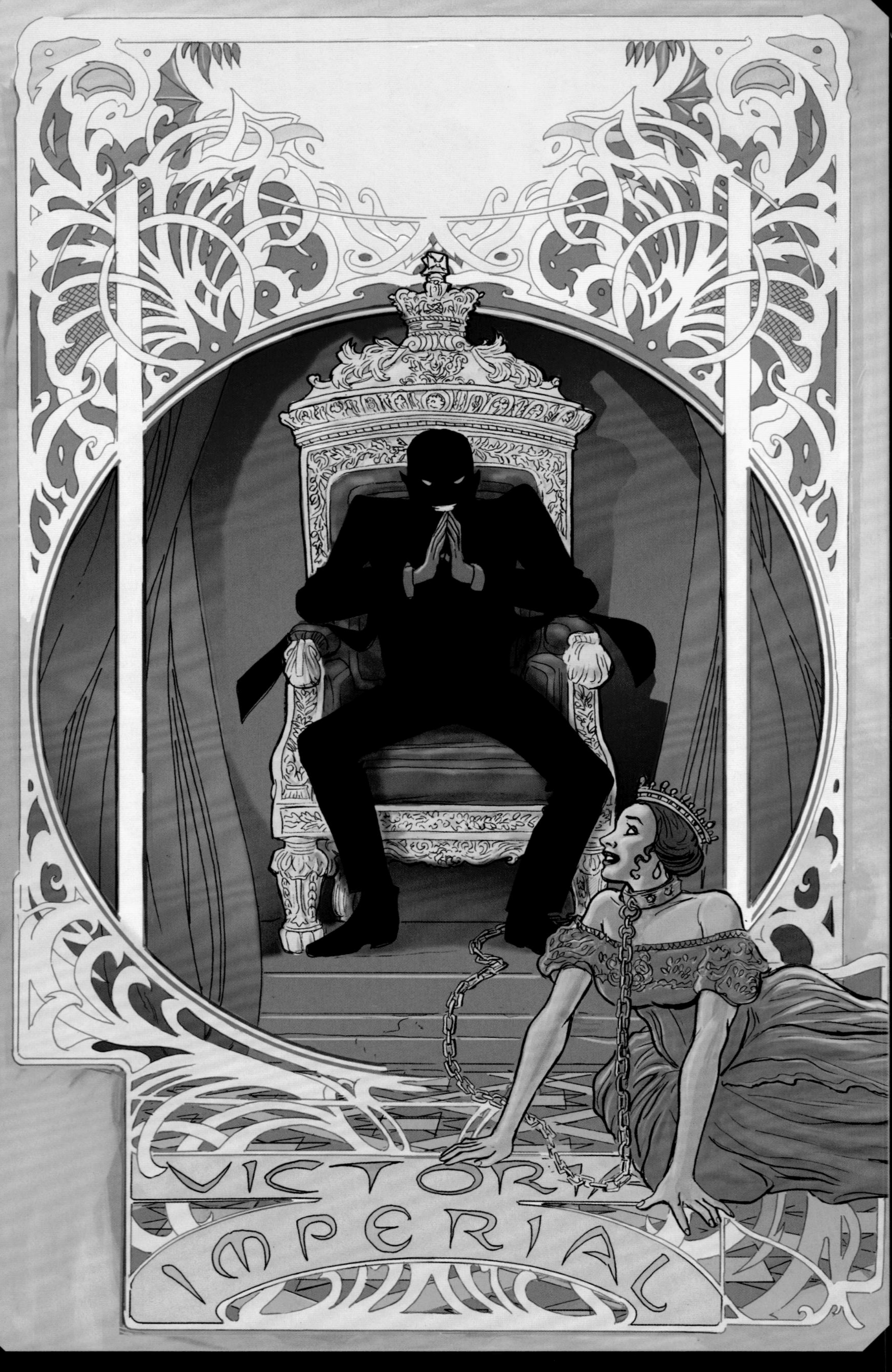
VICTORIA
IMPERIAL

Issue #1. Variant cover E by Mike Collins

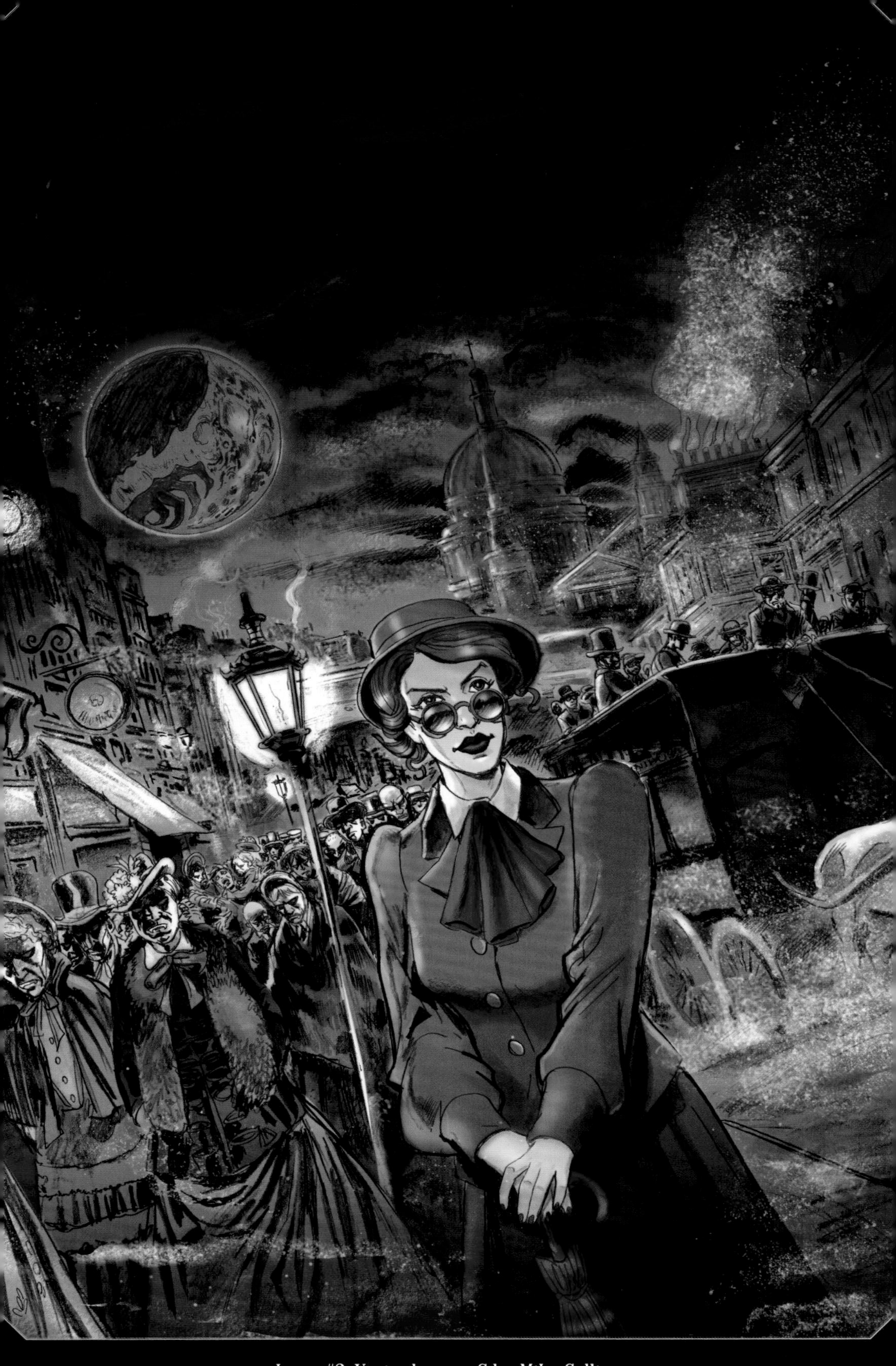

Issue #2 Variant cover C by Mike Collins

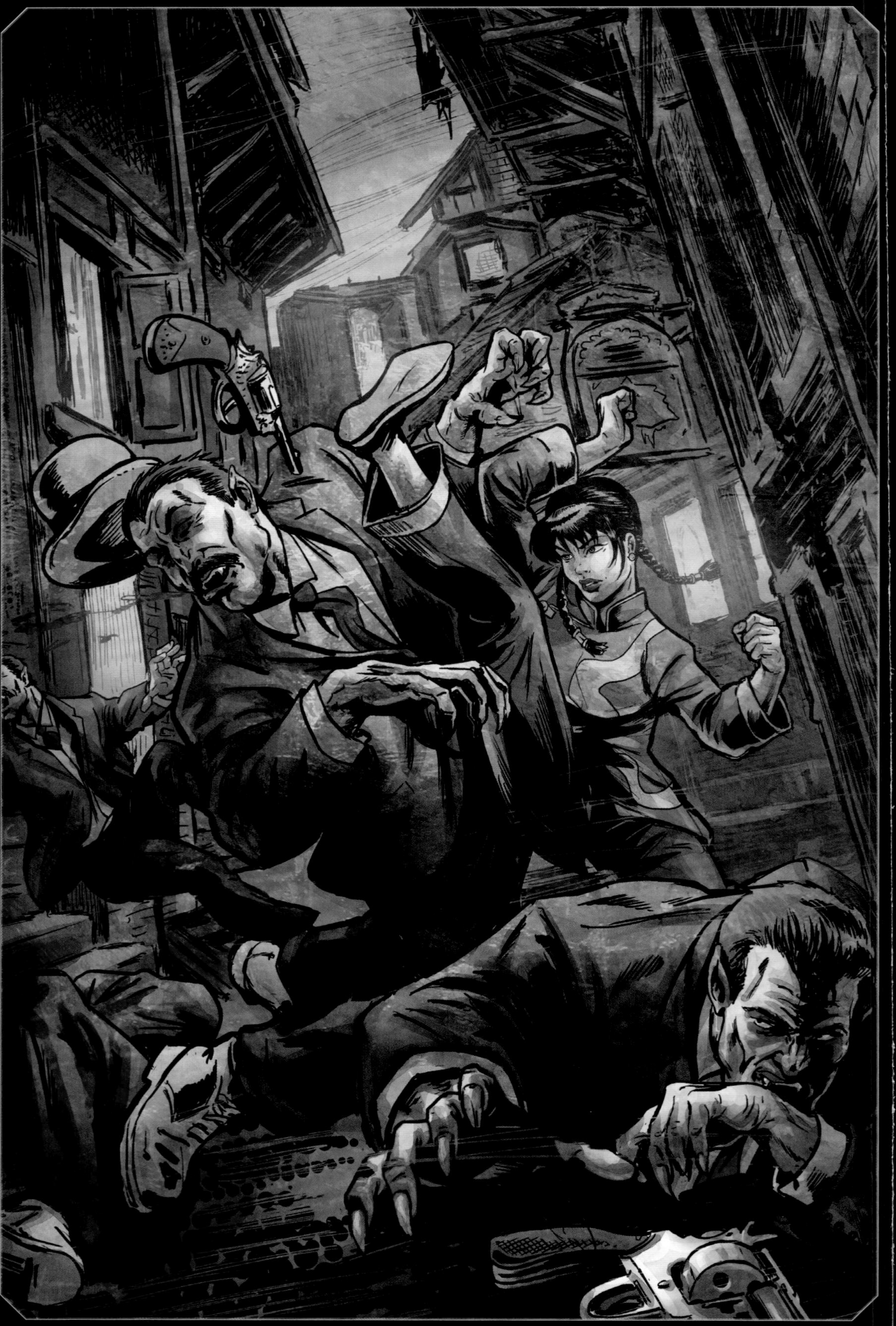

Issue #2. Variant cover D by Brian Williamson

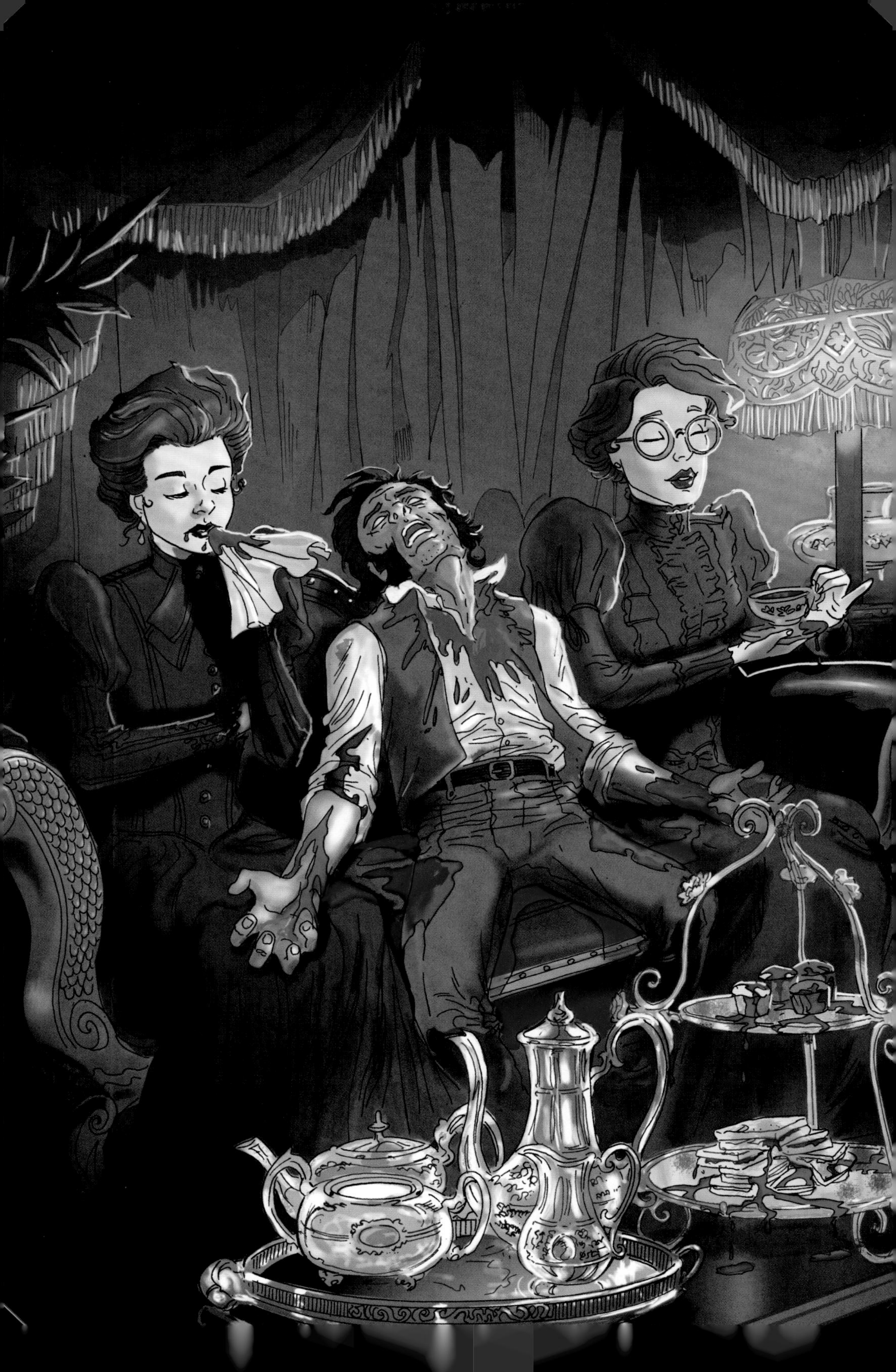

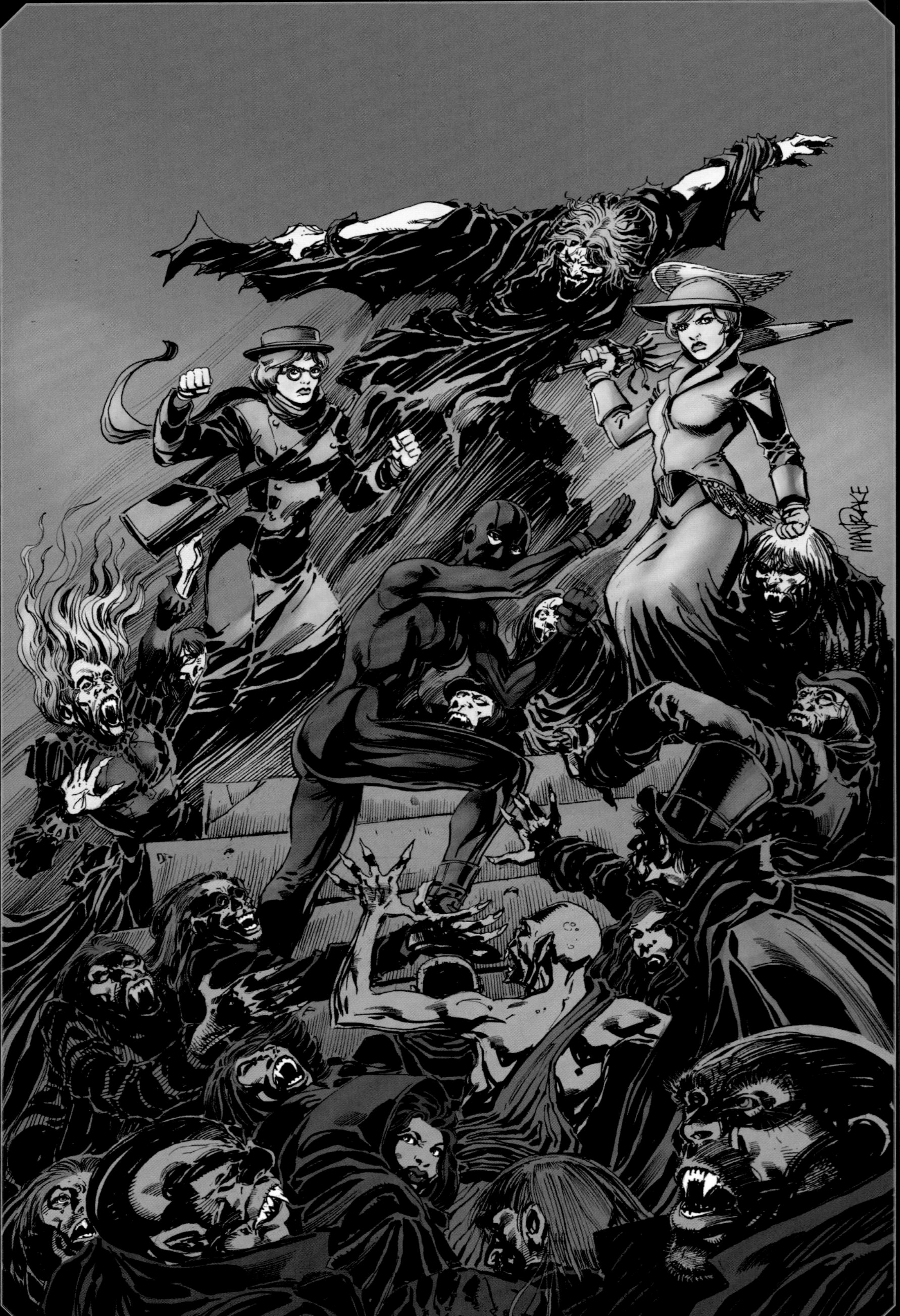
MANDRAKE

Issue #4. Variant cover C by Tom Mandrake. Colors by Sian Mandrake

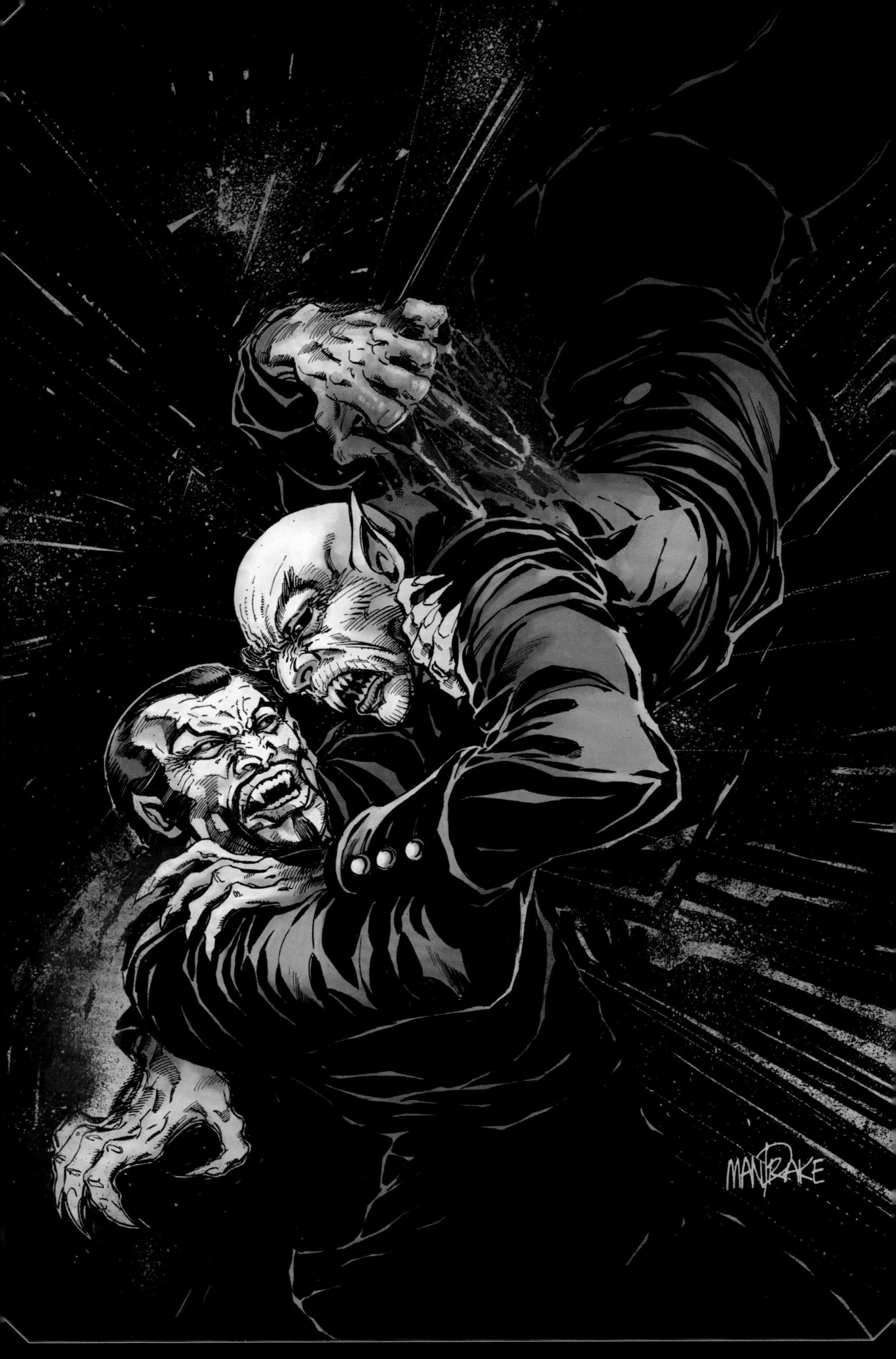
MANDRAKE

FROM PAUL MCCAFFREY'S

SKETCH BOOK

Presented for the first time ever, a small selection of some of Paul's character designs for Anno Dracula.

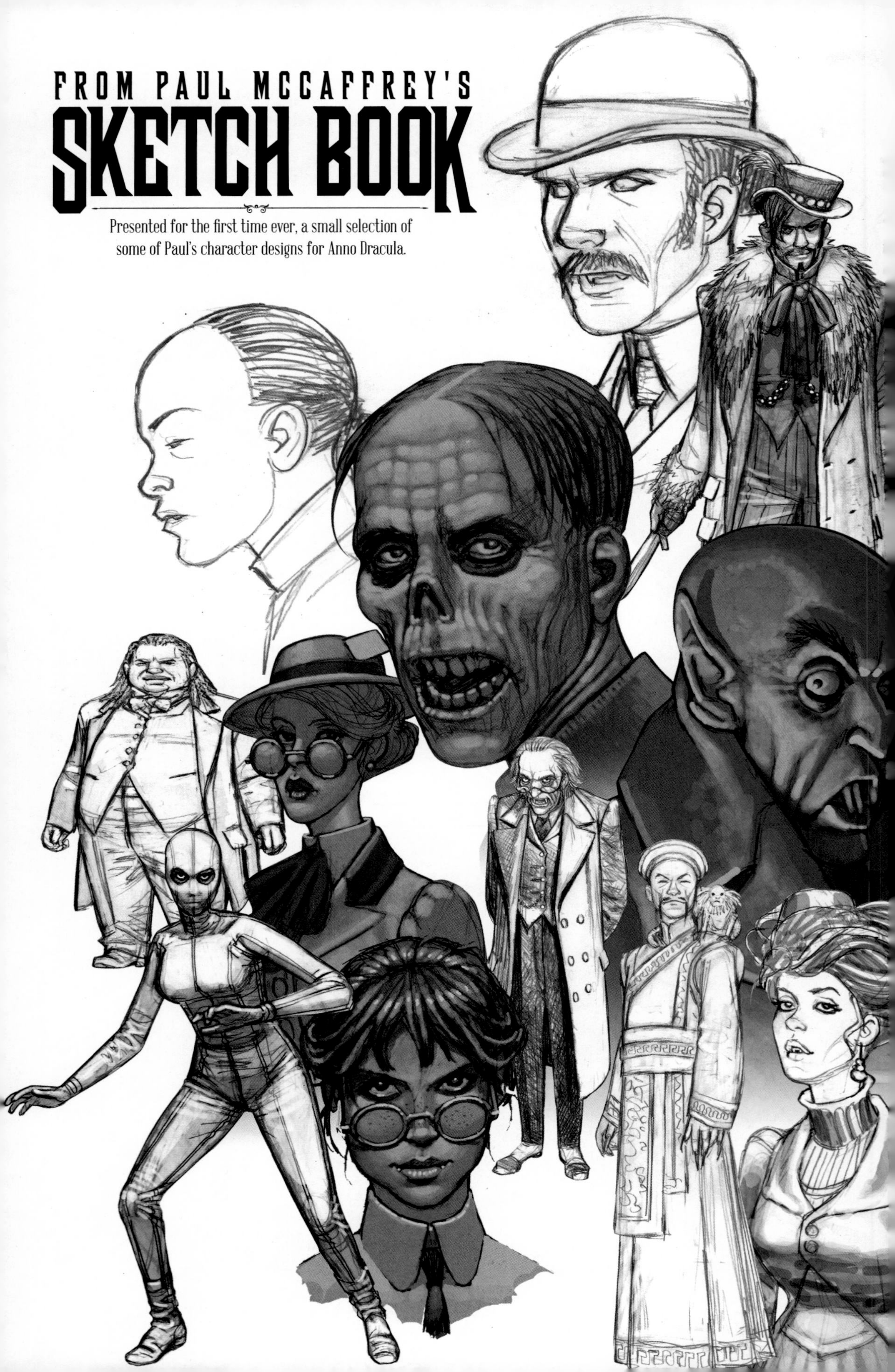

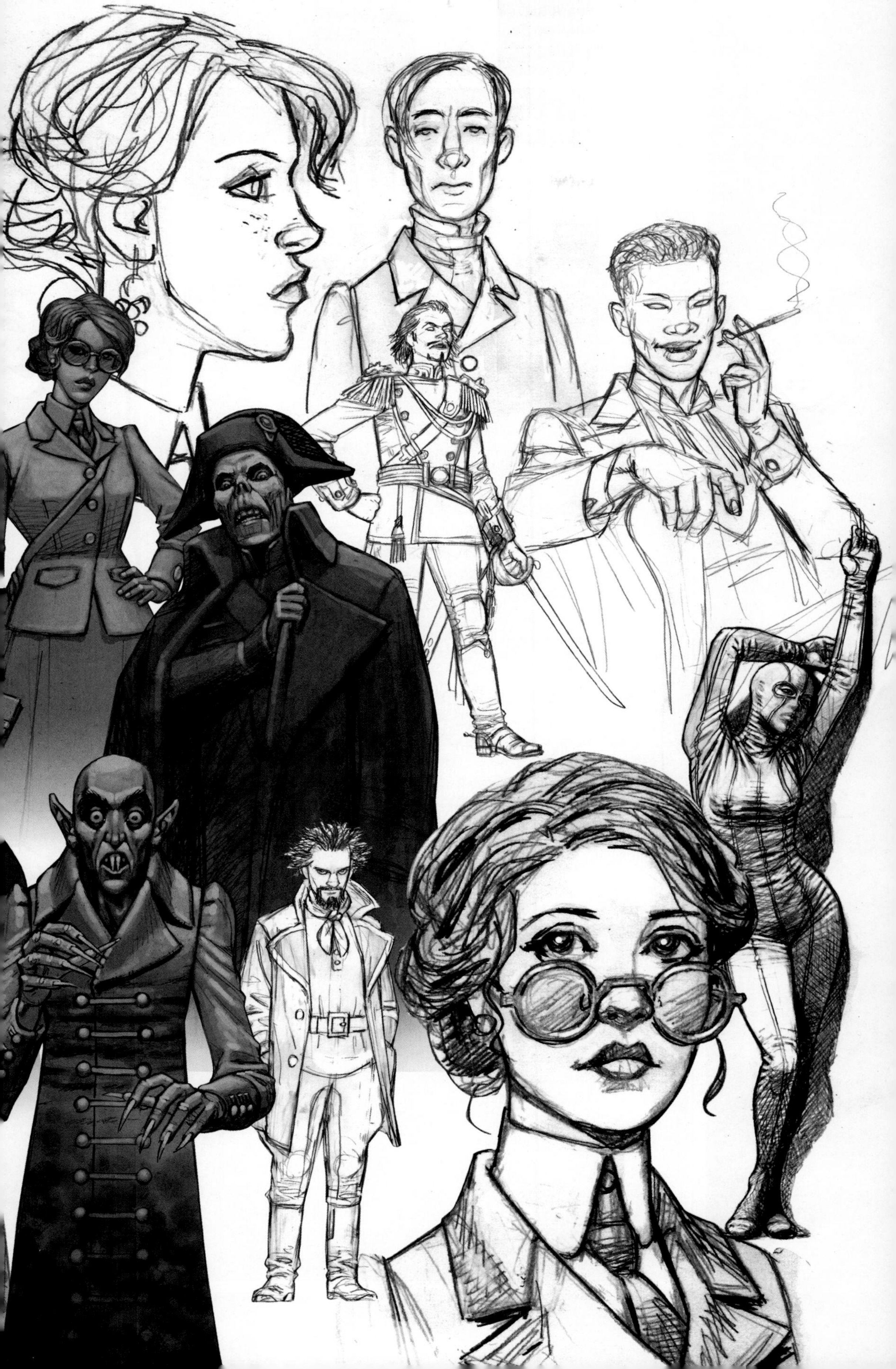

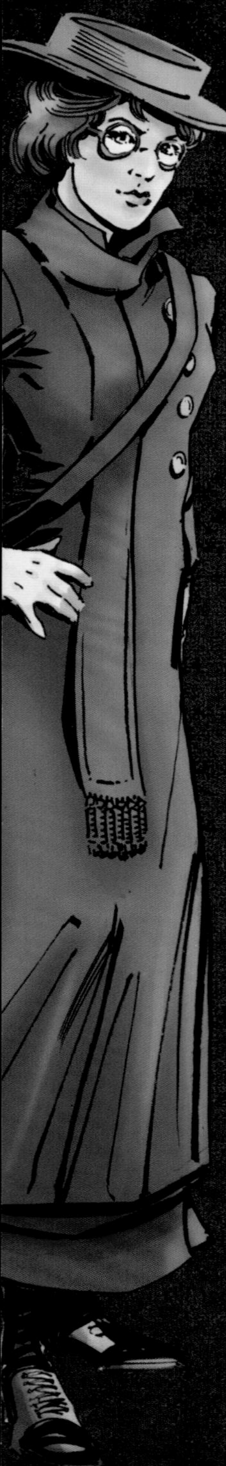

ANNO DRACULA

AFTERWORD

Anno Dracula 1895 Seven Days in Mayhem

It started as a footnote.

In 1978, at the University of Sussex, I took a course called Late Victorian Revolt, taught by Norman Mackenzie (co-author of the best biography of H.G. Wells, *The Time Traveller*) and the poet Laurence Lerner. In an essay about turn-of-the-century apocalyptic fiction, I wrote about war and invasion narratives, covering books like George Chesney's *The Battle of Dorking* (Germans invade Britain!), Wells' *War of the Worlds* (Martians invade Britain!) and Saki's *When William Came* (more Germans invade Britain!).

In a footnote, I suggested Bram Stoker's *Dracula* could be considered as an invasion narrative – with the vampire constituting a one-man occupation of London. His goal – British blood! – is the same as Wells' Martians, who drain human victims via transfusion. Dracula bigs up his military history and Van Helsing speculates that the Count intends to become 'father or furtherer of a new order of beings, whose road must lead through Death, not Life' …but Dracula gets distracted by the wife of a provincial solicitor and is chased off before his plans for Britain can develop.

…but what if he beat Van Helsing and conquered Britain, following in the path of Prince Albert to become Queen Victoria's second foreign consort? Albert was a vastly influential figure, encouraging technological change and importing European customs (like Christmas) to Britain. Even after his death, he was all over the 19th century and London is full of places like the Albert Hall and the Albert Memorial to this day. If Victoria's second husband was Count Dracula, how would that shape the country, the city, the Empire …the entire human race?

I began to explore the question with *Anno Dracula*, first published in 1992. More novels have followed, and my alternate world has expanded and continues to expand*. One of my initial inspirations was the comics genre of 'imaginary story' (DC) or What If …? (Marvel) – alternate histories which don't change the outcome of a war or an election but the course of a well-known story (what if Bruce Wayne's parents lived or Spider-Man joined the Fantastic Four). What if Dracula won?

So it's apt that now, there's an *Anno Dracula* comic too, with Paul McCaffrey putting faces to my characters… and, we trust, more to come.

Kim Newman

*Christina Light, introduced in *Seven Days in Mayhem*, continues into the novels *Anno Dracula 1899 One Thousand Monsters* (out now!) and *Anno Dracula 1999 Daikaiju* (forthcoming).

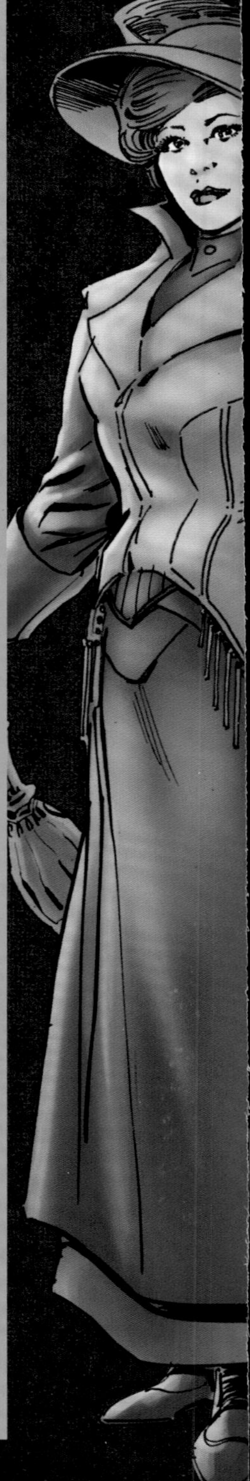

TIMELINE

CHRONOLOGICAL LIST OF THE ANNO DRACULA TITLES

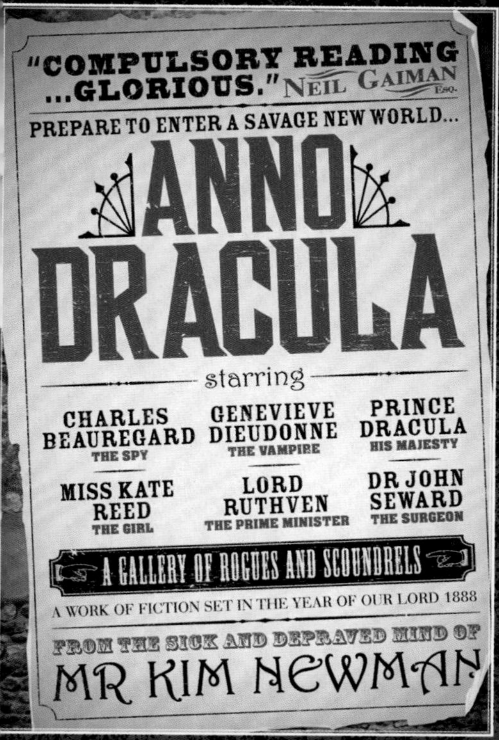

"COMPULSORY READING ...GLORIOUS." NEIL GAIMAN Esq.
PREPARE TO ENTER A SAVAGE NEW WORLD...
ANNO DRACULA
starring
CHARLES BEAUREGARD
THE SPY
GENEVIEVE DIEUDONNE
THE VAMPIRE
PRINCE DRACULA
HIS MAJESTY
MISS KATE REED
THE GIRL
LORD RUTHVEN
THE PRIME MINISTER
DR JOHN SEWARD
THE SURGEON
A GALLERY OF ROGUES AND SCOUNDRELS
A WORK OF FICTION SET IN THE YEAR OF OUR LORD 1888
FROM THE SICK AND DEPRAVED MIND OF
MR KIM NEWMAN

NNO DRACULA (1888)

Novel – first published in 1992.

t is 1888, Queen Victoria has remarried, taking as her new onsort Count Dracula. Van Helsing, Dracula's nemesis, s dead. The novel tells the story of vampire Geneviève Dieudonné and Charles Beauregard of the Diogenes Club as hey strive to solve the mystery of the Jack the Ripper murders.

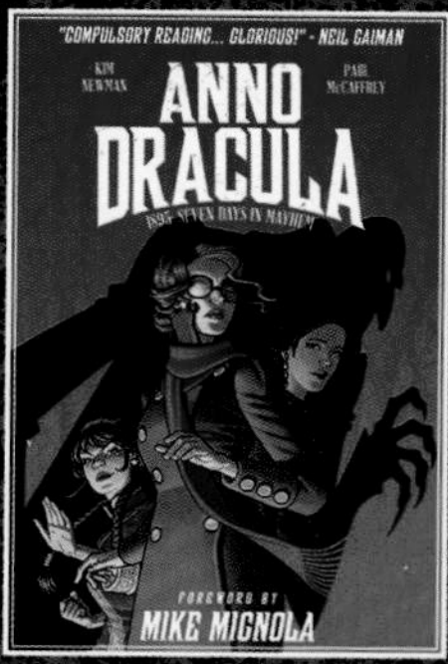

"COMPULSORY READING... GLORIOUS!" - NEIL GAIMAN
KIM NEWMAN
PAUL McCAFFREY
ANNO DRACULA
1895: SEVEN DAYS IN MAYHEM
FOREWORD BY
MIKE MIGNOLA

ANNO DRACULA 1895: SEVEN DAYS IN MAYHEM

Comic – first published in 2017.

As the British Empire prepares to celebrate Dracula's Tin Jubilee, a secret group known as the Council of the Seven Days – led by Christina Light – plots to sabotage the event and assassinate the Crown Prince.

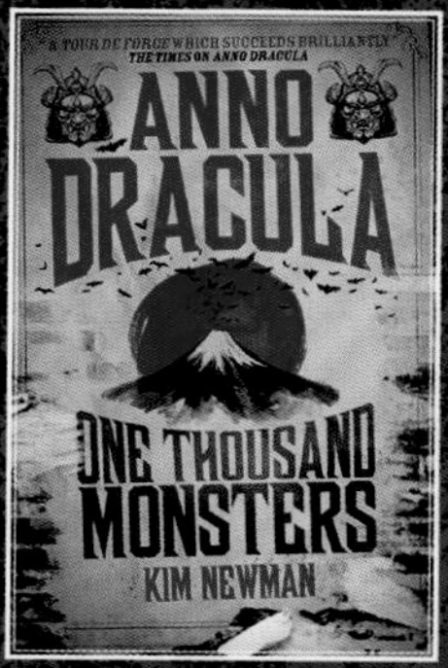

ANNO DRACULA
ONE THOUSAND MONSTERS
KIM NEWMAN

Anno Dracula: One Thousand Monsters

Novel – coming soon.

In 1899, a group of vampire exiles – including the revolutionary Christina Light – are banished to Japan where they discover the horrors within the Temple of One Thousand Monsters.

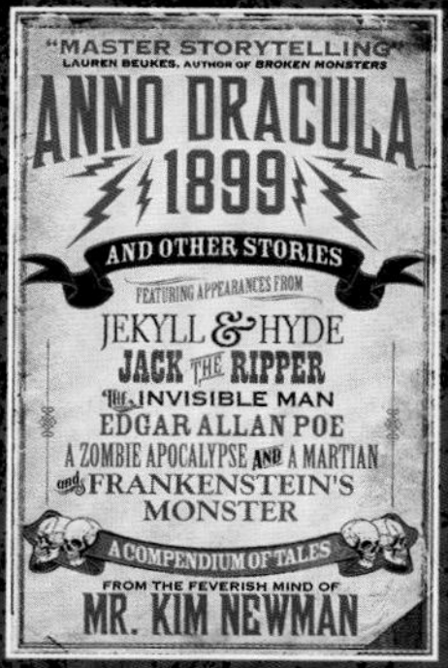

"MASTER STORYTELLING"
LAUREN BEUKES, AUTHOR OF BROKEN MONSTERS
ANNO DRACULA
1899
AND OTHER STORIES
FEATURING APPEARANCES FROM
JEKYLL & HYDE
JACK THE RIPPER
THE INVISIBLE MAN
EDGAR ALLAN POE
A ZOMBIE APOCALYPSE AND A MARTIAN
and FRANKENSTEIN'S MONSTER
A COMPENDIUM OF TALES
FROM THE FEVERISH MIND OF
MR. KIM NEWMAN

ANNO DRACULA 1899 AND OTHER STORIES

Novel – first published in 2017.

A collection of stories featuring the likes of Frankenstein's monster, Dr Jekyll and Mr Hyde, Jack the Ripper, the Invisible Man and Count Dracula himself.

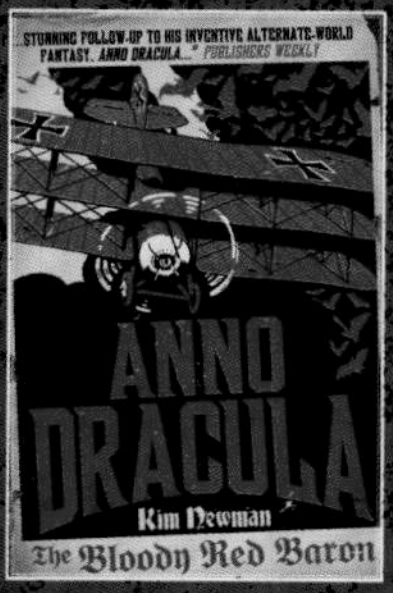

ANNO DRACULA
Kim Newman
The Bloody Red Baron

HE BLOODY RED BARON (1917)

Novel – first published in 1995.

t is WWI, Dracula, now xpelled from the British Empire, is raising a squadron of vampire pilots, led by the Red Baron to fight the allies..

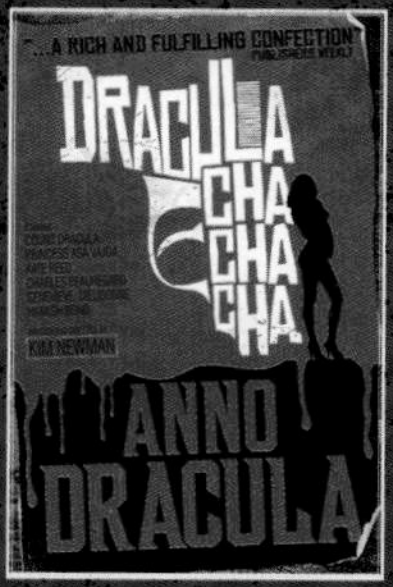

"...A RICH AND FULFILLING CONFECTION" PUBLISHERS WEEKLY
DRACULA CHA CHA CHA
KIM NEWMAN
ANNO DRACULA

DRACULA CHA CHA CHA (1959)

Novel – first published in 1988.

Dracula's nuptials in Rome brings every high-ranking vampire of note flocking to the wedding. However, a mysterious vampire killer threatens to spoil the day.

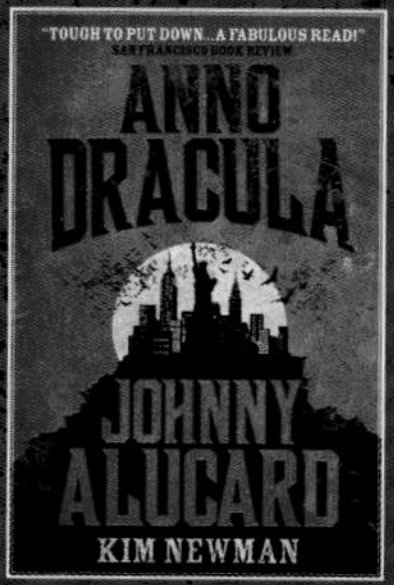

"TOUGH TO PUT DOWN...A FABULOUS READ!"
ANNO DRACULA
JOHNNY ALUCARD
KIM NEWMAN

JOHNNY ALUCARD (1970s–1980s)

Novel – first published in 2013.

A collection of short stories that follow the lives of vampires and humans alike, all of whom have been affected by a mysterious man called Johnny Alucard.

RIPPED FROM THE HAMMER VAULT!

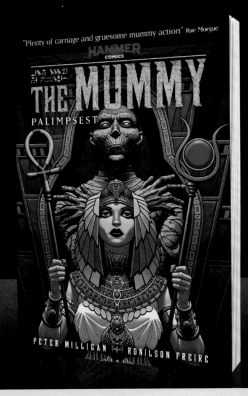

"Plenty of carnage and gruesome mummy action" Rue Morgue

HAMMER COMICS

THE MUMMY

PALIMPSEST

PETER MILLIGAN + RONILSON FREIRE

THE MUMMY

WRITTEN BY PETER MILLIGAN AND DRAWN BY RONILSON FRERE.

CAPTAIN KRONOS
VAMPIRE HUNTER

THE RETURN OF CAPTAIN KRONOS – VAMPIRE HUNTER!

BY DAN ABNETT AND TOM MANDRAKE

COMING SOON

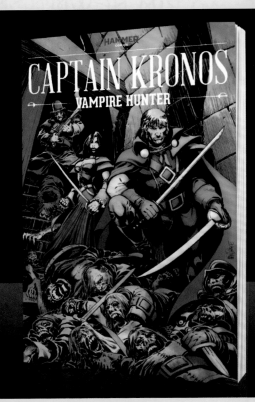

AVAILABLE IN PRINT AND DIGITALLY AT
WWW.TITAN-COMICS.COM

HAMMER
COMICS

TITAN
COMICS